On Creation

THOMAS AQUINAS IN TRANSLATION

ST. THOMAS AQUINAS

On Creation

[*Quaestiones Disputatae de Potentia Dei,* Q. 3]

Translated with introduction and notes by

S. C. Selner-Wright

The Catholic University of America Press
Washington, D.C.

The paper used in this publication meets the minimum
requirements of American National Standards for Information
Science—Permanence of Paper for Printed Library Materials,
ANSI Z39.48-1984.
∞

Library of Congress Cataloging-in-Publication Data
Thomas, Aquinas, Saint, 1225?–1274.
[Quaestiones disputatae de potentia Dei. Q. 3. English]
On creation : Quaestiones disputatae de potentia Dei, q. 3 /
St. Thomas Aquinas ; translated with introduction
and notes by S. C. Selner-Wright.
p. cm. — (Thomas Aquinas in translation)
Includes bibliographical references and index.
ISBN 978-0-8132-1798-7 (pbk. : alk. paper)
1. God (Christianity)—Omnipotence—History of doctrines—
Middle Ages, 600–1500. 2. Creation—History
of doctrines—Middle Ages, 600–1500.
I. Selner-Wright, S. C. (Susan Canty) II. Title.
B765.T53Q33713 2011
231.7'65—dc22
2010036187

CONTENTS

INTRODUCTION

Thomas Aquinas wrote his *Disputed Questions On the Power of God (Quaestiones disputatae de potentia Dei* or *De potentia)* in Rome in 1265–66. It was begun, but probably not completed, before he began the first part of his most famous work, the *Summa theologiae*, also composed during this time in Rome.[1] In the *De potentia*, Thomas takes up questions and ideas that evoked lively debate in his day and continue to do so in ours. In Question 3 these include divine and human freedom, the question whether or not the world is created, the problem of evil, and the status of the developing human embryo. This translation of Question 3 of the as-yet-unpublished Leonine edition of the *De potentia* is intended to make Thomas' contribution to current discussion more accessible.

In Question 3, Thomas first addresses what is meant by "creation" (aa. 1–3), and then the question of who is able to create (aa. 4–6). This is followed by articles on the nature of God's activity in creation (aa. 7–12, 15–16), including specific treatment of the relationship between divine and creaturely activity (aa. 7–12), and even more specifically, the relationship between them in the area of reproduction (aa. 9–12). Finally, Thomas treats the possibility that the world is eternal (aa. 13–14, 17) and the timing of the creation of angels (aa. 18–19). Before embarking on a study of Question 3 itself, the reader may find it helpful to pause briefly to consider its context and some of the main ideas Thomas addresses in it.

The *De potentia* was written during the time when Thomas was assigned to establish a new *studium* in Rome for the formation of men from the Roman province of the Order of Preachers. This assignment came on the heels of his work at the priory in Orvieto, where Thomas' primary teaching duty was to prepare men for their roles as preachers and confessors, and where Thomas had recourse to the manuals on moral theology prepared by earlier Dominicans. There is

1. See Jean-Pierre Torrell, O.P., *Saint Thomas Aquinas*, Vol. 1: *The Person and His Work*, trans. Robert Royal (Washington, D.C.: The Catholic University of America Press, 1996), 161–62, 335.

some speculation that Thomas' and others' dissatisfaction with these manuals, as lacking "the proper dogmatic formation in the great truths of the Christian faith,"[2] was part of the impetus for assigning him to found this new *studium,* where he could develop a course of studies which would lay a more adequate intellectual foundation for pastoral ministry. As part of that course of studies, Thomas offered his *De potentia.*

Given this context, the *De potentia* can be read as an indicator of the core concerns Thomas thought needed to be addressed in his students' intellectual formation. The content of the *De potentia* indicates that primary among these was a grasp of what we can know by natural means about the nature of God and of God's activity. This is a necessary starting point (and is also the focus of the first 45 questions of the *Summa theologiae*) because we must from the beginning make a radical shift in our understanding of causality, of the relation between cause and effect.

Our ordinary understanding of causality is rooted in our experience of the world, specifically in our experience of human impact on the world through our various technologies, and our experience of cause and effect in the natural world. In that experience, we find that all "causing," all "making," is fundamentally a reorganizing of something that is already there. When torrential rain causes a mudslide, the rain has caused earth which had been stable to lose its stability and fall, taking down also whatever might be rooted in it or built on it. When a dog has a litter of puppies, genetic material that already existed in her has been combined with genetic material from a male dog, and from that initial group of single cells, these puppies have developed. When a group of human beings construct a building, they use already existing concrete, wood, and steel to build it. In our ordinary experience, there is always something "out of which" a new thing comes, and if there is nothing "out of which"—if for example the contracted companies fail to deliver the concrete, wood, and steel to the building site—then nothing will come to be. This experience is captured in the ancient dictum: *"ex nihilo, nihil fit,"* literally, "from nothing, nothing is made," or "nothing comes from nothing."

2. Torrell, *Saint Thomas Aquinas,* vol. 1, 120.

But Genesis introduces a very different understanding of causality, and all subsequent thinkers, whether they believe Genesis reveals the truth or not, must contend with this understanding. The claim of Genesis that "In the beginning God created the heavens and the earth"[3] has been taken to mean that God causes the universe to exist in its entirety—there is nothing "out of which" it is made, nothing pre-existing which is reorganized by God's action. Creation is a violation of the dictum *"ex nihilo, nihil fit,"* an action entirely outside of our ordinary experience; and so from the beginning our understanding of causality has to be re-shaped if we are to grasp what creation means—whether we accept it as the truth about the origin of the universe or not. We cannot accept or reject the notion of creation on rational grounds unless we first understand what it means. And unless we understand the implications of creation, we cannot understand related claims about the nature of God's relation to and activity in the world. And so, much of the *De potentia* is taken up with the contrast as well as the analogy between generation and creation, between our ordinary understanding of causality and the understanding we will come to if we fully articulate the metaphysical roots of the ordinary world—for Thomas is convinced that the world itself can reveal to us that it comes from nothing, and that in teaching this Genesis is confirming a truth that is available to reason. In fact, Thomas begins Question 3 of the *De potentia* by explicitly arguing for creation *ex nihilo* in article 1 ("Whether God can make something out of nothing").

In the first part of the *Summa theologiae,* after clarifying his understanding of theology as distinct from philosophy, Thomas begins by arguing in Question 2 for the createdness of the world; he then goes on to draw inferences about the nature of the creator in Questions 3–26. In Question 25, he specifically treats *divina potentia,* the power of God, and he follows this with a treatment of the procession of the Trinity in Questions 28–43 and then a specific treatment of the creation of the world in Questions 44–49.

We find the same set of issues in the *De potentia,* but they are more woven together, and this interweaving can be both challenging and

3. Genesis 1:1.

illuminating. After giving a general treatment of God's power in the first question, Thomas focuses in the remaining questions on how the power of the one God can be manifest in the creation of a diverse universe (QQ. 3–6), and on how the one God can be manifest in the procession of the Trinity (QQ. 2, 7–10). The reader unfamiliar with Thomas and his milieu might wonder at this juxtaposition of the purely theological notion of the Trinity and the philosophical claim of the world's createdness. To understand this juxtaposition, I think we must grasp two things: first, the issues surrounding what philosophers call "the problem of the One and the Many," and, second, the Neoplatonic response to this problem. A primary purpose of the *De potentia* (and of the first part of the *Summa*) is to address the problem of the One and the Many; and Thomas is convinced that the Neoplatonic response to this problem has developed metaphysical tools which are crucial for philosophy and for Christian theology. But because there are serious philosophical errors in the Neoplatonic view, Thomas must show how these can be avoided without sacrificing the usefulness of underlying Neoplatonic principles. This project entails treating both creation and the procession of the Trinity.

In Question 3 of the *De potentia* Thomas responds again and again to the principle that "Nature is determined to one." When Neoplatonists (and, we shall see, the Islamic thinker Avicenna) consider the nature of the first cause of the universe, this principle leads them to the conclusion that because that first cause is utterly simple it can give rise only to another simple being, another "one." The problem then is to understand how the complex, multiple universe that is evident to our senses can have come to be from this first. Neoplatonism solves this problem by positing a series of "intermediates" between the first cause and the material universe, and assigning the diversity and evil that are evident in the world to a gradual decline from the simplicity and purity of the first cause.

Thomas argues that this view of creation via intermediaries is not only contrary to the revelation of Genesis (which maintains God's immediate creation of the universe and his assessment of it as good), it is also philosophically untenable, for only the infinite power of God is adequate to creation. He makes this case most explicitly here in article 4 ("Whether the power or even the act of creation is communicable to another") and article 5 ("Whether there can be anything that is not created by God"). But, someone might ask, does this not defy the principle of sufficient reason, which entails that the effect cannot manifest something that does not somehow pre-exist in the cause? Where do the multiplicity and imperfection among creatures come from if the cause of creatures is itself one perfect God? Thomas addresses these questions again and again, most specifically in article 6 ("Whether there is only one principle of creation") and article 16 ("Whether a multitude can proceed from one first thing").

Because Thomas is at pains to respond to the Neoplatonic vision of creation via intermediaries, he must also concern himself with the Neoplatonic claim of three "divine hypostases" which might easily and disastrously be confused with the three persons of the Trinity revealed in Christianity. According to Plotinus, the first "hypostasis," the One, naturally and involuntarily "emanates" the second hypostasis, the Intelligence, which has its own simplicity as an intelligence but not the radical simplicity of the One. The Intelligence, in turn, emanates the third hypostasis, World-Soul, which then emanates the Nature of the material world. There are two points here that a Christian theologian must counter. First is Plotinus' view that the second and third hypostases are lesser than the first, which might lead someone to the mistaken notion that the second and third persons of the Trinity are not equal to the first person. While Thomas treats this more completely elsewhere in the *De potentia,* he does address it here in Question 3 in article 13 ("Whether something which is from another can be eternal"). The second mistake in the Neoplatonic view (especially as that view is articulated by Avicenna) is the claim that the simplicity of the One is incompatible with free action. Thomas argues against this view repeatedly in Question 3, and his most sustained treatment of it is found in article 15 ("Whether things proceeded from God by natural necessity or by the decree of his will").

The question of God's freedom to create is a critical one for Thomas, both philosophically and theologically. We shall see him argue again and again that God is a person with intellect and will and that creation is a deliberately chosen divine action. In the course of Question 3, this position leads Thomas to treat two very important ideas, one coming from the Neoplatonic view of the world and the other from Aristotle. The first is the dictum "The good is diffusive of itself," most clearly formulated by Pseudo-Dionysius. This principle shapes our understanding of God's efficient causality; Thomas must show how it is true without allowing it to be pushed to the point of saying that because God is good he is compelled to create. The second idea is what Thomas calls "necessity of supposition," or "necessity of the end," a view of final causality that he adopts from Aristotle. In article 17, Thomas argues that this is the one kind of necessity under which God does operate: If God's goal is X, then God must do what is necessary to X. For example, Thomas maintains that if God wants to cause a universe of finite beings that manifests his infinite goodness, then that universe must be composed of a diversity of creatures. This is not a constraint on God's freedom, because of that initial "if": God is free to create or not to create. But given God's choice of an "end," what is entailed by that end becomes necessary.

This form of necessity bears on another central preoccupation of Question 3, namely God's "responsibility" for evil in the created universe. The underlying question of article 6 ("Whether there is only one principle of creation") is how to account for the existence of evil if God is the sole creator of the universe. We shall see Thomas argue that the necessity of diversity in creation entails that some creatures "lack" what other creatures "have," and this lack can be experienced as an evil. Further, Thomas argues that God chooses for his creatures to be efficacious, to have their own share of authentic causality, and one creature's action can entail another creature's evil, as for example the lion's hunting means the gazelle's death.

In article 7 ("Whether God works in all the operations of nature") and article 8 ("Whether God operates in nature by creating, which is to ask whether creation is mingled with the work of nature"), Thomas focuses on the relation between God's creative activity and the activity of his creatures; and he goes on in articles 9 through 12 to focus specifically on the relation between divine and creaturely activity in producing new creatures. Thomas argues that while the activity of creatures is founded on God's creative activity, we should not understand this dependence as robbing creatures of any authentic efficient causality, an error which we now refer to as occasionalism. This is just one instance of another theme we see throughout Question 3: that creatures, while radically dependent, have been given the dignity of a real and vital role to play within creation.

A point of intersection between divine and human activity which is developed at length here in Question 3 is in the activity of producing new human beings. In article 9 Thomas poses the question, "Whether the rational soul is brought into being by creation or by the transmission of semen." That is, do human parents cause both the soul and body of their children, or is the soul of each child directly created by God? Thomas' arguments in response to this question assume an understanding of Aristotle's hylomorphism and the difference between the human soul and the forms of other living beings. Every material being is composed of matter and form with the potency of the matter actualized by the form. In living beings the form is called a soul. But among living beings, only the human acts in a way that indicates immaterial operation. Every other living being is informed by a soul whose actuality is entirely directed toward actualizing the potency of matter. In our experience to date, only human beings operate in a way that shows that while our form is the form of matter, actualizing the potency of matter, its actuality is not exhausted by its relation to matter. Unlike any other form of matter, the human soul is itself subsistent, having the capacity for existence independent of the condition or even the existence of the body. Therefore, Thomas argues in article 9, the human soul cannot be materially generated but rather must be individually and immediately created. With Thomas' earlier arguments that only God can create, the conclusion follows that while human parents cause the body of the human child, only God can cause the soul; and so production of a new human being is an act entailing the cooperation of three agents: a father, a mother, and God.

The ninth objection to Thomas' view that God creates each human soul focuses on the activity of the early embryo, arguing that it can be explained only if there is a rational soul in the semen which begins to direct the operation of the embryo as soon as conception occurs. Thomas' reply to this objection is unusually lengthy and the position he articulates has had an important impact on current philosophical debate about the status to be accorded to early embryos. It is very important to know that Thomas' understanding of embryonic development is almost entirely derived from Aristotle's biology, developed in the fourth century B.C. Thomas' view is that the early development of the human embryo takes place under the direction of a "formative power" which is not itself a soul but which is derived from the father's soul and transmitted with the father's semen. The developing embryo is informed by a succession of souls until, under the direction of the formative power, it finally has sufficient material organization to be informed by a human soul. At that point, Thomas thinks, God acts to create a human soul which informs the now human body, and together these constitute a human being. This theory, which is called "delayed hominization," has received a great deal of attention recently, with some going so far as to claim that because he holds this theory, Thomas could support the case for abortion of the early embryo.[4] Given the fact that there is no indication in Thomas' work that he regards intentional abortion as anything other than a serious crime,[5] it is strange to see him recruited in this cause. Even more important, given biology's current understanding of the self-organization that marks the activity of the zygote immediately upon the fusion of human sperm and egg, the specifically human organization that Aristotle's biology observed only after weeks of embryonic development is actually present from fertilization on; and so the same line of reasoning that led Thomas to hold delayed hominization would now lead him to conclude to immediate hominization.[6] In that case, Thomas would conclude that intentional killing of the embryo is not only a crime but the crime of homicide, and that exploitation of the embryo for another's benefit is slavery.

4. Cf. Stephen Asma, "Abortion and the Embarrassing Saint," *The Humanist* 54 (1994): 30-33, and Robert Pasnau, *Thomas Aquinas on Human Nature* (Cambridge: Cambridge University Press, 2002) 100–130.

5. In fact, Thomas refers to the abortion of a pregnancy only three times in his entire corpus and then only as indirectly related to the question at hand. See *Summa theologiae* II-II Q. 64, a. 8 and III Q. 68, a. 11; and *Commentary on the Sentences* IV, d. 6, q. 1, ad 4. For a discussion of these texts, see John Haldane and Patrick Lee, "Aquinas on Human Ensoulment and the Value of Life," *Philosophy* 78 (2003): 256–57.

6. Maureen L. Condic, "When Does Human Life Begin? A Scientific Perspective," *National Catholic Bioethics Quarterly* 9 (2009): 131–49. See article 9, note 55.

Given that Question 3 stretches from an examination of the meaning of creation itself to the creation of individual human beings, it will not surprise the reader that Thomas also takes up the creation of angels, devoting the last two articles to that subject. Because angels are not part of our natural human experience, belief in their existence depends on a belief in the veracity of Scripture, which refers to them many times. For the philosopher, angels are interesting hypothetical beings, whose possible existence leads to many interesting questions: What would a purely formal creature be like? What would be the purpose of such a creature? What would its activity be like? Thomas treats the angels here in the context of the questions whether they were, and whether they could have been, created before the material universe. Thomas argues that angels could have been created prior to the material universe (a. 19), but it seems more fitting in light of what we know of God's ordering of creation to conclude that in fact angels were created at the same time that the material world began to be (a. 18).

Given our modern predilection for strictly separating the realms of naturally attainable truth and revealed truth, it may seem odd, even "unprofessional," that Thomas presents philosophical arguments on various topics along with discussions of purely theological notions such as the Trinity and angels. But Thomas is convinced that philosophy and theology, while distinct in their range and method, are nonetheless complementary in their operation; and his work shows that attention to the use of philosophical principles in response to theological questions can shed much light on the meaning of these principles in the properly philosophical realm.

On the other hand, philosophy and theology are distinct disciplines and Thomas is careful not to blur the lines between them, either by improperly extending philosophical arguments into matters of revealed truth, or by improperly applying revealed theological principles to philosophical questions. There are limits to reason's capacity to "prove" truths of faith; and while there are some positions held in faith which can also be concluded to rationally, there are many others which cannot. In Question 3 of the *De potentia,* we see an excellent example of Thomas' commitment to these limits in his discussion of whether we can prove rationally that the world is co-eternal with God or whether we can prove the contrary, that it has a beginning. In article 14 ("Whether that which is from God, differing in essence from him, can have always been") and article 17 ("Whether the world has always existed"), Thomas shows that both of these positions are in error. He argues that reason cannot prove either of these positions with certainty, and so philosophy cannot be used here to destroy faith or to prove the tenets of faith.

Given the remarkable range of ideas taken up in the *De potentia,* the reader may not be surprised at the enormous number of sources on which Thomas is drawing and to which he is responding. Question 3 alone contains references to more than 50 different works other than sacred Scripture (which is referred to about 40 times). There are more than 120 references to 11 of Aristotle's works, more than 50 references to 12 of Augustine's, and 24 references to the *Book of Causes,* a very important Neoplatonic source, to name only the most frequently cited. This is much more than a display of erudition: it is a sign of Thomas' remarkable curiosity and commitment to entering into conversation with any serious thinker, whether pagan, Christian, Muslim, or Jewish, who takes up topics cogent to the questions arising here. The bibliography which follows the translation gives contemporary citations for these sources for the reader who wishes to continue that project.

A NOTE ON THE TRANSLATION

This is an English translation of the as-yet-unpublished Leonine edition of Question 3 of the *De potentia* that Fr. R.-A. Gauthier, O.P., had been working on prior to his death in 1999. Fr. Adriano Oliva, O.P., current chairman of the Leonine Commission, has very graciously granted permission for use of the unpublished text of Question 3 as established by Fr. Gauthier.

The 10 questions which make up the *De potentia* are focused on the nature of God's power (Q. 1) and the manifestation of that power in creation of a diverse universe (QQ. 3–6) and in the procession of the Trinity (QQ. 2, 7–10). Question 3 was chosen for this translation for several reasons: it is the first of the three questions which are most specifically philosophical; it offers a comprehensive treatment of creation and shows Thomas' metaphysics and anthropology at work in his consideration of the general creation of the universe and the particular creation of each human being; and at roughly 200 pages it constitutes a focused but extended example of Thomas' work at the height of his intellectual powers. In order to make this important text available to a wide audience, this translation has been undertaken with the goal of philosophical clarity in combination with accessibility to the reader who is not trained specifically in Thomistic or even medieval philosophy.

The English translation of the *De potentia* currently in print is Wipf & Stock Publishers' 2004 reprint of Fr. Lawrence Shapcote's translation of the Marietti edition, published by the Newman Press in 1952. It contains all 10 questions and numbers more than 700 pages. Because the Leonine edition of Question 3 is largely in agreement with the Marietti, and because Fr. Shapcote's translation of the Marietti is very capably executed, the reader of both translations will find them mostly in agreement about the meaning of Thomas' text. My method has been to compare the Leonine with the Marietti, then to translate the Leonine, and finally to consult Fr. Shapcote's translation of the Marietti.

My comparison of the Marietti and Leonine editions revealed

many differences, but almost all of the variation is in word order or in word choice where the meaning of the passage is not, in my view, significantly altered. In Question 3 (the only part of the Leonine edition to which I have had access) I have found differences that I think alter the meaning of the text in only a handful of instances, all of which are indicated in the footnotes. Where Fr. Shapcote and I differ on the best translation, I have noted that difference only in places where I think the Latin reader might find the difference interesting or provocative.

The translation itself was completed in the fall of 1999 during a sabbatical leave granted by Mount Saint Mary's College in Emmitsburg, Maryland. During that time, I felt myself to be the only student in a very special seminar: the teacher, Thomas Aquinas O.P.; the post-doctoral assistant, Lawrence Shapcote, O.P.; and myself, the lowly student. I was there to learn directly from St. Thomas and felt free to disagree with Fr. Shapcote's understanding of him, but I felt myself frequently glancing at Fr. Shapcote to exchange looks of amazement at our mutual good fortune to be present to the teaching of St. Thomas and occasionally to ask him a question to get his take on what St. Thomas was saying. I am deeply grateful for Fr. Shapcote's careful work in his translation of the Marietti edition (not to mention his other work as a translator of St. Thomas), and this translation owes a great deal to his work.

The greatest difference between this translation and Fr. Shapcote's is also a main reason for the great delay between the completion of the translation and the publication of this book: the footnotes. It has been my goal to serve the reader not only through an accessible translation but also by doing the basic groundwork that will allow him or her to enter into fruitful study and research with this important text. To that end, several kinds of footnotes are included, which may be broadly categorized as research notes, philosophical notes, and translation notes.

Research notes have been the most laborious part of this undertaking and, among these, by far the most hours have been spent on those which attempt to trace St. Thomas's own sources. My goal has been to identify as specifically as possible the source of every text that is clearly in some way beholden to a source. With the exception of fourteen vexing texts which I am sure are paraphrases or even quotations of source material, this goal has been achieved. Of course, I am certain there are many influences which I have not recognized, and I ask any who identify these to communicate with me about them. But anyone who can illuminate me regarding the texts where I have had finally to surrender I beg to come to my assistance. These fourteen are marked with the concession, "I have been unable to trace this reference."

Other research notes point to other works of St. Thomas that give parallel or, on occasion, significantly different discussions of something in this text. And finally there are notes referring readers to contemporary secondary scholarship on specific texts in the *De potentia* or on specific topics that arise in it.

The reader will also find footnotes giving philosophical background for particular claims or arguments in this text, and others tracing certain important philosophical principles at work throughout the text. These notes are intended to help the reader who is not already conversant with these principles, claims, or arguments to understand them and to see the continuity of Thomas' thinking over the span of the 19 articles of Question 3. Where appropriate, these notes also refer readers to contemporary secondary scholarship that can further enrich their understanding of St. Thomas' text and what is at stake in it.

Finally, there are "translation" footnotes, which give the Latin word or phrase (or, very occasionally, an entire passage) for passages where seeing the Latin might give the Latin reader a more nuanced sense of the text, or where I thought it possible that a Latin reader might disagree with my translation. My goal in these notes has been to give full disclosure to the Latin reader without unduly distracting the reader who lacks Latin. The reader who is trained in classical Latin may notice in these notes that the Leonine edition preserves the medieval practice of abbreviating the diphthong "ae" to a simple "e."

Within the text itself, the following conventions are observed: italicized words were also italicized in the Leonine edition, indicating that they are paraphrases or quotations of source material; angle brackets (< >) are used in this text, and in the Leonine edition, to indicate words added by Fr. Gauthier, the editor of the Leonine; square brackets ([ ]) are used in this text to indicate words I have added as an aid to understanding.

I would like to thank Kevin White for his help in communicating with the Leonine commission and securing the Leonine text of Q. 3 and permission to use it for this translation. It would have been simply impossible to do this work without his help. I am very grateful for Susan Barnes' work in editing the manuscript. I also wish to thank David McGonagle, director of the Catholic University of America Press, for suggesting this project in the first place and for his patience with a process that we had projected to be completed long ago. I have two beautiful children and much better footnotes to show for the delay! I owe my understanding of St. Thomas and of his role in the history of philosophy to many. My gratitude to my teachers is profound and extends to many more than I can mention here: Msgr. John Wippel; Fr. W. Norris Clarke, S.J.; Dr. B. Carlos Bazán; Dr. Thérèse Druart; Dr. Thomas Prufer; Dr. David L. Schindler; and Dr. Janet Smith. Finally, I must thank my children and extended family and above all my husband: their support has been the *sine qua non* for anything I have done. To them I say, God makes me necessary, but you make me possible.

ABBREVIATIONS

CCSL	Corpus Christianorum, Series Latina
CSEL	Corpus Scriptorum Ecclesiasticorum Latinorum
FOTC	Fathers of the Church
NPNF	Nicene and Post Nicene Fathers of the Christian Church
PG	Patrologia Gracea
PL	Patrologia Latina
ST	*Summa theologiae*, Thomas Aquinas
SCG	*Summa contra gentiles*, Thomas Aquinas

ST. THOMAS AQUINAS

On Creation

[*Quaestiones Disputatae de Potentia Dei,* Q. 3]

The question concerns creation, which
is the first effect of the divine power.

ARTICLE 1

And the first thing to be asked is whether God can make something out of nothing. And it seems that he cannot.[1]

OBJ. 1. For God cannot act counter to first principles,[2] as for example the whole cannot be greater than its part. But as the Philosopher says in Physics I,[3] it is a first principle and axiom of physics that nothing comes out of nothing. Therefore God cannot make something out of nothing.

OBJ. 2. Everything which comes to be was possible before it came to be, for if it were impossible it could not come to be, for nothing is changed to that which is impossible. But the potency by which something is able to be, cannot be except in some subject, since an accident cannot be without a subject. Therefore everything that comes to be comes from matter or a subject. Therefore it is impossible for something to come from nothing.

OBJ. 3. An infinite distance cannot be crossed. But from absolute non-being to being is an infinite distance, which is clear because the less that potency is disposed to act the more distant it is from act. And so if there is no potency at all, the distance will be infinite. Therefore it is impossible for something to pass from absolute non-being into being.

OBJ. 4. In On Generation I, the Philosopher says that things which are completely dissimilar do not act on each other, for it is necessary that agent and patient have genus and matter in common.[4] But absolute non-being and God have nothing in common. Therefore God is not able to act on absolute non-being, and thus cannot make something from nothing.

OBJ. 5. But it may be said that the preceding argument concerns an agent whose action differs from its substance, and which there-

1. For parallel discussions of this question, see *Summa theologiae (ST)* I Q. 44, a. 2 and *Summa contra gentiles (SCG)* II 16.

2. *communem animi conceptionem.*

3. Aristotle, *Physics,* I 4, 187a29, 33–34.

4. Aristotle, *On Generation and Corruption,* I 7, 323b33 and 324b7–8.

fore requires some receiving subject. On the contrary, Avicenna says that if heat were separated from matter, it would act of itself without matter; but nevertheless its action would not be its substance.[5] Therefore the fact that God's action is his essence does not show that he does not require matter.

OBJ. 6. It is a principle of reason that nothing is concluded from nothing. But rational being follows natural being. Therefore also in nature, nothing can come from nothing.

OBJ. 7. If something were made from nothing, the preposition "from" would connote either cause or order. With reference to causes, it seems to connote only the efficient or the material cause. But "nothing" can be neither the efficient nor the material cause of a being, and so in this proposition "from" does not denote cause. Likewise with order since, as Boethius says, there is no order of being to non-being.[6] Therefore in no way can something come to be from nothing.

OBJ. 8. According to the Philosopher in Metaphysics V, active potency is the *cause of change in another thing insofar as it is other.*[7] But God has only active potency. Therefore he requires some subject of change, and thus cannot make something from nothing.

OBJ. 9. Diversity is found in things inasmuch as one thing is more perfect than another. But the cause of such diversity is not God, who is one and simple. Therefore the cause of this diversity must be matter, and so it is necessary to hold that things which are made are from matter and not from nothing.

OBJ. 10. That which is made from nothing has being after non-being. Therefore we can consider an instant which is the last of its non-being, from which point it ceases not being, and an instant which is the first of its being, from which point it begins to be. These are either one and the same instant or distinct instants. If the same, then it follows that two contradictories exist at the same instant. If they are distinct, then since *between two instants there is an intermediate time,*[8] it follows that there would be an intermediate between affirmation and negation, for it cannot be said that it is not after the

5. Cf. Avicenna, *Liber de Philosophia Prima sive Scientia Divina,* IX 5.
6. This may be a reference to Boethius, *De Hebdomadibus,* Axiom 4.
7. Aristotle, *Metaphysics,* V 12, 1019a15–20.
8. I have been unable to trace this reference.

last instant in which it was not, nor that it is before the first instant in which it is. But both of these are impossible, namely that contradictories are true simultaneously and that there is an intermediate between them. Therefore it is impossible for something to come to be from nothing.

OBJ. 11. That which is made necessarily was being made at some time, and that which is created was being created at some time. Therefore either that which is created is both being made and already made simultaneously or not simultaneously. But it cannot be said that these are not simultaneous, since before it is made a creature is not. Therefore if its being made preceded its having been made, some subject of the making would be necessary, which is contrary to the notion of creation. But if being made and having been made are simultaneous, it follows that being made and not being made are simultaneous, since in things which are not purely transient[9] that which has been made is, while that which is being made is not. But this is impossible. Therefore it is impossible for something to be made from nothing or to be created.

OBJ. 12. *Every agent produces its like.*[10] But *every agent acts insofar as*

9. I am following Fr. Shapcote in translating *"in permanentibus"* as "in things which are not purely transient." See Aquinas, *On the Power of God,* trans. English Dominican Fathers (Westminster, MD: Newman Press, 1952), 81.

10. This maxim, "Omne agens agit simile sibi," is often referred to as the principle of similitude or, sometimes, the law of similarity. In his work on the *Summa contra gentiles,* R.-A. Gauthier says the principle of similitude was given this particular formulation by Michael the Scot in his translation of Averroes' Great Commentary on the *De Anima,* II, com. 118 (*Saint Thomas d'Aquin, Somme contre les gentils. Introduction* [Paris: Éditions Universitaires, 1993], 96). Gauthier is cited by John F. Wippel, who examines Thomas' justification and application of this principle in his "Thomas Aquinas on Our Knowledge of God and the Axiom That Every Agent Produces Something Like Itself," *Proceedings of the American Catholic Philosophical Association* 74 (2001): 81–101; reprinted in *Metaphysical Themes in Thomas Aquinas II* (Washington, D.C.: The Catholic University of America Press, 2007), 152–71. According to Philipp Rosemann, Aristotle gives the "first explicit formulation of the law of similarity in the history of philosophy" in *Metaphysics* XII 3, 1070a4. P. Rosemann, *Omne Agens Agit Sibi Simile: A "Repetition" of Scholastic Metaphysics* (Leuven: Leuven University Press, 1996), 54.

Here in obj. 12, as in many other places in the *De potentia* and elsewhere in Thomas' corpus, the principle of similitude is juxtaposed with another maxim: every agent acts insofar as it is in act *(omne agens agit secundum quod est in actu).* On the source of this principle, see note 14 below. In his article on the principle of similitude, Msgr. Wippel presents these two maxims as components of an argument implicit or explicit in many texts that culminate in the claim that *it is in act.* Therefore nothing is made except insofar as it is in act. But prime matter is not in act. Therefore it cannot be made, especially by God, who is pure act. And so whatever is made, is made from pre-existing matter and not from nothing.

OBJ. 13. Whatever God makes he effects according to an idea, just as an artificer also produces works of art according to a form of art. But there is no idea of prime matter in God, because an idea is a form and is a likeness of what it is an idea of. But since the notion of the essence of prime matter entails that it is without any form, no form can be a likeness of it. Therefore prime matter cannot be made by God and thus the same conclusion follows.

OBJ. 14. The same thing cannot be the principle of both perfection and imperfection. But imperfection is found in things when certain things are better than others, which happens only through the imperfection of the inferior. Therefore since God is the principle of perfection, imperfection must be traced to another cause. But there is no other except for matter. Therefore it must be that things are made from some sort of matter and not from nothing.

OBJ. 15. If something is made from nothing, it is from nothing either as from a subject, just as a statue is from bronze, or as from its opposite, just as a shaped thing is from something unshaped, or as from the composite, just as a statue is from unshaped bronze. But something cannot be from nothing as a subject, since non-being cannot be the matter of being. Nor [can it be from nothing] as from the composite, for thus non-being would be converted into being, just as unshaped bronze is converted into shaped bronze. This in turn would require that there be something common to being and non-being, which is impossible. Nor [can something come from nothing] as its opposite, since absolute non-being is more different from being than two beings of diverse genus are, and one of these cannot be made into the other. Shape, for example, cannot become color, except perhaps accidentally. Therefore something can in no way be made from nothing.

---

perfections present in creatures pre-exist in their surpassingly perfect creator. See "Thomas Aquinas on Our Knowledge of God," 91–95. In Q. 3 of the *De potentia,* Thomas weaves the two principles most closely together in the respondeo of article 8.

OBJ. 16. Everything which is accidentally is traced to that which is *per se*. But a thing is made from its opposite accidentally, and from a subject *per se*, as for example a statue is made accidentally from what is unshaped but *per se* from bronze, since to be unshaped is an accident of bronze. If therefore something were made from nothing, this would be accidentally. Therefore it is necessary that it be made *per se* from some subject, and so not made from nothing.

OBJ. 17. A maker gives being to that which is made. If, therefore, God makes a thing from nothing, God gives that thing being. Therefore, there must either be something which receives being or nothing. If nothing, then nothing is constituted in being by this act, and thus nothing is made. If, however, there is something which receives being, this will be distinct from God, since receiver and received are not the same. Therefore God makes from something pre-existing and thus not from nothing.

On the contrary (1) Genesis I says, In the beginning God created heaven and earth.[11] According to the Gloss,[12] to create is to make something from nothing. Therefore God can make something from nothing.

Further (2) Avicenna says that *an agent which acts accidentally* requires matter *on which to act.*[13] But God does not act accidentally, but rather his action is his substance. Therefore he does not require matter on which to act, and so is able to make something from nothing.

Again (3) Divine power is greater than natural power. But natural power makes a being from that which was in potency. The divine power, therefore, does something more, and makes from nothing.

I answer that we must firmly hold that God can and does make something from nothing. To make this evident we should understand that *every agent acts insofar as it is in act,*[14] and so it is necessary

11. Genesis 1:1.

12. Bede, *In Genesim* I 1.

13. Avicenna, *Liber de Philosophia Prima sive Scientia Divina,* VII 2.

14. I have been unable to determine a source text for this principle. The most promising possibility I can find is in Proposition 20 of the *Book of Causes.* There, while discussing the agent that acts as a creator, the author says, "it rules things through the mode in which it acts, and it acts only through its being" (Aquinas, *Commentary on the Book of Causes,* trans. V. A. Guagliardo, O.P., C. R. Hess, O.P., and R. C. Taylor [Washington D.C.: The Catholic University of America Press, 1996], 111). Earlier in the *De potentia,* Thomas argues, "it is in

that action be attributed to an agent according to the way in which it is in act. Now a natural thing is in act in a particular way, and this in two senses. First, in comparison to itself, because its whole substance is not in act, since this sort of thing is composed of matter and form. And because of this a natural thing does not act by its whole self, but by virtue of its form, through which it is in act. Second, in comparison with things which are in act, because no natural thing includes the acts and perfections of everything which is in act, but each has act confined to one genus and one species. And so it is that none of these acts [simply] as a being, but rather each acts as a particular being confined to this or that species, for *an agent produces its like.*[15] And so the action of a natural agent does not produce being absolutely, but determines pre-existing being to this or to that, as for example to the species of fire or whiteness or something of that sort. And because of this the natural agent acts by moving something, and so requires matter, which is the subject of change or motion. And so [the natural agent] cannot make something from nothing.

On the other hand, God is all act, both in comparison to himself, since he is pure act without any admixture of potency, and in comparison to things which are in act, since in him is found the perfection of every being as the most complete and first source of [those] beings. Thus, through his action he produces the whole subsistent being, without anything pre-existing, since he is the principle of all being and [acts] according to his whole being.[16] And because of this he is able to make something from nothing and this action of his is called creation.

And so the Book of Causes says that being is by way of creation, but life and the like are by way of form.[17] For the causation of being

---

the nature of every act to communicate itself as far as possible. Wherefore every agent acts forasmuch as it is in act: while to act is nothing else than to communicate as far as possible that whereby the agent is in act" (Q. 2, a. 1, resp. This is Fr. Shapcote's translation of the Marietti edition). W. Norris Clarke, S.J., cites this passage and analyzes it in juxtaposition with other crucial texts from Thomas, in the section of his *Person and Being* titled "Being as Active and Self-Communicative." *Person and Being* (Marquette University Press, 1993), 6–13.

15. See note 10.

16. *utpote qui est totius esse principium et secundum se totum.*

17. *Book of Causes,* Prop. 18. I am following Fr. Guagliardo et al. in translating *"per informationem"* as "by way of form" (*Commentary on the Book of Causes,* 111).

is to be traced entirely to the first universal cause, while the causation of all that is added to being or those things which specify being, pertains to secondary causes, which act by way of form, presupposing the effect of the first cause.[18] And so it is that no thing gives being except insofar as it participates in divine power. Because of this the Book of Causes says that the *noble soul* has a divine operation insofar as it gives being.[19]

AD 1. The Philosopher says that "nothing comes out of nothing" is a first principle or opinion of natural philosophers because the natural agent which they investigate acts only through motion, and so it is necessary that there be some subject of motion or change.[20] In a supernatural agent this is not necessary, as has been said above.

AD 2. Before the world was, it was possible for the world to come to be, but it is not necessary that some material thing existed as the ground of that potency. For [as] it is said in Metaphysics V, sometimes a thing is said to be possible *not with regard to potency* but because it involves no contradiction of terms, in the way that the possible is opposed to the impossible.[21] Therefore it is said that before the world was it was possible for the world to come to be, because there was no contradiction between the predicate and subject. Or it can be said that it was possible on account of the active potency of the agent, rather than some passive potency of matter. The philosopher uses this argument in Metaphysics VII regarding natural generation [when he argues] against the Platonists, who said separate forms are the principles of natural generation.[22]

18. *cause universalis.* Note that the medieval spelling abbreviates the diphthong "ae" to "e" so that where classical Latin would have "causae" the Leonine text has "cause."

19. This is a reference to *Book of Causes,* Prop. 3. However, the passage Thomas is citing does not say that the noble soul *"dat esse,"* as Thomas puts it here. After saying that the noble soul has a divine operation, the text goes on to specify, *"Operatio autem divina est quoniam ipsa praeparat naturam cum virtute quae est in ipsa a causa prima"* (*Super librum de causis expositio,* ed. H.-D. Saffrey [Fribourg, 1954], 17. Fr. Guagliardo translates: "The activity [of soul] is divine because soul provides for nature with the power present in it from the first cause" (*Commentary on the Book of Causes,* 19).

20. Aristotle, *Physics,* I 4, 187a29 and I 8, 191b13–17.

21. Aristotle, *Metaphysics,* V 12, 1019b28–32.

22. Aristotle, *Metaphysics,* VII 13, 1038b1–1039a22. For a fuller articulation of the point at issue in this reply, see article 14.

AD 3. Between being and absolute non-being there is always an infinite distance in some way, but not always in the same way. Sometimes it is infinite on both parts, as when non-being is compared to divine being, which is infinite, or if infinite whiteness were compared to infinite blackness. Sometimes however [the distance] is infinite only on one part, as when absolute non-being is compared to created being, which is finite, or if infinite blackness were compared to finite whiteness. Therefore it is impossible to pass from non-being to that being which is infinite, but it is possible to pass [from non-being] to that being which is finite, inasmuch as the distance from non-being to that being is determinate on one part, although there is no passage properly speaking, as there is in continuous movements through which one part passes after another.[23] In that sense, the infinite cannot in any way be crossed.

AD 4. When something comes from nothing, non-being or nothing is not a patient, but is the opposite of that which comes to be through the action. And in natural things the opposite is not a patient, except accidentally, but rather the subject is [a patient].

AD 5. If heat were separated from matter, it would indeed act without matter being required on the part of the agent, but not without the matter required on the part of the patient.

AD 6. "To be concluded" is in rational actions as "to be moved" is in natural actions, because, in concluding, reason moves from one thing to another and so just as every natural motion is from something, so is every rational conclusion. Indeed, just as understanding first principles, which is the starting point for any conclusion, is not concluded from something, so is creation, which is the starting point for all motion, is not from anything.

AD 7. When something is said to come from nothing, this has two senses, as Anselm makes plain in his Monologion.[24] For the negation conveyed by "nothing" can negate the preposition "from" or it can be included under that preposition. But if it negates the preposition, again this can be in two senses. First, when the negation bears on the whole and not only the preposition but also the verb is negated,

23. *quamvis non sit transitus proprie, sicut est in motibus continuis per quos transit pars post partem.*

24. Anselm, *Monologion,* 8.

and in this way something might be said to come to be from nothing because it does not come to be. In this way we say of a silent person that he speaks of nothing. And in this sense we can say of God that he comes to be from nothing, since he in no way comes to be, although this way of speaking is not customary. The other sense is when the verb remains affirmed and the negation bears only on the preposition, and thus something might be said to come to be from nothing because it indeed comes to be but there is no pre-existing thing from which it comes to be, just as we say someone grieves for nothing because his grief has no cause. And in this way in creation something is said to come to be from nothing. If, however, the preposition includes the negation, then there are two senses, one true and the other false. It is certainly false if the preposition conveys the sense of cause, for non-being can in no way be the cause of being. But it is true if it conveys only order, as when it is said that something comes to be from nothing because it comes to be after nothing, which also is true in creation. When Boethius says that there is no order of non-being to being,[25] this refers to the order of definite proportion or the order of real relation, which cannot exist between being and non-being, as Avicenna says.[26]

AD 8. The definition cited applies to natural active potency.

AD 9. God produces things not from natural necessity but from the order of his wisdom, and so the diversity of things need not be from matter but from the order of divine wisdom, which established diverse natures to complete the universe.

AD 10. When something comes to be from nothing, its being does begin in some instant, but its non-being is not in that instant or in any real instant but only in an imagined one. For just as beyond the universe there is no real dimension but only imaginary dimension, in terms of which we can say that God can make something beyond the universe at this or that distance from the universe, in this way before the beginning of the world there was not any real time but only imaginary, and in that sense it is possible to imagine a last instant of its non-being. It does not follow that between these two in-

25. Again, this may be a reference to Boethius, *De Hebdomadibus,* Axiom 4.
26. Avicenna, *Liber de Philosophia Prima sive Scientia Divina,* III 10.

stants there is an intermediate time, since real time and imaginary time are not continuous.

AD 11. That which comes to be from nothing is simultaneously being made and already made. And the same is true in all instantaneous changes, as for example the air is being illuminated and is illuminated simultaneously. For in such things, having been made means being made inasmuch as the thing is from the first instant of its being made.

We may also say that that which is made from nothing is said to be being made when it is already made, not in terms of motion, which is from one point to another, but in terms of outflow[27] from the agent into the thing made. For these two are seen in natural generation, namely transition from one point to another and outflow from agent into thing made, of which only the latter is proper to creation.

AD 12. Neither matter nor form nor accident is properly said to be made; rather what is made is the subsisting thing. For since to be made terminates in being, to be made properly belongs to that to which being properly[28] belongs, namely the subsisting thing. And so neither matter nor form nor accident is properly said to be created, but to be concreated, while a subsisting thing, whatever it is, is properly created. Nevertheless, as long as it is not taken too far, we might say that prime matter bears a likeness to God insofar as it partakes of being. For just as a stone is like God insofar as it is a being, although it has no intellect as God does, in this way prime matter bears a likeness to God insofar as it is a being, [though] not a being in act. For being is in a certain way common to potency and act.

And so the response to the thirteenth objection is also made clear: for properly speaking there is an idea not of matter but of the composite, since the idea is the form by which something is made. Nevertheless, there can be said to be some idea of matter insofar as matter in some way imitates the divine essence.

AD 14. If one creature is of greater worth than another, it is not necessarily the case that the creature of lesser worth has some im-

27. *effluxum.*
28. *per se.*

perfection, for imperfection denotes the lack of something which is natural or due to a thing. And so even in glory, although one of the saints may be above another, none are imperfect. But if some imperfection is in creatures, it is not necessary that it be from God or from matter, but from the fact that the creature is from nothing.

AD 15. Something is said to be made from nothing [as] from its opposite, in terms of one of the senses explained above. It does not follow, however, that a being of one genus may be made into a being of another genus, like color being made into shape, because being and non-being cannot exist simultaneously, while color and shape can. But that from which something is made must be in contact with the thing made, as is said in Physics I,[29] yet they are not simultaneous.

AD 16. If "from" denotes cause, something cannot be made from its opposite except accidentally, by relation to a subject.[30] But if it denotes order, then something is made from its opposite even *per se*. Thus even privation is said to be a principle of becoming but not of being. In this way something is said to be made from nothing, as was said above.

AD 17. God simultaneously gives being and produces that which receives being. And so it is not necessary that he act with something pre-existing.

29. This may be a reference to a discussion in Aristotle's *Physics*, III 2–3, 202a2–202b9.

30. *ratione scilicet subjecti.*

ARTICLE 2

The second thing to be asked is whether creation is a change. And it seems that it is.[1]

OBJ. 1. The word "change" denotes that one thing comes after another, as is plain in Physics V.[2] But this is true of creation, for being comes after non-being. Therefore creation is a change.

OBJ. 2. Everything which is made, comes to be in some way from non-being, since that which [already] is does not come to be. Therefore just as generation (through which a thing is made with respect to part of its substance) is related to the privation of form (which is a kind of non-being), so is creation (through which a thing is made with respect to its whole substance) related to absolute non-being. But privation properly speaking is one term[3] of generation. Therefore, absolute non-being also properly speaking is a term of creation. And so creation properly speaking is a change.

OBJ. 3. The greater the distance between the terms, the greater the change. Indeed, the change from white to black is greater than the change from white to pale. But absolute non-being is further from being than contraries are from each other, or than relative non-being is from being. Therefore, since transition from contrary to contrary or from relative non-being to being is a change, much more is creation, the transition from absolute non-being to being, a change.

OBJ. 4. That which is not *in the same condition now as it was before*[4] is moved or changed. But that which is created is not in the same condition now as it was before, since before it was absolute non-being and then it became a being. Therefore that which is created is moved or changed.

OBJ. 5. That which *passes from potency to act*[5] is changed. Now that which is created passes from potency to act, since before creation it

1. For parallel discussions of whether creation is a change, see *ST* I Q. 45, a. 2, ad 2 and *SCG* II 17.

2. Aristotle, *Physics*, V 1, 224b35–225a3.

3. *terminus*.

4. I have been unable to trace this reference.

5. Cf. Aristotle, *Physics*, III 1, 201a10–201b5.

was only in the potency of the maker, but now it is in act. Therefore that which is created is changed, and so creation is a change.

On the contrary, according to the Philosopher in the Categories, *there are six kinds of motion*[6] or change, but none of these is creation, as is plain by taking them one by one. Therefore creation is not a change.

I answer that every change requires some one thing common to both terms of the change. For if the opposing terms of a change had nothing in common, then it could not be called a change from one to the other. For the words "change" and "transition" signify that some one thing is otherwise now than before. Indeed the terms of a change are not themselves incompatible (as is required in relation to their being the terms of a change) except in reference to one thing. For two contraries, if referred to different subjects, may exist simultaneously.

Therefore it sometimes happens that there is one common actually existing subject of both terms of a change, and then it can be properly called motion, as for example in alteration or in increase and decrease or in local motion. For in all of these motions some subject, [while] actually remaining one and the same, is moved from one contrary to another.

Sometimes both terms have the same common subject, but instead of an actual being, it is only a potential being, as happens in simple generation and corruption. For the subject of the substantial being and its privation is prime matter, which is not actual being.[7] Hence neither generation nor corruption is properly called motion, but each is a kind of change.

And sometimes there is no common subject existing actually or potentially, but there is one continuous period of time, in the first part of which is one contrary and in the second the other, as when we say that this is made from that, i.e. after that, as for example noon comes from the morning. But this is not properly called change, ex-

6. Aristotle, *Categories*, 14, 15a14.

7. For a discussion of prime matter in the context of contemporary understanding of matter, see W. Norris Clarke, S.J., *The One and the Many: A Contemporary Thomistic Metaphysics* (Notre Dame: University of Notre Dame Press, 2001), 145–47. Also see Joseph Bobik, *Aquinas on Matter and Form and the Elements* (Notre Dame: University of Notre Dame Press, 1998), 3–6, 25–33.

cept metaphorically speaking, insofar as we imagine time to be the subject of those things which occur in time.

In creation, however, there is nothing common in any of the ways we have discussed. For there is no common subject existing either actually or potentially. And there is no continuous time when we speak of the creation of the universe, for before the world there was no time. However, we do find something in common, but only on the imaginary level, namely when we imagine one common time when the world was not and afterwards when the world had been brought into being. For just as we can imagine some magnitude beyond the universe even though there is none in reality, so is it possible to imagine some time before the beginning of the world, even though there was none. And so, properly speaking, creation does not in truth have the nature[8] of a change, but only on the level of imagination, when we speak not properly but metaphorically.

AD 1. The word "change" denotes that one thing comes after another in some one thing, as was said above. But this is not the case in creation.

AD 2. In generation, through which something is made with respect to part of its substance, there is some common subject of privation and form, even if it is not actually existent. And so just as two terms are properly found [in generation], so also is transition properly found there. But these are not found in creation, as has been said.

AD 3. Where there is greater distance between the terms there is greater change, if there is a single subject.

AD 4. That which is not in the same condition now as it was before is changed, if there is a consistent subject. Otherwise absolute non-being would be changed, since absolute non-being is neither in the same condition now as it was before nor in a different condition. But for there to be a change there must be some one thing which is in a different condition now than it was in before.

AD 5. Passive potency, not active, is the subject of change. And so that which passes from passive potency to act is changed, but not that which proceeds from active potency. Thus the objection proves nothing.

8. *rationem*.

ARTICLE 3

The third thing to be asked is whether creation is something real in the creature, and, if it is, what it is. And it seems that it is not something real in the creature.[1]

OBJ. 1. For as the Book of Causes says, *anything which is received in something is in it according to the mode of the receiver.*[2] But God's creative action is received in absolute non-being, since in creating God makes something from nothing. Therefore creation posits nothing real in the creature.

OBJ. 2. Everything that is real[3] is either the creator or the created. But creation is not the creator, or it would be eternal. Neither is it a creature, since then creation would need to be created by another creation, and so on to infinity. Therefore, creation is not something real.

OBJ. 3. Everything that is is either a substance or an accident. But creation is not a substance, since it is neither matter nor form nor composite, as can easily be made plain. Neither indeed is it an accident, since an accident follows its subject, while creation is naturally prior to the created, which alone can be posited a subject. Therefore, creation is not something real.

1. For parallel discussions of the question whether creation is something really or only logically in the creature or in God, see *ST* I Q. 13, a. 7 and Q. 45, a. 3 and *SCG* II 11–14.

2. *Book of Causes,* Prop. 10. See also Props. 12, 19, 20, 22, and 24. This metaphysical principle is extremely important for Aquinas. See John F. Wippel's "Thomas Aquinas and the Axiom 'What Is Received Is Received according to the Mode of the Receiver," in *A Straight Path: Studies in Medieval Philosophy and Culture,* ed. R. Link-Salinger (Washington, D.C.: The Catholic University of America Press, 1988) 279–89; reprinted in *Metaphysical Themes in Thomas Aquinas II,* 113–22. For a comprehensive collection of the texts in which Aquinas uses this principle, see John Tomarchio's "Four Indices for the Thomistic Principle Quod recipitur in aliquo est in eo per modum recipientis," *Medieval Studies* 60 (1998): 315–67. Also see his "The Modus Principle in the Writings of St. Thomas Aquinas," Ph.D. thesis (The Catholic University of America, Department of Philosophy, 1997). For a study of Thomas' use of the word "mode," see Tomarchio, "Aquinas's Division of Being according to Modes of Existing," *Review of Metaphysics* 54 (2001): 585–613.

3. I am following Fr. Shapcote in thus translating "omne quod est in rerum natura."

OBJ. 4. As generation is to the thing generated, so is creation to the thing created. But the thing generated is not the subject of generation, but rather its term, for its subject is prime matter, as is said in On Generation I.[4] Therefore neither is the created thing the subject of creation. Nor can it be said that its subject is some matter, since the created thing is not created from any matter. Therefore creation does not have any subject, and thus it is not an accident. Moreover, it is clear that it is not a substance. Therefore it is not a real thing.

OBJ. 5. If creation is something real, then since it is not a change, as was said above,[5] it seems most likely to be a relation. But it is not a relation, since it cannot belong to any of the species of relations: for absolute being is neither superior nor subject nor equal to absolute non-being, from which creation proceeds. Therefore, creation is not something real.

OBJ. 6 If creation implies a relation of the created being to God, from whom it has being, then since this relation would remain in the creature always, not only when it begins to be, it follows that creation would be not only when the thing begins to be, but throughout its existence. And thus something would be continually created, which seems absurd. Therefore creation is not a relation, and thus the same conclusion follows.

OBJ. 7. Every relation which is really in existing things derives from something which is distinct from that relation itself, as for example equality is distinct from quantity and likeness is distinct from quality. Therefore, if creation were some relation really existing in the creature, it would necessarily be distinct from that from which the relation derives. But this is what is received through creation. It follows, therefore, that creation itself would not be received through creation, and thus it would follow that it would be something uncreated, which is impossible.

OBJ. 8. Every change is reduced to that genus in which it terminates, as for example alteration is reduced to quality and increase to quantity. And because of this it is said in Physics III that there are as many species of motion as there are of being.[6] Now creation termi-

4. Aristotle, *On Generation and Corruption,* I 1, 314b27.
5. In article 2.
6. Aristotle, *Physics,* III 1, 201a7.

nates in substance but nevertheless it cannot be said that it is in the genus of substance, as was said above.[7] Therefore it does not seem that it is something real.

On the contrary (1) if creation is not some thing, then neither is anything really created. But this is clearly false. Therefore creation is something real.

Further (2) God is the lord[8] of the creature because he produces it in being by creating it. But dominion is a certain relation really existing in the creature. Therefore much more is creation.

I answer that some have said that creation is something real, a medium or mean between creator and creature.[9] And, since the mean is neither of the extremes, it would follow that *creation would be neither the creator nor the creature.*[10] But this was judged to be erroneous by the masters, since everything that in any way exists has its being only from God and thus *is a creature.*[11]

And so others have said that creation itself does not posit anything real on the part of the creature. But this also seems unreasonable. For in all those things which are referred to each other by their names [and] in which one depends on the other but not conversely, in the one which depends on the other a real relation is found, while in the other there is only a logical relation, as is clear in knowledge and the thing known, as the Philosopher says in Metaphysics V.[12] But the creature is referred to the creator by its name, and the creature depends on the creator and not conversely. Whence it must be that the relation by which the creature is referred to the creator is real, but in God it is only a logical relation. And this the Master expressly says in Sentences I, distinction 30.[13]

7. In obj. 3.

8. *dominus.*

9. *quidam dixerunt creationem aliquid esse in rerum natura, medium inter creatorem et creaturam.*

10. I have been unable to trace this reference.

11. I have been unable to trace this reference.

12. Aristotle, *Metaphysics,* V 15, 1021a27–31.

13. Peter Lombard, *The Sentences,* I, d. 30, ch. 1. Many have found this idea challenging and provocative. See Susan Selner-Wright, "Aquinas on Acts of Creation and Procreation," *National Catholic Bioethics Quarterly* 3 (2003): 707–16; Martin J. de Nys, "Aquinas and Kierkegaard on the Relation between God and Creatures," *American Catholic Philosophical Quarterly* 75 (2001): 389–407; Michael-Thomas Liske, "Kann Gott reale Beziehungen zu den Geschopfen

And so we must say that creation can be taken actively or passively. If it is taken actively, then it designates God's action, which is his essence, with relation to the creature, which is not a real relation but only a logical one. But if it is taken passively, since creation properly speaking is not a change, as has already been said above, it cannot be said that it is something in the genus of passion but [rather it is something] in the genus of relation.

This can be made more clear as follows. In every true change or motion we find a sort of twofold process: one from one term of motion to the other, as for example from whiteness to blackness; the other from agent to patient, as from the maker to the thing made. But these processes are not the same during the motion itself and when the term has been reached. For during the motion itself, that which is moved recedes from one term of motion and approaches the other. But this is not the case when the term has been reached, for at that point [the thing] begins to be what it has been moving toward.[14] This is clear in that which is moved from whiteness to blackness, since at the term of the motion it no longer approaches blackness but begins to be black. Similarly, while it is in motion the patient or thing made is being changed by the agent, but when the term has been reached it is no longer being changed by the agent, but the thing made attains a certain relation to the agent, inasmuch as it has being from it and is similar to it in some way, as for example at the term of human generation the child attains membership in the family.[15] But as was said above, creation cannot be taken as a motion

haben? Logisch-theologische Betrachtungen im Anschluss an Thomas von Aquin," *Theologie und Philosophie* 68 (1993): 208–28; Montague Brown, "The Relation between God and Human Beings: The Difference It Makes to Human Happiness," *Proceedings of the American Catholic Philosophical Association* 66 (1992): 163–73; Frederick D. Wilhelmsen, "Creation as a Relation in St. Thomas Aquinas," *Modern Schoolman* 56 (1979): 107–33. Wilhelmsen and I both discuss the connection between the distinction of logical from real relation and the distinction of immanent from transitive action. In Wilhelmsen, see esp. p. 111. Here in Q. 3 of the *De potentia,* Thomas takes up the distinction between immanent and transitive action in article 15, where he connects these modes of action to modes of relation.

14. *set tunc iam incipit mobile esse in ultimo termino motus.* Note that these words do not appear in the Marietti edition, which skips them and moves straight on to the example.

15. *consequitur natus filiationem.* This example must be understood in light of

which precedes the term of the motion, but is understood as the accomplished fact. Whence creation itself implies neither an approach to being nor a change worked by the creator, but only a beginning of being and a relation to the creator, from whom it has being. And so creation is really nothing other than a certain relation to God with newness of being.

AD 1. In creation it is not non-being which receives the divine action but that which is created, as was said above.

AD 2. Creation taken actively signifies the divine essence with a certain relation understood, and thus in this sense created.[16] But taken passively, as was said, it signifies a certain real relation according to the mode of change because of the newness or beginning that it implies. Moreover this relation is a kind of creature, taking the word "creature" in the general sense of "anything which is from God." Nor must this proceed to infinity, since the relation of creation is not referred to God by another real relation, but by itself: for no relation is referred by another relation, as Avicenna says in his Metaphysics.[17] But if we take the word "creature" in a stricter sense to include only that which subsists (which properly speaking is [what is] made and created since it properly has being), then the relation mentioned is not something created, but concreated, just as properly speaking it is not a being but something inherent. And it is likewise with all accidents.

AD 3. This relation is an accident, and considered in its being, as inhering in a subject, is posterior to the created thing just as an accident is posterior to its subject both logically and naturally. It is not, however, the sort of accident which is caused by the principles of its subject. But if it is considered according to its nature,[18] just as the relation mentioned arises from the action of an agent, so is it in a certain way prior to the subject, as is the divine action itself which is its proximate cause.

Thomas' theory of delayed hominization, which he develops at length in article 9.

16. *creatio active accepta significat divinam essenciam cum quadam relatione cointellecta, et sic est ibi creatum.*

17. Avicenna, *Liber de Philosophia Prima sive Scientia Divina,* III 10.

18. *rationem.*

AD 4. In generation there is both a change and a relation by which the generated thing is referred to the generator. Therefore, with regard to change, its subject is not the generated thing itself, but its matter. But with regard to relation, its subject is the generated thing itself. In creation, however, there is relation but not change properly speaking, as has been said,[19] and so the cases are not the same.

AD 5. This relation is not to be understood as one of being to non-being, since such a relation cannot be real, as Avicenna says.[20] Rather it is [a relation] of created being to the creator, whence it is plain that it is a relation of subjection.

AD 6. Creation implies this relation with newness of being, whence it is not necessary that a thing is being created whenever it exists, though it is always related to God. Nevertheless, it would not be unfitting to say that, just as air is being illuminated by the sun as long as it is light, so is the creature being made by God as long as it has being, as Augustine says in On the Literal Interpretation of Genesis.[21] But this is only a semantic distinction, since the word "creation" can be understood with newness [of being] or without it.

AD 7. That from which the relation of creation is derived is principally the subsisting thing, which is distinct from the relation of creation itself, which is itself created, not principally but secondarily, because it is concreated.

AD 8. Motion is reduced to the genus of its term insofar as there is a process from potency to act. For in motion itself the term of motion is in potency, and potency and act are reduced to the same genus. But in creation there is no passage from potency to act, and so the cases are not the same.

19. In article 2.
20. Avicenna, *Liber de Philosophia Prima sive Scientia Divina,* III 10.
21. Augustine, *De Genesi ad litteram libri XII,* VIII 12.

ARTICLE 4

The fourth thing to be asked is whether the power or even the act of creation is communicable to another, that is, to a creature. And it seems that it is.[1]

OBJ. 1. For things are ordered to their ultimate end in the same mode and order in which they come from their first principle, since one thing is [both] their first principle and ultimate end. But lower creatures are ordered to God as their end through mediating higher creatures because, as Dionysius says, *it is the law of the divine to draw* the last things to himself *through the first.*[2] Therefore lower creatures also come from the first principle by creation through mediating higher creatures, and thus the act of creation is communicated to a creature.

OBJ. 2. That which can be communicated to a creature without taking it beyond the limits of a creature is communicable to a creature by the power of the creator, who is even able to make new kinds of creatures. But if the ability to create were communicated to a creature, it would not push it beyond the limits of a creature. Therefore the ability to create is communicable to a creature. The proof of the second premise is as follows. To push beyond the limits of a creature is to posit something of it which is incompatible with the notion[3] of a creature. But the ability to create is not incompatible with the notion of a creature except for the infinite power which seems to be required for creation. But it seems that this is not [in fact] required, for however distant something is from one opposite, it partakes to that extent in the nature of the other. Thus the further a thing is from being black, the more white it is. Now, created being shares in the nature of being in a finite way, and so it is a finite distance from absolute non-being. But to bring something to be from a finite distance does not demonstrate infinite power. And so it follows that the act of

1. For a parallel discussion of this question, see *ST* I Q. 45, a. 5 and *SCG* II 21.
2. Pseudo-Dionysius, *The Celestial Hierarchy,* 5.
3. *rationi.*

creation can be an act of a finite power. Thus the ability to create is not incompatible with the notion of a creature and it does not push it beyond the limits of a creature.

OBJ. 3. Regarding what was said above, that however distant something is from one opposite, it partakes to that extent in the other, it might be said that this applies to those opposites in which both are natures, as contraries are, but not to those in which only one is a nature, as is the case in privation and habit or affirmation and negation. But on the contrary, this proposition applies to contraries because of their distance from each other, which exists inasmuch as they are opposites. But the cause and root of opposition in contraries is the opposition of affirmation and negation, as is proved in Metaphysics IV.[4] Therefore, the proposition applies especially to affirmation and negation.

OBJ. 4. According to Augustine's On the Literal Interpretation of Genesis, things are said to be made in three ways: in the Word, in the angelic intelligence, and in their proper nature,[5] on account of which in Genesis 1 it is said, *He said, let it be made, and it was made.*[6] Now the way in which things are said to be made in the angelic intelligence is intermediate between the other two ways. Therefore it seems that created things proceed into their proper natures from the Word by means of mediating angelic intelligence, and so it seems that things are created by mediating angels.

OBJ. 5. Nothing and something are more distant than something and being because nothing and something have nothing in common, while something is part of being. Now in creating, God makes what was nothing become something and consequently [he makes] no potency become some potency. Therefore much more is he able to make some determinate potency, like the potency of a creature, become omnipotence, which includes the power to create. And so the power to create can be communicated to a creature.

OBJ. 6. Spiritual light is more noble and powerful than corporeal light. But corporeal light multiplies itself. Therefore an angel, who is spiritual light according to Augustine's On the Literal Interpretation

4. Aristotle, *Metaphysics,* IV 6, 1011b17–20.
5. Augustine, *De Genesi ad litteram libri XII,* II 8.
6. Genesis 1.

of Genesis,[7] is able to multiply itself. But this cannot be done except by creating. Therefore an angel is able to create.

OBJ. 7. Substantial forms are not generated because only the composite is generated, as the Philosopher proves in Metaphysics VII.[8] Therefore substantial forms cannot be brought into being except through creation. But created nature disposes matter to form. Therefore something [i.e. created nature] operates ministerially in creation, and so it can be communicated to a creature that it have a role[9] in creation.

OBJ. 8. The work of justification is more noble than the work of creation, since grace is superior to nature, whence Augustine also says that to justify the sinner is greater than to create heaven and earth.[10] But the creature renders service[11] in the justification of the sinner, for the priest is said to act as a minister in justifying or forgiving sins. Therefore, much more is the creature able to render service in the act of creation.

OBJ. 9. A made thing must be like the agent, as is proved in Metaphysics VII.[12] But the corporeal creature is like God in neither species nor genus. Therefore it cannot proceed from God through creation except through the mediation of some creature which is like it at least in genus. And so it seems that corporeal things are created by God through mediating higher creatures.

OBJ. 10. In the Book of Causes it is said that that *which is merely intelligence receives from the first goodnesses which proceed from the first cause only through a mediating* higher *intelligence.*[13] But being itself is one of the first goods. Therefore the second intelligence does not receive being from God except through the mediating first intelligence,

7. Augustine, *De Genesi ad litteram libri XII,* IV 22.
8. Aristotle, *Metaphysics,* VII 8 and 9.
9. *ministerium.*
10. Augustine, *Tractates on the Gospel of John,* Tractate 72, no. 3.
11. *exhibet ministerium.*
12. The most likely reference for this in *Metaphysics* VII seems to be ch. 8, 1033b30. The Latin here is "oportet factum simile esse agenti," which is a corollary of the principle of similitude: "omne agens agit simile sibi." See article 1, note 10.
13. *"que est intelligencia tantum non recipit ex bonitatibus primis ... nisi mediante intelligencia superiori." Book of Causes,* Prop. 19. I am here following the translation of Fr. Guagliardo et al., *Commentary on the Book of Causes,* 116.

and so it seems that God communicates the act of creation to a creature.

OBJ. 11. In the same book it is said that *an intelligence knows what is beneath it according to the mode of its substance* insofar as *it is the cause of it.*[14] But one intelligence knows another which is beneath it. Therefore, it is its cause. But since [the lower intelligence] is not composed it is caused through creation. Therefore, an intelligence can create.

OBJ. 12. In his book On the Immortality of the Soul, Augustine says that spiritual creatures communicate species and being to corporeal creatures,[15] and so it seems that corporeal creatures are created through mediating spiritual creatures.

OBJ. 13. There are two kinds of knowledge, one from which things derive, and another which is derived from things. Now an angel's knowledge of corporeal things is not derived from things, since he does not have the sensitive powers through whose mediation knowledge of sensible things reaches the intellect. Therefore, he knows things with the sort of knowledge from which things derive, which is like the divine knowledge. Therefore, just as God through his knowledge is the cause of things, so also does the knowledge of the angel seem to be a cause of things.

OBJ. 14. Things come into being in two ways: one by passing from pure non-being into being, which happens through creation; and the other by passing from potency into act. Now material power, which is the power of natural things, can produce things in the second way, namely by drawing things from potency into act. Immaterial power, such as that of the angel, is more powerful, and so it can produce something in being in the first way, which belongs to the greater power, that is, [by drawing it] from pure non-being into being, which is to create. And so it seems that an angel is able to create.

OBJ. 15. There is nothing greater than the infinite. But an infinite power is required in order to educe something from nothing into being; otherwise nothing would prevent creatures from creating. Therefore, no power can be greater than this one, and so to make a creature from nothing and give it the power to create is no

14. *Book of Causes,* Prop. 8.
15. Augustine, *The Immortality of the Soul,* 16.

more than to create. But God can do the latter; therefore he can also do the former.

OBJ. 16. The greater the opposition of the patient to the agent, the greater the difficulty of the action. But a contrary puts up more opposition than non-being, for non-being is not able to act as a contrary can. Therefore, since a creature is able to make something from its contrary, it seems it would be much more able to make something from nothing, which is to create. Therefore a creature is able to create.

On the contrary (1) being and non-being are infinitely distant. Now it requires an infinite power to operate at an infinite distance. Therefore, to create requires an infinite power and thus it cannot be communicated to a creature.

Further (2) according to Dionysius' book On the Celestial Hierarchy, the higher creatures, such as the angels, *are divided into essence, power, and operation*[16] from which we can conclude that no power of a creature is its essence, and thus no creature acts by its whole self, since that by which a thing acts is it power. But insofar as an agent acts, an effect is produced. Therefore, no creature can produce an effect in its entirety, and so it cannot create, but always presupposes matter in its action.

Further (3) in On the Trinity III, Augustine says that angels, whether good or bad, are not able to be the creators of anything.[17] But of all creatures, the angels are the most noble. Much less, therefore, can any other creature create.

Further (4) it belongs to the same power to create and to conserve creatures in being. But creatures cannot be conserved in being except by divine power, at the withdrawal of which they would immediately cease to be, according to Augustine's On the Literal Interpretation of Genesis IV.[18] Therefore things cannot be created except by divine power.

Further (5) that which is proper to one thing cannot also be proper to another. But to create is commonly said to be proper to God. Therefore, to create cannot belong to another.

16. Pseudo-Dionysius, *The Celestial Hierarchy,* 11, no. 12.
17. Augustine, *The Trinity,* III 8.
18. Augustine, *De Genesi ad litteram libri XII,* IV 12.

I answer that certain philosophers held that God created lower creatures through the mediation of higher creatures, as is plain in the Book of Causes, in Avicenna's Metaphysics, and in Algazel.[19] They were led to this conclusion through supposing that *from one simple being only one being*[20] can be immediately produced, and that by the mediation of that being, a multitude of things proceeded from the one first being. They spoke thus as though God acted from natural necessity, whereby from one simple thing only one [other] thing can come.[21]

We, on the other hand, hold that things proceed from God by way of knowledge and intelligence, whereby a multitude of things can proceed immediately from the one first and simple God, inasmuch as his wisdom contains all things. Hence according to the Catholic faith we hold that God immediately created all spiritual substances and corporeal matter, and deem it heresy to say that anything was created by an angel or by any other creature. Wherefore Damascene declares: Whosoever shall say that an angel created anything, let him be anathema.[22]

Certain Catholic writers, however, have maintained that, although no creature can create, it could be communicated to a creature that through its service[23] God create something. The Master maintains this in Distinction 5, Book 4 of the Sentences.[24] Some on the other hand hold that the creative act cannot in any sense be communicated to a creature, and this is the more common opinion.

In order to make this point clear, we must observe that creation

19. In the *Book of Causes*, see Props. 3 and 9; for Avicenna, *Liber de Philosophia Prima sive Scientia Divina*, IX 4; for Algazel, *Tahâfot al-falâsifat* (*The Incoherence of the Philosophers*).

20. On the sources of this principle, see Wayne Hankey, *"Ab uno simplici non est nisi unum,"* in *Divine Creation in Ancient, Medieval, and Early Modern Thought*, ed. M. Treschow et al. (Leiden: Brill, 2007), 316–28. Also see A. Hyman, "From What Is One and Simple Only What Is One and Simple Can Come," in *Neoplatonism and Jewish Thought*, ed. L. E. Goodman, Studies in Neoplatonism 7 (Albany: State University of New York Press, 1992), 111–35.

21. Hankey examines the connection Avicenna draws between the *"ab uno simplici"* principle and his characterization of God as necessitated in *"Ab uno simplici non est nisi unum,"* 323–28.

22. John Damascene, *Exposition of the Orthodox Faith*, II 3.

23. *ministerium*.

24. Peter Lombard, *The Sentences*, IV, d. 5, ch. 3.

denotes the first act whereby things are brought into being, and so it requires no pre-existing matter or previous agency, which are the only causes that are pre-requisite for [subsequent] action. For the form of the thing generated is the term of the generator's action, and it is also the end of generation which, with respect to its being, does not precede but follows the action. Now it is clear from its very definition that creation does not presuppose matter, since to be created is to come from nothing. And that it does not presuppose a previous active cause is clear when Augustine proves in On the Trinity III that the angels cannot create because they work by means of nature's implanted seeds, which are the active forces of nature.[25] Accordingly, if creation is taken in this strict sense, it is evident that creation is proper only to the first agent, since a second cause does not act save through the influence[26] of the first: so that every action of a second cause presupposes that of the [first] active cause.

Nor did the philosophers maintain that angels or intelligences create, except through a divine power existing in them, in the sense that a second cause can have a twofold action, one proceeding from its own nature, the other from the power of a prior cause. For it is not possible that a second cause by its own power be the principle of being as such. This belongs to the first cause, since the order of effects follows the order of causes. Now the first of all effects is being itself, which is presupposed by all other effects, and which does not presuppose any other effect.[27] It must follow that only the first cause gives being as such by its own power, and whatever other cause gives being does so insofar as the power and operation of the first cause is in it, not by its own power. Thus an instrument performs an in-

25. Augustine, *The Trinity,* III 8.

26. *influencia.* Thomas clearly has the teaching of the *Liber de causis* in mind here (cf. Prop. 1). In Fr. Guagliardo's translation of Thomas' *Commentary on the Book of Causes, "influencia"* is usually translated as "infusion," and only occasionally as "influence." I have chosen the latter because it highlights the connection to the Neoplatonic notion of emanation as it is transformed in the *Book of Causes* into the dual notions of creation and influence. On this see Leo Sweeney, S.J., "Doctrine of Creation in *Liber de Causis*" in *An Etienne Gilson Tribute,* ed. C. J. O'Neil (Milwaukee: Marquette University Press, 1959), 280–82. For Fr. Guagliardo's reasons for translating *"influencia"* as he does, see Thomas' *Commentary,* xxxiv.

27. *Book of Causes,* Prop. 4.

strumental operation not by the power of its own nature but by the power of the one who moves it. And thus natural heat engenders living flesh by the power of the soul, while by the power of its own nature it merely heats and dissolves.

In this sense then, certain philosophers have held that the first intelligences create the second in that they give them being by the power of the first cause existing in them. For being is by creation, while goodness, life, and so forth are by way of form, as stated in the Book of Causes.[28] This was the foundation of idolatry, in that divine worship was accorded to created substances as though they were the creators of other things. Even the Master holds that this [power to create] is communicable to a creature, not however by its own power, as if it were the source, but ministerially, as an instrument.[29] But if we look into the question carefully, it will be clear that this is impossible. For the action of a thing, even when it is acting as an instrument, must arise from that thing's power. And since the power of every creature is finite, no creature can possibly create anything, not even as an instrument, since creation requires infinite strength in the power from which it proceeds. This is made clear by the five following arguments.

The first is based on the fact that the power of a maker is proportionate to the distance between the thing made and the opposite thing from which it is made. Thus the colder a thing is, and therefore the more distant it is from being hot, the greater will be the strength of the heat required to make that cold thing hot. Now absolute non-being is infinitely distant from being, because non-being is further distant from any particular being than any being is from another, however far apart any beings may be. And consequently something could produce being from absolute non-being only by means of infinite power.

The second reason is that the way a made thing is made is in accord with the way the maker acts. Now the agent acts inasmuch as it is in act: wherefore that alone acts by its whole self which is wholly in act, and this belongs to none but the infinite act who is the first

28. *Book of Causes,* Prop. 18.
29. Peter Lombard, *The Sentences,* IV, d. 5, ch. 3.

act. And consequently only something with infinite power can make a thing with respect to its whole substance.

The third reason is that since every accident must be in a subject, and the subject of an action is the recipient of that action, only that agent whose action is not an accident but its very substance requires no recipient matter when it makes a thing. Only God is such an agent, and therefore he alone can create.

The fourth reason is that because all second causes derive their action from the first cause, as is proved in the Book of Causes,[30] it follows that mode and order are imposed on all second agents by the first agent, while neither mode nor order is imposed on [the first agent] by another. Now, since the mode of an action depends on the matter which receives the action of the agent, the first agent alone will be competent to act without presupposing matter from another agent, and to provide matter for all second agents.

The fifth argument is a reduction to absurdity. The power of something which reduces a thing from potency to act is proportionate to the distance between the potency and the act; the further the potentiality is from the act, the greater is the power required. Hence if there were some finite power which effected something without any presupposed potentiality, there would be some proportion between it and that active power that educes a thing from potentiality to act; and thus there would be proportion between no potentiality and some potentiality, which is impossible. For there is no proportion between non-being and being, as is held in Physics IV.[31] We conclude therefore that no power of a creature can create something, either by its own strength or as the instrument of another.

AD 1. In drawing things to their end, those things which conduce to the end already exist, and so it is possible for a creature to cooperate with God in drawing something to its last end. But nothing already exists in the universal eduction of things into being, and so the cases are not the same.

AD 2. Nothing prevents our imagining a distance which is infinite <on both parts or infinite> on one part and finite on the other.

30. *Book of Causes,* Prop. 1.

31. Thomas seems to be inferring this principle from what Aristotle says in *Physics,* IV 8, at 215a10 and 216a11.

We imagine a distance infinite on both parts when both of the opposites are infinite, for instance if there were infinite heat and cold. But [we imagine a distance which is infinite only] on one part when one is finite and the other infinite, as for example if there were infinite heat and finite cold. Therefore, the distance of an infinite being from absolute non-being is infinite on both parts, while the distance of a finite being from absolute non-being is infinite only on one part, but nevertheless it requires infinite active power.

The third objection we concede, for it makes no difference whether both opposites are natures or only one.

AD 4. Things are said to be made in the angelic intelligence only in terms of knowledge, not in terms of operative power. And so things are not produced by God by means of mediating angels; rather, angels merely have knowledge of creation.

AD 5. Something is said to be impossible for someone to do not only because of the distance of the extremes, but also because it is entirely impossible to do. We might say for example that God cannot be made from any body, because it is entirely impossible for God to be made. It should, therefore, be said that omnipotence cannot be made from some [lesser] potency not only because of the distance between them, but also because it is entirely impossible to make omnipotence. For anything which is made cannot be pure act, since from the very fact that it has being from another, potency is discovered in it, and so it cannot be infinite power.

AD 6. Corporeal light multiplies itself not by creation of new light, but by diffusing itself over matter. This cannot be said of angels, since they are self-subsistent substances.[32]

AD 7. Form can be understood in two ways. First, insofar as it is in potency, and in this way it is concreated by God with matter, without any intervening action of nature for the disposition [of the matter]. Secondly, insofar as it is in act, and in this way it is not created, but is educed from the potency of matter by the natural agent. And so it is not necessary that nature act dispositively in order for something to be created. Nevertheless, because there is a natural form produced in being through creation whose matter nature does

32. *substancie per se stantes.*

dispose, namely the rational soul, we must note that, since the work of creation is independent of matter,[33] something can be said to be created in two ways. For certain things are created without any pre-existing matter from which or in which they are made, as for example angels and the heavenly bodies, and nature can have no dispositive work in the creation of these. But other things are created which, while they require no pre-existing matter from which they are made, nevertheless do require matter in which they are made, as for example, the human soul. In the sense then that they have matter in which they exist, nature can work dispositively, although not to the extent that the action of nature extends to the very substance of the created thing.[34]

AD 8. Man has some role in the work of justification, but only as a minister employing the sacraments. And so, because the sacraments are said to justify instrumentally and dispositively, the solution is the same as the one given above.

AD 9. Although there can be no likeness of genus or species between God and creatures, nevertheless there is a certain analogous likeness, as there is between potency and act and between substance and accident. And this in two ways. First, insofar as created things imitate in their own way an idea in the divine mind, just as the form which is in the mind of the artificer [is imitated by his work]. And in a second way, in that created things are in a certain way like the very nature of God, insofar as they have their being from the first being, and their goodness from the [first] good, and so on. Nevertheless, this objection is not to the point since, even granting that creatures ultimately proceed from God through the mediation of some created potency, the same difficulty will still remain, namely how this first creature can be from God without any existing likeness [to God].

AD 10. The Book of Causes does explicitly contain this error that lower creatures are created by God through mediating higher creatures. And so in this case the authority of that book is not to be accepted.

We can reply in the same way to the eleventh objection.

33. *cum creationis opus materiam tollat.* I am following Fr. Shapcote's translation of *tollat.*

34. For a recent overview and discussion of Thomas' view of the human

AD 12. Augustine is speaking there of the soul, which does communicate being and species to the body, but by way of form, not by way of creation.

AD 13. Although an angel's knowledge of things is not derived from them, it is not therefore necessary that its knowledge is the cause of these things. For its knowledge is a mean between the two kinds mentioned, since it knows things by natural knowledge through likenesses[35] of things in its intellect which flow[36] from the divine intellect. And so its knowledge is not directed to things as the cause of [those] things, but it is a likeness of the divine knowledge, which is their cause.

AD 14. In the eduction of things from potency to act, many degrees can be observed, inasmuch as something can be brought into act from a more or less remote potency and it may also be brought more or less easily. And so it need not be that if the power of an angel exceed that of material nature it can make something from pure non-being while nature educes something from potency into act. Rather, the angel can do this much more easily than nature. And so Augustine says in On the Trinity III that demons work the seeds of nature more secretly and efficaciously than we can.[37]

AD 15. There is no greater power than the power to create. Nevertheless, it does not follow that the power of creation extends to the communication of the power to create to a creature, for that is in no way communicable to a creature. That something is impossible may be due not only to a defect in the power of the agent, but sometimes also to the fact that the very nature of the thing[38] is such that it cannot be done. Thus, for example, God cannot make God, not because of a defect in his power, but because God can in no way be made. Likewise, the power to create cannot be finite, nor can it be communicated to a creature, because it is infinite.

AD 16. There are two ways an action may be difficult. First, it may be because the patient resists the action. This does not happen

---

being as composed of a human soul and human body, see Jason Eberl, "Aquinas on the Nature of Human Beings," *Review of Metaphysics* 58 (2004): 333–65.

35. *similitudines,* which Fr. Shapcote translates as "ideas."

36. *effluxas.*

37. Augustine, *The Trinity,* III 8 and 9.

38. *ex ipsa ratione rei.*

in every case but only in those in which there is a mutual relation of action and reaction, in which the agent is subject to the contrary action of the patient. And so the heavenly bodies, whose action is in no way subject to the actions of others, have no difficulty in acting arising from any contrary action of the patient.[39] Much less would God. The second way, which is universal, is because the patient is removed from the act. For when the potency is found to be further removed from the act, the difficulty of the agent's action is proportionately greater. And so, since pure non-being is further removed from act than matter subject to any contrary however intense, it is evident that it requires a greater power to produce something from nothing than to make one contrary from another.

39. On Thomas' understanding of the nature of the heavenly bodies, see Bobik, *Aquinas on Matter and Form and the Elements,* 199–219; Oliva Blanchette, *The Perfection of the Universe according to Aquinas: A Teleological Cosmology* (University Park, PA: The Pennsylvania State University Press, 1992), 206–16; and Thomas Litt, *Les corps célestes dan l'univers de Saint Thomas d'Aquin* (Louvain: Publications Universitaires, 1963).

ARTICLE 5

The fifth point of inquiry is whether there can be anything that is not created by God. And it seems that this is possible.[1]

OBJ. 1. Since the cause is more powerful than its effect, that which is possible to our intellect, which takes its knowledge from things, would seem yet more possible to nature. Now our intellect can understand a thing apart from understanding that it is from God, because its efficient cause is not part of a thing's essence, so that the thing can be understood without it. Much more therefore can there be a real thing[2] that is not from God.

OBJ. 2. All things made by God are called his creatures. Now creation terminates at being, for *the first of created things is being,* as is held in the Book of Causes.[3] Since the quiddity of a thing is in addition to its being, it would seem that the quiddity of a thing is not from God.

OBJ. 3. Every action terminates in an act, just as it proceeds from an act, because *every agent acts insofar as it is in act,*[4] and *every agent produces its like in nature.*[5] But prime matter is pure potentiality. Therefore the creative act cannot terminate in it, and so not all things are created by God.

On the contrary, it is said in Romans 11, *From him and through him and in him are all things.*[6]

I answer that the ancients proceeded in accordance with the order of human knowledge in their examination of the nature of things. Thus as human knowledge reaches the intellect by beginning with the senses, the early philosophers were engrossed with the domain of the sensible, and from there gradually reached the intelligible. And because accidental forms are in themselves sensible, while substantial forms are not, the first philosophers said that all forms were accidents, and that matter alone was a substance. And because substance suffices to cause accidents that are caused through principles

1. For parallel discussions of this question, see *ST* I Q. 44, a. 1 and *SCG* II 15.
2. I am following Fr. Shapcote in translating *"in rerum natura."*
3. *Book of Causes,* Prop. 4.
4. See article 1, note 14.
5. See article 1, note 10.
6. Romans 11:36.

of substance, the first philosophers held that there is no other cause besides matter, and that matter is the cause of all we observe in the sensible world. Consequently they were forced to state that matter has no cause, and to deny absolutely the existence of an efficient cause.

The later philosophers, however, began to take some notice of substantial forms. Yet they did not attain to the knowledge of universals, but were wholly intent on the consideration of special forms.[7] And so they did posit some active causes, not however such as confer being to things universally, but such as transmute matter to this or that form. Among these were intelligence, friendship, and strife, whose action they assumed in separation and adhesion.[8] And so, according to them, not all beings proceeded from an efficient cause, but matter was presupposed in the action of an agent cause.

Later philosophers, like Plato, Aristotle, and their followers, attained to the consideration of universal being itself, and so they alone posited some universal cause of things, from which all others came into being, as Augustine states in The City of God VIII.[9] Cer-

7. *formas speciales.*

8. In article 16, Thomas makes clear that he is thinking of Anaxagoras and Empedocles. In the *respondeo* he says, "Anaxagoras held that the divine intellect produced different things by separating them from commixture with matter" (see Diels-Kranz 59B12–13). "And thus," Thomas continues, "Empedocles held that different effects were distinguished and conjoined in various ways through friendship and strife according to the diversity of matter" (see Diels-Kranz 31B17, 21, 22, 26, 35).

9. Augustine, *City of God,* VIII 4. Augustine does not mention Aristotle by name in this text. On the question of whether Thomas means to attribute a doctrine of creation to Aristotle, see Mark Johnson, "Did St. Thomas Attribute a Doctrine of Creation to Aristotle?" *New Scholasticism* 63 (1989): 129–55; James Weisheipl, O.P., "The Date and Context of Aquinas' De aeternitate mundi," in *Graceful Reason: Essays in Ancient and Medieval Philosophy presented to Joseph Owens, CSsR,* ed. L. P. Gerson (Toronto: Pontifical Institue of Mediaeval Studies, 1983), 239–71; and Etienne Gilson, *The Spirit of Mediaeval Philosophy,* trans. A. Downes (New York: Charles Scribner's Sons, 1940), 438–41, n. 4. On the accuracy of the history of philosophy that Thomas offers here, see Fernand van Steenberghen, "Le problème de l'existence de Dieu dans les questions disputées 'De potentia Dei,'" *Pensamiento* 25 (1969): 252 and his later *Le problème de l'existence de Dieu dans les Écrits de S. Thomas d'Aquin* (Louvain-la-neuve: l'Institut Supérieur de Philosophie, 1980), 138. Joseph de Finance compares this history to the ones Thomas gives in the *De substantiis separatis* IX and *ST* I Q. 44, a. 2 in *Etre et agir dans la philosophie de Saint Thomas,* 3rd ed. (Rome: Presses de l'Université Grégorienne, 1965), 127–29, n. 18. Johnson's article compares it with *ST* I Q. 44, a. 2 and with *In VIII Physicorum* lect. 2 ("Did St. Thomas," 142–46, 148–50).

tainly this position is in accord with the Catholic faith. And it can be demonstrated with three arguments.

First, if something is found to be common to many things, it is necessary that it be caused in them by some one cause. For it is not possible that that [common feature] belongs in common to each one in itself, since each one, according to what it is in itself, is distinct from the others, and diversity of causes would produce diverse effects. Therefore, since being is found to be common to all things, which are in themselves distinct from one another, it necessarily follows that it is to be attributed to them not as from them in themselves, but from some one cause. And this seems to be the argument of Plato, who was of the opinion that *prior to every multitude* there must be some unity, not only in number but in the nature of things.[10]

The second argument is that when something is found to be participated by many things in various ways, it must be attributed to all those in which it is found more imperfectly by virtue of that in which it is found most perfectly. For those things which have something predicated of them to a greater or lesser degree, have this in reference to one thing which they approach, one nearer than another, because if it belonged to each one in itself, there would be no reason why it would be found more perfectly in one than in another. Thus we see that *fire,* which is *the extreme of hotness,*[11] is the cause of heat in all hot things. Now this is to posit one being which is most perfect and most true, which follows from the fact that there is a mover wholly immobile and perfect, as philosophers have proved. Therefore, it is necessary that all other less perfect things receive being from it. And this is the proof of the Philosopher in Metaphysics II.[12]

The third argument is that that which is through another, is reduced as to a cause to that which is through itself. Thus if there were

10. R. J. Henle, S.J., traces this reference to Pseudo-Dionysius' *Divine Names* 13, no. 2 and Aristotle's *Metaphysics,* I 6, 987b1–8. See his *Saint Thomas and Platonism* (The Hague: Martinus Nijhoff, 1956), 24–25.

11. Aristotle, *Metaphysics,* II 1, 993b25.

12. Aristotle, *Metaphysics,* II 1, 993b19–30. On this text from the *Metaphysics,* see John Wippel, "Truth in Thomas Aquinas," *Review of Metaphysics* 43 (1989): 298, n. 8; reprinted in *Metaphysical Themes in Thomas Aquinas II,* 65–112. Also see H. H. Berger, "Der Partizipations-gedanke im Metaphysik-Kommentar des Thomas von Aquin," *Vivarium* 1 (1963): 130–32 and de Finance, *Etre et agir,* 125–26.

one heat existing through itself, it would be necessary that it be the cause of all hot things which have heat by way of participation. Now this is to posit some being which is its own being, which is proved from the fact that there must be some first being which is pure act, in which there is no composition. Hence it is necessary that all other beings which are not their own being, but have being by way of participation, are by that one being. This is the argument of Avicenna.[13] Thus reason proves and faith holds that all things are created by God.

AD 1. Although the first cause, which is God, does not enter into the essence of creatures, yet the being which is in creatures cannot be understood except as derived from the divine being, just as a proper effect cannot be understood except as derived from its proper cause.

AD 2. From the very fact that being is attributed to a quiddity, not only being but the quiddity itself is said to be created, since before it has being it is nothing, except perhaps in the intellect of the creator, where it is not a creature but the creating essence.

AD 3. This argument proves that prime matter is not created *per se,* but it does not follow that it is not created under a form, for it is thus that it has actual being.

13. Avicenna, *Liber de Philosophia Prima sive Scientia Divina,* VIII 6.

ARTICLE 6

The sixth thing to be asked is whether there is only one principle of creation. And it seems not.[1]

OBJ. 1. In the fourth chapter of the Divine Names, Dionysius says, Good is not the cause of evil.[2] But there is evil in the world. Therefore it is either caused by some cause which is not good or it is in no way caused but is [itself] a first cause. But in either case we must posit multiple principles of creation, for it is certain that the first principle of creation of good things is good.

OBJ. 2. Someone might reply that good causes evil not *per se* but accidentally. On the contrary, every effect which comes from some cause accidentally, comes from another cause *per se,* since every accident is traced to something *per se.* If therefore evil is an accidental effect of the good, it will be the *per se* effect of something else, and so the same conclusion follows as before.

OBJ. 3. An accidental effect of a cause occurs without the intention of the cause and is not made.[3] Therefore if good causes evil accidentally, it will follow that evil would not be something made. But nothing is uncreated except the principle of creation, as was shown above.[4] Therefore evil will be a principle of creation.

OBJ. 4. No harm[5] occurs in an effect without the intention of the agent except because of either the ignorance of an agent which lacks foresight or the impotence [of an agent] that cannot avoid [the effect]. But in God, who is the creator of good, there is neither impotence nor ignorance. Therefore evil, which is harmful, cannot occur in God's effects without his intention, for Augustine says that something is called evil because it does harm.[6]

OBJ. 5. That which is accidental happens *in few cases,* as is main-

1. While most of the objections in this article argue that God cannot be the source of the evil in creation, it is also argued that he cannot be the source of multiplicity. For parallel discussions of God and evil, see *ST* I Q. 47, a. 2 and Q. 49. On God as source of multiplicity, see *ST* I Q. 47, a. 2 and *SCG* II 45.

2. Pseudo-Dionysius, *The Divine Names,* 4, no. 19.

3. I.e. it is not properly speaking an effect.

4. Article 5.

5. *nocumentum.*

6. Augustine, *Faith, Hope and Charity,* 3, no. 11.

tained in Physics II.[7] But evil happens *in many cases,* as is maintained in Topics II.[8] Therefore evil is not caused accidentally.

OBJ. 6. According to Augustine, evil has not an efficient but a deficient cause.[9] But an accidental cause is an efficient cause. Therefore good does not cause evil accidentally.

OBJ. 7. That which is not has no cause, since what is not is neither cause nor effect. But according to Augustine evil is nothing.[10] Therefore evil has neither a *per se* nor an accidental cause. Therefore it is false to say that good is the accidental cause of evil.

OBJ. 8. According to the Philosopher in Metaphysics II, that in which a [feature] is first, is the cause of all else in which that [feature] is subsequently found.[11] For example, fire is the cause of heat in all hot things. But malice was first in the devil. Therefore he is the cause of malice in all evil things. And so there is one principle of all evil things just as there is of all good.

OBJ. 9. According to Dionysius, in the fourth chapter of the Divine Names, *good happens in one way, but evil in many ways.*[12] Evil therefore is closer to being than good. Therefore if good is a nature which requires a creator, evil also needs a creator. And so the same conclusion follows.

OBJ. 10. That which is not cannot be either a genus or a species. But evil is taken to be a genus, for it is said in the Categories that *good and evil are not in a genus but are genera* of other things.[13] Therefore evil is a being and so it requires a creator. Whence, since it is not created by a good, it seems that we must posit something evil which is a principle of creation.

OBJ. 11. Each of a pair of contraries is a positive nature, for *contraries are in the same genus,*[14] but that which is not cannot be in a genus. Now good and evil are contraries. Therefore evil is a nature, and the same conclusion follows.

7. Actually, this seems to refer to Aristotle, *Metaphysics,* V or VI. See 1025a13–21 and 1026b32.

8. Aristotle, *Topics,* II 6, 112b12.

9. Augustine, *City of God,* XII 7.

10. Augustine, *Tractates on the Gospel of John,* Tractate 1, no. 3.

11. Aristotle, *Metaphysics,* II 1, 993b24.

12. Pseudo-Dionysius, *The Divine Names,* 4, no. 31.

13. Aristotle, *Categories,* 11, 14a24–25.

14. Aristotle, *Categories,* 11, 14a20; *On Generation and Corruption,* I 7, 324a1–4.

OBJ. 12. Differences which constitute species signify a nature, and so in one way *nature is* that which *gives* [something its] *specific difference,*[15] as Boethius says in his book On Two Natures.[16] But evil is the constitutive difference of a species, for good and evil differentiate habits. Therefore evil is a nature, and the same conclusion follows.

OBJ. 13 <19>.[17] Just as generation is a natural movement, so is corruption. But corruption terminates in privation just as generation does in form. Therefore, just as form is induced because of the intention of nature, so is privation. And so it must be that evil, which is a privation, has a *per se* active cause, just as form does.

OBJ. 14 <13>. According to Ecclesiasticus XXXIII, *Evil is set against good and life against death, just as the sinner is against the just man.*[18] If therefore there is one good principle of creation, there must be another evil [principle] which is contrary to it.

OBJ. 15 <14>. Increase and remission[19] connote relation to some term. Now one thing is found to be worse than another. Therefore there must be something which is the worst, which would be the term of evil, and this must be the principle of all evil things, just as the highest good is the principle of all good things.

OBJ. 16 <16>. According to Genesis I, *in the beginning* of the creation of things, *darkness was over the face of the abyss.*[20] But the good, which has the nature of light, cannot create darkness. Therefore the creation described [in Genesis] is not from a good principle but from an evil one.

15. *natura est unumquodque informans specifica differencia.*

16. Boethius, *De Persona et Duabus Naturis,* 1.

17. In the Leonine edition, in article 14 the reader finds objs. 1–12 (and their respective replies) as usual and then is presented with objections (and replies) with the following numeration and in the following order: 14, 15, 17, 16, 19, 20, 13, 23, 21, 22, 18, 24, 25, 26. The Marietti edition has the text of the objections (and their respective replies) in the same order as the Leonine but renumbers them to follow normal numerical order. So the text which is designated obj. 14 in the Leonine is designated obj. 13 in the Marietti, what is 15 in the Leonine is 14 in the Marietti, and so on. In this translation of the Leonine, I have given the text of each objection with the number assigned to it by the Leonine edition but I have re-ordered the texts so that they follow normal numerical order. Because of the difference between the Leonine and Marietti, translations based on the Marietti will give a different numbering for objs. 13–23. The numbering as the Marietti has it is given here in angle brackets.

18. Ecclesiasticus 33:14.

19. *intensio et remissio.*

20. Genesis 1:2.

OBJ. 17 <15>. According to Matthew VII, *A good tree cannot bear bad fruit.*[21] But evil is found in the world. Therefore it cannot be the fruit or effect of a good, which the good tree represents. And so it is necessary that some first evil be the cause of all evils.

OBJ. 18 <22>. *From one simple thing only one*[22] simple thing may proceed. But God is wholly simple. Therefore these composite things are not from him, but from some other agent.

OBJ. 19 <17>. Every effect attests to its cause insofar as it is similar to it. But evil in no way attests to God, nor does it have any similarity to him. Therefore it cannot be from him, but from another principle.

OBJ. 20 <18>. Nothing comes from a thing unless it is [already] in it potentially. But evil is in God neither actually nor potentially. Therefore it is not in God, and so the same conclusion follows.

OBJ. 21 <20>. The action of every agent presupposes the first agent. But when the free will sins, its act does not presuppose the divine action, for some sins, like fornication and adultery, cannot be separated from their deformity, which cannot be from God. Therefore it must be that either the free will is a first agent or it is traced to some first agent other than God.

OBJ. 22 <21>. One might claim that the substance of the sinful act is from God but not the deformity. On the contrary, in Metaphysics VII the Commentator says, It is impossible for the action of one agent to terminate in the matter and that of another in the form.[23] But deformity is a sort of form of the sinful act. Therefore it cannot be that the deformity of the sin is from one agent and the substance is from another.

OBJ. 23. The stain [of sin] places something in the soul. For if it were merely the privation of grace, then through any mortal sin a man would have the stain of all sin. But the stain of sin is not from God, for God is not the agent of that which he punishes, according to Fulgentius.[24] And since [the stain] is not from eternity it must have

21. Matthew 7:18.

22. See article 4, note 20.

23. Averroës, *Commentarium in Aristotelis Metaphysicorum libri XIV,* VII 8, com. 28.

24. Fulgentius, *To Monimus,* I 17, no. 1.

a cause. Therefore it must be traced to some first cause which is not God.

OBJ. 24. Ecclesiastes III says, *I have learned that all the works that God has made continue eternally.*[25] But corruptible things do not continue eternally. Therefore they are not works of God but must be traced to another principle.

OBJ. 25. *Every agent produces its like.*[26] But corporeal things are not like God, for God is <spirit>, as John 4 maintains.[27] Therefore corporeal things are not from God, and so the same conclusion follows.

OBJ. 26. *Nature always does what is better,* according to the Philosopher,[28] and this is because of the goodness of nature. But the goodness of God is more perfect than that of nature. Therefore God makes things as good as he can. But spiritual things are better than corporeal things. Therefore he did not make corporeal things, because if he had made them, he would have given them spiritual goodness. And so it follows that we must posit multiple principles of creation.

On the contrary (1) is what we find in Isaiah XLV: *I am the Lord and there is no other God. I form the light and create darkness, make peace and create evil. I the Lord do all these things.*[29]

Further (2), evil does not take root except in the nature of good,[30] as Dionysius shows in the fourth chapter of the Divine Names.[31] But this would not be the case if evil had a principle of creation contrary to that which creates good things. Also the principle of evil things would be more powerful than the principle of good, because it induces its effect in the good itself. Therefore evil is not from a principle of creation other than [the principle] of good.

Further (3), the Philosopher proves in Physics VIII that there is one first mover. But this would not be if there were different first principles of creation, for one principle would not govern and move creatures of another contrary principle. There is, therefore, only one principle of creation.

25. Ecclesiastes 3:14.

26. See article 1, note 10.

27. John 4:24.

28. Aristotle, *On the Heavens,* II 5, 288a3. Cf. *On the Progression of Animals,* 12, 711a19; *On Generation and Corruption,* II 10, 336b27.

29. Isaiah 45:6–7.

30. *malum non radicatur nisi in natura boni.*

31. Pseudo-Dionysius, *The Divine Names,* 4, especially no. 20.

I answer that, because they considered only particular things[32] in nature, when the ancient philosophers considered material things they fell into the error of believing that not all natural things are created. Thus, upon consideration of contraries, which they posit with matter as the principles of nature, they arrived at the conclusion that there are two first principles of things. And this was due to a threefold fault which deceived them in their consideration of contraries.[33]

The first was that, although *contraries* are *in the same genus,*[34] they considered contraries only insofar as they differ in species, but not insofar as there is something one in them from the nature of [their common] genus. And so they ascribed a cause to contraries not in terms of what they have in common, but in terms of their differences, and because of this they reduced all contraries to two first contraries as two first causes, as is shown in Physics I.[35] Among these, Empedocles even posited first contraries, namely love and strife, as first active causes, and he was the first to posit good and evil principles, according to Metaphysics I.[36]

The second fault was that they judged each contrary equally, whereas one of two contraries must always bring the privation of the other,[37] and because of this one [can be taken] as perfect and the other as imperfect, and one better and the other worse, according to Physics I.[38] From there they proceeded to posit that good and evil, which seemed to be the most general contraries, were each distinct natures. And thus it was that Pythagoras posited two genera of things, namely good and evil, and in the genus of good he placed all perfections, including light, the masculine, rest, and things of that sort, while in the genus of evil he put all imperfections, including darkness, the feminine, and the like.

The third fault was that they judged things only in reference to

32. *specialia.*

33. For a detailed discussion of Thomas' analysis of these errors regarding the contraries, see Blanchette, *The Perfection of the Universe according to Aquinas,* 108–18.

34. Aristotle, *Categories,* 11, 14a20; *On Generation and Corruption,* I 7, 324a1–4.

35. Aristotle, *Physics* I, especially chs. 4 and 5.

36. Aristotle, *Metaphysics,* I 4, 985a4–9.

37. Aristotle, *Physics,* I 7, 191a14.

38. This is Thomas' interpretation of *Physics,* I 5, 188b37. See his commentary on *Physics I,* lect. 10, no. 81.

the things themselves or according to the order of one thing to another particular thing, but not in comparison with the whole order of the universe. And so it was that if they found something to be harmful to another or to be imperfect in comparison with other perfect things, they judged it to be absolutely evil in its nature and not to originate from the cause of good. And because of this Pythagoras places the feminine, which is imperfect in this way,[39] in the genus of evil.

And this is also the root of the Manichean error that [since] the corruptible in comparison with the incorruptible, and the visible in comparison with the invisible, and the Old Testament in comparison with the New Testament, are [all] imperfect, they may not be held to be from the good God, but from a contrary principle, especially since [the Manicheans] saw that some good creatures, like man, suffer harm from some visible and corruptible creatures.

Now this error is wholly impossible, and all things must be traced to one first principle which is good. For the moment this may be shown by three arguments.

The first is that whenever something is found to be common to diverse things, it is necessary to trace them to one cause with respect to that common [feature], for either one is the cause of the other or there is one common cause of both of them. For it cannot be that that one common [feature] belongs to each as that which is proper to each of them, as was maintained in the preceding article. Now all contraries and diverse things in the world have something in common, either in the nature[40] of [their] species or of [their] genus, or at least in the common nature[41] of being. Whence it must be that there is one principle of all these things, which is the cause of being in all of them. Now being, as such, is good. This is plain from the fact that everything desires to be and this is the nature[42] of the good, namely that it be desirable. And so it is clear that above all diverse causes we must place some one cause, just as above those contrary agents in nature the natural philosophers place one first agent, namely the heaven, which is the cause of the diverse motions in these inferior

39. *que est quid inperfectum.*
40. *natura.*
41. *ratione.*
42. *ratio.*

things. But since diversity of place is found even in the heaven itself, which is the cause of the contrariety of the inferior bodies, we must have recourse further to a first mover which is moved neither *per se* nor accidentally.

The second argument is that *every agent acts insofar as it is in act*[43] and consequently [every agent acts] insofar as it is in some way perfect. Now insofar as a thing is evil, it is not actual, since something is said to be evil because it is potential and deprived of its proper and due act. But insofar as something is actual it is good, because it is according to [its actuality] that it has perfection and entity, in which the nature[44] of the good consists. Therefore nothing acts insofar as it is evil, but every agent acts insofar as it is good. Therefore it is impossible to posit an active principle of things other than the good. And indeed, since *every agent produces its like,*[45] nothing is made except insofar as it is good. And so with respect to both [cause and effect] it is impossible to maintain that evil is the principle of creation of evils.[46] And this argument is in accord with that of Dionysius, who says that *evil does not act except by virtue of a good* and that *evil is beyond intention* and generation.[47]

The third argument is that if diverse beings were to be traced entirely to contrary principles without these being traced to one supreme principle, then they could not concur in one order except accidentally. For many things cannot be coordinated except by some orderer, unless many things chance accidentally to concur in the same order. Now we see that corruptible and incorruptible, spiritual and corporeal, perfect and imperfect [all] concur in one order: for the spiritual moves the corruptible, which is apparent at least in man; and the corruptible is disposed by incorruptible bodies, as is plain in the alterations of the elements by the heavenly bodies. Nor can this be said to happen accidentally, for then it would happen not always or *for the most part* but only *in a few cases.*[48] Therefore it is

43. See article 1, note 14 above.

44. *ratio.*

45. See article 1, note 10 above.

46. Thomas offers an argument against the Manicheans with many of the same elements in his *Treatise on Separate Substances* XVII, in *Sancti Thomae de Aquino opera omnia,* Leonine ed., vol. 40 (Rome: 1969), D 70.

47. Pseudo-Dionysius, *The Divine Names,* 4, especially nos. 19, 20, 28, 31, 32.

48. Aristotle, *Metaphysics,* VI 2, 1026b32.

necessary to trace all these diverse things to some one principle by which they are ordered into one [order]. And so in Metaphysics XI the Philosopher concludes that the sovereign is one.[49]

AD 1. We have already shown that since evil is not being but a lack of being it follows that it cannot be made *per se.* And in this sense Dionysius says that good is not the cause of evil. He does not mean that evil is to be traced to another first cause.

AD 2. This objection concerns an effect which can have a *per se* cause. But evil is not of this sort, whence neither can it properly be called an effect.

AD 3. Evil is incidental to effects, but is not properly speaking a made thing,[50] which is clear from the fact that it is not intended. Nevertheless it does not follow that it is a first principle, unless we add that evil is a certain nature.[51] For just as evil, because it is not a being but a privation of being, lacks the proper nature[52] of an effect, much more does it lack the nature[53] of a cause, as has been proved.

AD 4. According to Augustine's Enchiridion, God is so good that he would never permit any evil to be unless he were so powerful that he could draw good from evil.[54] And so evils occur in the world not because of impotence or ignorance in God but by the order of his wisdom and the magnitude of his goodness, because of which the various degrees of goodness in things are multiplied, many of which would be absent if no evil were permitted. For the good of patience would not be if it were not for the evil of persecution, nor could there be the good of a lion's continued life if it were not for the evil of the destruction of the animals on which it lives.

AD 5. Evil is found only in a few cases, if effects are referred to their proper causes. Indeed this is clear in natural things, for fault or evil does not occur in actions of nature except when the active cause is affected by an impediment, which happens only in a few cases, as in the case of monsters in nature and things of that sort. Now in voluntary matters evil seems to be more in things done than in things made, inasmuch as art fails only in a few instances, for it *imitates*

49. Aristotle, *Metaphysics,* XII 10, 1076a4.

50. I.e. an effect.

51. *natura.*

52. *ratione.*

53. *ratione.*

54. Augustine, *Faith, Hope and Charity,* 24, no. 96.

nature.[55] Now in actions in the realm of virtue and vice, there is a twofold appetite at work, namely the rational and the sensual, and that which is good according to one appetite is evil according to the other, as for example to pursue pleasures is good according the sensible appetite, which is called sensuality, while it is evil according to the rational appetite. And since more follow the senses than reason, there are more evil men than good. Nevertheless the person who follows the rational appetite behaves well in most instances and ill in only a few.

AD 6. The accidental cause is twofold. One does something toward the effect, but is said to cause it accidentally because the effect which follows is not intended by the cause. This is clear for example in the case of the man who finds treasure while digging a grave. The other accidental cause does nothing toward the effect, but is called an accidental cause because it is an accident of the acting cause. For example, white is said to be the accidental cause of a house because it is an accident of the builder. Likewise the accidental effect is twofold. One can be the term of the action of the cause, but it occurs without its intention. For example, the discovery of the treasure, and effects like this, although accidental for this cause, may be the *per se* effect of another cause. But evil does not have an accidental cause in this way, since, as we just said, it cannot be the term of any action. The other accidental effect is one which is not the term of an agent's action, but it is called an accidental effect because it is an accident of an effect. For example, white that is accidental to a house may be said to be the accidental effect of the builder. And in this sense nothing prevents evil from having an accidental cause.

AD 7. Although evil is not a nature, it is nevertheless not a pure negation, but a privation, which, according to the Philosopher, is a negation inherent in a subject. For, according to the Philosopher in Metaphysics IV, privation is negation in a substance.[56] And so, because it is an accident of something, we can assign an accidental cause to [evil] in this sense.

AD 8. Evil was in the devil before it was in others with respect to

55. Aristotle, *Meterology,* IV 3, 381b6 and *On the Heavens,* 5, 396b11.
56. Aristotle, *Metaphysics,* IV 2, 1004a12–16.

time but not with respect to nature, as though malice were his essence or an accident derived from the principles of his proper nature. Nor, if he is worse than others, does that count against this position, since this is not because malice is connatural to him, but rather it is an accident of his having committed the greater sin. But things which are principles of others are those which have a feature to the highest degree *per se,* not accidentally.

AD 9. It is because of the perfection of the good that it happens only in one way. For something cannot be perfect unless everything which is integral to its perfection comes together, and if any of these is absent then it is imperfect and therefore evil. And so it is because of the imperfection of evil that it happens in many ways, and therefore evil has less of the nature[57] of a being than good does.

AD 10. The Philosopher's words refer to the opinion of Pythagoras, who posited good and evil to be genera, as was said above. Nevertheless, that opinion has some truth in it for, since good is said positively while evil is said privatively, as was said above, just as every form has the nature of a good, so does every privation have the nature of an evil, and so good and evil are in a certain sense interchangeable with being and privation of being. But privation and habit are included in all contraries, as is proved in Metaphysics X.[58] And so the contrary which is more perfect is always reduced to the good and the one which is less perfect is reduced to evil. And so in Physics I the Philosopher says that *one of two contraries* tends to *wickedness.*[59] And in this sense good and evil can be called genera of contraries.

AD 11. The evil that is contrary to a good bespeaks not only privation, but [also] a certain habit with the privation. This habit has the nature of an evil, not insofar as it has being, but insofar as it has the adjoined privation of a due perfection.

AD 12. Evil differentiates the vicious habit, not insofar as it is merely a privation, but inasmuch as that [privation] is combined

57. The word here is *"ratione."* It seems odd to refer to evil, a privation, as having a positive "nature." Thomas addresses this concern in objection 11 and the reply to it, below.

58. Aristotle, *Metaphysics,* X 4, 1055a34–38. See also V 12, 1019b5–10.

59. Aristotle, *Physics,* I 9, 192a18.

with the intention of an undue end. And the notion[60] of evil is not found in this intention except when the intended end is inconsistent with a due end, as for example the end of carnal pleasure is inconsistent with the good of reason. Good and evil differentiate the species of the habits of the soul because moral acts, and consequently habits, are specified by the end, which is a sort of form of the will, which is the proper principle of moral acts. Things are called good or evil in relation to the end.

AD 13 <19>. Nature is not related to generation and to corruption in the same way. For form, which is the term of generation, is directly[61] intended by both universal and particular nature. Privation, on the other hand, is beyond the intention of a particular nature, while it is intended by universal nature, although not directly[62] intended, but inasmuch as, without the privation of one form, another form cannot be introduced. And so generation is natural in every way, while we sometimes say corruption is against nature, in relation to a particular nature.

AD 14 <13>. Good is to be understood as against evil not in the way that one first principle is against another first principle, but in the way that two things proceeding from one first principle are when one proceeds from it *per se* and the other accidentally. This is clear from what follows: *And so look upon all the works of the Most High,* etc.[63]

AD 15 <14>. Evil is increased not by approach to a certain term but by withdrawal from a term. For just as something is said to be good through participation in the good, so is it said to be evil through withdrawal from the good.

AD 16 <16>. The darkness which is spoken of at the beginning of creation was not some creature but only a lack of light in the air. It was not however an evil, since lack of good is evil only when that good can and ought to be in something. For it is not an evil in a stone that it has no senses, or in a newborn child that it does not walk. Nor was it because of imperfection of the agent that air was created without light, but because of its wisdom, whose order requires that things be drawn from imperfection to perfection.

60. *ratio.*
61. *per se.*
62. *per se.*
63. Ecclesiasticus 33:15.

AD 17 <15>. By the good tree the Lord means a cause of good, not the first cause, however, but the cause proximate to some particular effect. The case of the bad tree is the same, and so by the bad tree he means heretics, who are known by their works as a tree [is known] by its fruit. Indeed, this is clear if we attend to the similarity. For the first cause of the fruit is not the tree but the root. If, however, we take the tree to represent universally every cause, as Dionysius apparently does, then we should say that the good is not the *per se* cause of evil, as was said in response to the first objection.

AD 18 <22>. This argument presumes an agent acting from natural necessity, for which it is the case that if there is one, it produces one effect. Nor is it necessary that an effect be simple because its cause is simple, since an effect need not be equal to its cause in unity or simplicity. But God acts not from natural necessity but voluntarily. And so he can make both simple and composite, both mutable and immutable.

AD 19 <17>. This objection presumes that evil has a cause *per se*, which we have shown above to be false.

And the same can be said to the twentieth <eighteenth> objection.

AD 21 <20>. Whatever there is of entity or action in a sinful act is traced to God as first cause, while the deformity in it is traced to the free will as its cause. Thus what there is of a step in limping is traced to the motive power as its first cause, while what there is of walking off course comes from the curvature of the leg.

AD 22 <21>. This argument applies to two wholly disparate agents, but does not apply when one agent operates in the other, for in that case one effect can come from them. But God operates in every nature and will, and so the argument fails.

AD 23. The stain [of sin] places in the soul not some nature, but only the privation of grace. This privation is related to the sinful act committed which caused or might have caused it. And so it cannot be that someone who has not committed the act of a certain sin has the stain of that sin.

AD 24. The works of God continue eternally, not individually[64]

64. *secundum numerum.*

but as a species or genus, and [they continue] with respect to substance, not with respect to their mode of being. *For the manner of this world passes away,* as is said in I Corinthians 7.[65]

AD 25. Although God is spirit, he has nevertheless in his wisdom the ideas[66] of bodies, to which bodies are likened in the way that artifacts are likened to their artificer in terms of his art. However, bodies are likened to God [also] with respect to his nature insofar as they are, and are good, and have some unity.

AD 26. Nature always does what is better relative to the whole, not the part. Otherwise the whole human body would be eye or heart, for this would be better for the part, but not for the whole. Likewise, although it would be better for a particular thing that it be placed in higher order, this would not be better for the universe, which would remain imperfect if all creatures were of one order.

65. Corinthians 7:31.
66. *rationes.*

ARTICLE 7

The seventh thing to be asked is whether God works in all the operations of nature. And it seems that he does not.[1]

OBJ. 1. For *nature neither lacks necessary things nor abounds in superfluous ones.*[2] But the active power on the part of the agent and the passive on the part of the recipient suffice for natural action. Therefore there is no need for divine power operating in things.

OBJ. 2. One might reply that the active power of nature depends in its operation on divine operation. On the contrary, just as the operation of created nature depends on divine operation, so does the operation of an elemental body depend on the operation of a heavenly body. For a heavenly body is related to an elemental body as first cause to second. However, we do not say that the heavenly body operates in every action of an elemental body. Therefore we cannot say that God operates in every operation of nature.

OBJ. 3. If God operates in every operation of nature, then the operation of God and nature are either one and the same operation or distinct operations. But they are not one and the same, for unity of operation attests to unity of nature (which is why there are two operations in Christ because there are two natures in him), and it is certain that God and creature are not of one nature. Likewise, neither is it possible that they are distinct operations. For distinct operations do not seem to terminate in the same product,[3] since motions and operations are distinguished by their terms. Therefore in no way is it possible that God operates in nature.

OBJ. 4. One might reply that two operations can have the same termination when they are related as prior and posterior.[4] On the contrary, things which are immediately related to one thing are not

1. For parallel discussions of this question, see *ST* I Q. 105, a. 5 and *SCG* III 67. Msgr. Wippel discusses this article and these parallel texts in his "Thomas Aquinas on Creatures as Causes of *esse*," *International Philosophical Quarterly* 50 (2000): 81–101; reprinted in *Metaphysical Themes in Thomas Aquinas II*, 172–93.

2. Cf. Aristotle, *Parts of Animals*, IV 2, 691b5.

3. *factum*.

4. I.e. when one is subordinate to the other.

ordered to each other. But both God and nature immediately produce[5] a natural effect. Therefore the operation of God and the operation of nature cannot be related as prior and posterior.

OBJ. 5. Whenever God establishes a nature, by that very fact he gives to it everything which is essential[6] to that nature, as for example, from the very fact that he makes a human being he gives him a rational soul.[7] But it is essential to power that it be the principle of action, since power is the *ultimate potency*[8] and potency is the *principle* of acting *on another insofar as it is other,* as is maintained in Metaphysics V.[9] Therefore, from the very fact that he implants natural powers in things, he gives them the ability to complete their natural operations. Therefore there is no need for anything else to operate in natural things.

OBJ. 6. One might reply that natural powers, like all other beings, cannot endure unless they are maintained by the divine power. On the contrary, to operate on a thing is not the same as to operate in it. But the operation of God, which either makes a natural power or preserves it in being, is an operation on the very power established or preserved. Therefore it does not follow from this that God operates in natural operation.

OBJ. 7. If God operates in nature's operation, it must be that by this operation he imparts something to the natural thing. For in acting an agent makes something in act. Therefore this [something] either suffices to make nature able to operate *per se* or it does not. If it suffices, then since God imparted that very natural power, for the same reason we can say that natural power sufficed for action. Nor will it be necessary for God to do anything further toward its operation after giving power to nature. But if [what is imparted to the thing] does not suffice, then [God] must do something else in addition and, if that does not suffice, then something else, and so on to infinity. But that is impossible, for one effect cannot depend on

5. *operatur.*

6. *de ratione.* Here and in the next sentence "essential" is translating *"de ratione."*

7. Thomas develops the claim that God is constrained by this "necessity of the end" or "necessity of supposition" in the respondeo of article 16, below.

8. *virtus sit ultimum potencie.* I have been unable to trace this reference.

9. Aristotle, *Metaphysics,* V 12, 1019a15–20.

an infinite number of actions because, since an infinite cannot be crossed, it would never come to be. Therefore we are left with the first alternative, that natural power suffices for natural action without God operating further in it.

OBJ. 8. Because *nature is determined to one* [effect],[10] given a cause acting out of natural necessity, its action follows unless it is impeded accidentally. Therefore if the heat of fire acts out of natural necessity, then given heat, heating follows and no other higher power acting in it is required.

OBJ. 9. Things which are entirely distinct can be separated from each other. But God's action and the action of nature are entirely distinct, since God acts voluntarily while nature acts out of necessity. Therefore God's action can be separated from the action of nature, and so there is no need for God to operate in natural action.

OBJ. 10. Considered in itself, a creature has a likeness to God insofar as it actually is and actually acts, and in this way it participates in the divine goodness. But this would not be the case if its power did not suffice for action. Therefore a creature [has what] suffices for action without God operating in it.

OBJ. 11. Two angels cannot be in one place, as some say, lest confusion of operation follow, since *where* the angel *is, there he operates.*[11] But God is more distant from nature than one angel is from another. Therefore God cannot operate simultaneously with nature in the same [action].

OBJ. 12. Ecclesiasticus 15 says that *God* made *man and left him in the hand of his own counsel.*[12] But he would not have left [us] if he always operated in the will. Therefore he does not operate in voluntary operation.

OBJ. 13. *The will is master of its own act.*[13] But this would not be if it could not act without God operating in it, since our will is not the

10. I have been unable to find a source text for this principle. For interesting discussions of it, see the respondeo of article 13 and of article 15.

11. I have been unable to determine a source text for this principle. For a discussion of this line of reasoning, see J. Collins, *The Thomistic Philosophy of the Angels,* in The Catholic University of America Philosophical Studies, vol. 89 (Washington, D.C.: The Catholic University of America Press, 1947), 319.

12. Ecclesiasticus 15:14.

13. Cf. Augustine, *City of God,* V 9.

master of divine operation. Therefore God does not operate in the operation of our will.

OBJ. 14. A free thing is one which is a cause for itself, as is said at the beginning of the Metaphysics.[14] Therefore that which cannot act unless [another] cause is acting in it is not free in action. But our will is free in action. Therefore it can act without another cause operating in it, and so the same conclusion follows.

OBJ. 15. The first *cause has more power*[15] over the effect than the second cause. Therefore if God operated in the will and nature as a first cause in a second, it would follow that defects which occur in the operation of the will and nature should be attributed more to God than to nature or the will. But this is absurd.

OBJ. 16. Given a cause operating sufficiently, it is superfluous to posit the operation of another cause. But it is certain that if God operates in nature and the will, he operates sufficiently, for *the works of God are perfect.*[16] Therefore all operation of nature and will would be superfluous. Therefore, since *nothing in nature is superfluous,*[17] neither nature nor will would operate at all, but only God. But this is absurd and so the first [premise], namely that God operates in nature and the will, is as well.

On the contrary (1) is what is said in Isaiah XXVI: All our work you do in us, O Lord.[18]

Further (2) just as art presupposes nature, so does nature presuppose God. But nature operates in the operation of art. For the operation of art cannot be accomplished without the operation of nature, as for example iron is softened by fire so that it may be forged by the

14. Fr. Shapcote translates *"liberum est quod causa sui est"* as "to be free is to be the cause of one's own action," which fits the context of this objection quite well, but does not seem to be strong enough. The text Thomas is referring to is Aristotle, *Metaphysics,* I 2, 982b25, and the Latin as it appears in Thomas' commentary is, *"homo liber, qui suimet, et non alterius causa est, sic et haec sola libera est scientiarum: sola namque haec suimet causa est"* (*Metaphysicorum Aristotelis Expositio,* ed. M. R. Cathala, O.P., and R. M. Spiazzi, O.P. [Turin: Marietti, 1950], 17).

15. I am translating *"plus est influens"* as "has more power." This phrase comes from the *Book of Causes,* Prop. 1. On the difficulty of translating it, see Fr. Guagliardo's translation of Thomas' commentary, p. 5, n. 2.

16. Deuteronomy 32:4.

17. Aristotle, *Parts of Animals,* IV 2, 691b5.

18. Isaiah 26:12.

stroke of the smith. Therefore God also operates in the operation of nature.

Further (3) according to the Philosopher in Physics II, *man and the sun generate man*.[19] But just as in generation the operation of man depends on the action of the sun, thus and much more does the action of nature depend on the action of God. Therefore everything nature does, God also does.

Further (4) nothing can operate unless it exists. But nature cannot exist except by God's operation, for it would fall into nothingness without God operating to maintain it in being, as Augustine's On the Literal Interpretation of Genesis makes clear.[20] Therefore nature cannot act except by God's action.

Further (5) the power of God is in every natural thing, since he is said to be in everything by his essence, power, and presence. But it cannot be said that the divine power is idle insofar as it is in things. Therefore it operates insofar as it is in nature. Nor can it be said that it operates on something other than what nature operates on, since there is apparently only one operation. Therefore God operates in every operation of nature.

I answer that we must absolutely concede that God operates in natural and voluntary operations. But some, not understanding this correctly, fell into error, attributing <to God> every operation of nature in such a way that the natural thing would do nothing on its own[21] by [its own] proper power. And they were led to hold this view by various arguments. Indeed, according to Rabbi Moses, some of those recorded in the law of the Moors said all natural forms of this kind are accidents[22] and, since an accident cannot pass from one subject to another, they considered it impossible for a natural thing, through its own form, in any way to induce the same form in another subject. And so they said that fire does not heat but rather God causes heat in the heated thing. And if it were objected against them

19. Aristotle, *Physics*, II 2, 194b14. Thomas comments on this text in some detail in his *Treatise on Separate Substances*, X 58. See also Blanchette, *The Perfection of the Universe according to Aquinas*, 166–67 and Bobik, *Aquinas on Matter and Form and the Elements*, 206.

20. Augustine, *De Genesi ad litteram libri XII*, IV, no. 12.

21. *penitus*.

22. Moses Maimonides, *The Guide of the Perplexed*, I, 73, 8th premise.

that heating always follows from the application of fire to a heatable thing unless something accidentally is in the way, which shows fire itself[23] is the cause of heat, they would say that God established that an order be maintained in things such that he would cause heat only in the presence of fire, not that the presence of fire would have any part in heating things.

But this position is manifestly opposed to the senses. For, since a sense does not sense unless it is acted upon by a sensible object (which is manifest in touch and the other senses except in sight, about which there is a doubt according to those who say that sight works by extending itself), it follows that man would not sense the heat of the fire if the action of the fire did not cause a likeness[24] of the heat of fire in the sensing organ. Indeed, if this heat-species[25] were produced in the organ by another agent, then touch, though it sensed heat, would not sense the heat of the fire, nor would it sense fire to be hot. And yet the sense does judge this to be the case, and its judgment cannot err about its proper object.[26]

It is opposed also to reason, which shows that nothing in nature is useless. But unless natural things do something, the natural forms and powers in them would be useless, just as a knife's edge is useless if the knife does not cut. It would also be useless to require that fire be applied to wood if God could cause it to burn without fire.

Moreover it is opposed also to the divine goodness, which communicates itself, resulting in things being made like God not only in being but also in acting.

Indeed, the argument they propose is entirely frivolous. For, when it is said that an accident does not pass from one subject into another subject, this must be understood to apply to an accident which is the same numerically, and it does not mean that an accident which is specifically the same cannot be induced in another subject by virtue of an accident which is in some natural subject. Indeed, this necessarily happens in every natural action. Moreover, their supposition that all forms are accidents is false, since if they were then in natural things there would be no substantial being, the principle of which

23. *per se.*

24. *similitude.*

25. *species caloris.*

26. Cf. Aristotle, *On the Soul,* II 6, 418a15.

cannot be accidental form but only substantial form. This would also bring an end to[27] generation and corruption, and many other absurdities would follow.

Indeed, in his book Font of Life, Avicebron says that no corporeal substance acts but rather a spiritual power penetrating all bodies acts in them, and so a body is more active the more pure and subtle and therefore penetrable by spiritual power it is. And he offers three arguments for this.[28] The first is that every agent after God requires subject matter on which to act. But corporeal substance does not have matter subjected to it, and so it seems that it cannot act. The second is that since quantity impedes action and motion (in proof of which he points out that multiplication of quantity retards activity and adds weight to a body), corporeal substance, which is implicitly quantitative, cannot act. The third argument is that corporeal substance is most remote from the first agent, which is active only and in no way passive, while intermediate substances are [both] active and passive. And so it must be that corporeal substance, which is last, is passive only and not active.

But this is manifestly erroneous in that he takes all corporeal substance as numerically one and the same substance, as if it were not distinguished with respect to substantial being but only accidentally. For if different corporeal substances are taken to be substantially distinct, then not every corporeal substance will be the lowest of beings and most remote from the first agent, but one will be higher than another and closer to the first agent and so one will be able to act on another.

Moreover, in these arguments corporeal substance is considered only with respect to matter and not with respect to its form, whereas it is composed of both. Corporeal substance is indeed the lowest of beings and does not have a substance beneath it, but this is because of its matter, not its form, since, with respect to a thing's form, any substance whose matter has the potency for the form which this thing has in act is a subject beneath [this thing]. And so it follows that there is mutual action in corporeal substances, since in the mat-

27. *periret.*
28. Avicebron, *The Fountain of Life,* II 9.

ter of one there is the potential for the form of the other and conversely. And if this form is not sufficient for action, then for the same reason neither would the power of a spiritual substance [suffice], [for] it must be received by a corporeal substance according to the mode of the latter.

Nor does quantity hinder movement and action, since nothing moves unless it has quantity, as is proved in Physics VI.[29] Nor is it true that quantity is the cause of weight, a claim which is rejected in On the Heavens and Earth IV.[30] In fact, quantity increases the velocity of natural motion, for the heavier a body is the more quickly it falls downward, and likewise for a light thing [moving] upward. And although quantity itself is not a principle of action, no reason can be given why it would impede action (since it is more a certain subject[31] of an active quality), except to the extent that active forms, received in matter [also] subject[32] to quantity, receive being which has certain limits and is individuated to that matter, and thus they cannot extend themselves to act on other matter. But although they acquire being individuated in matter, they do not lose the nature[33] of [their] species, and because of this they can produce their like in species, although they cannot themselves be in another subject.

Therefore we should understand that God operates in every natural thing not in the sense that the natural thing does nothing, but because God operates in the very operation of nature and will. How this can be understood must now be shown.

We must observe that one thing can be said to be the cause of the action of another thing in several ways. The first way is by giving it the power to operate, as for example Physics VIII notes that the generator moves light and heavy things inasmuch as it gives the power which results in such motion.[34] And in this way God acts in all natural actions, since he gives natural things the powers through which they are able to act, not merely as the generator gives power to light

29. Aristotle, *Physics,* VI 10, 241a6.

30. Aristotle, *On the Heavens,* IV 2, 308a34–b29.

31. *stramentum.* I am following Fr. Guagliardo in translating this as "subject." See *Commentary on the Book of Causes,* p. 19, n. 5.

32. *subjecta.*

33. *rationem.*

34. Aristotle, *Physics,* VIII 4, 255a1–256a4.

and heavy things but does not preserve it further, but as continuously maintaining the power in being, since he is the cause of the power bestowed not only with respect to becoming, as in the case of the generator, but also with respect to being. And so God can be called the cause of action insofar as he causes and preserves natural power in being.

For indeed another way [in which one thing can be said to cause the action of another] occurs when a preserver of power is said to perform the action, as a medicine which preserves vision is said to cause someone to see.

But since nothing moves or acts through its own self unless it is an unmoved mover, a third way in which one thing may be said to cause the action of another is insofar as it moves [the other] to act, by which we mean not the bestowal or preservation of active power, but the application of power to action, as for example a man is the cause of the cutting of the knife because he applies the edge of the knife to cutting by moving it. And since a lower natural agent does not act except by being moved, because lower bodies of this sort both alter others and are altered, while the heaven alters others without being altered but nevertheless does not move unless it is moved, and this is the case all the way back to God,[35] it necessarily follows that God is the cause of the action of every natural thing by moving and applying [its] power to action.

Moreover we find that the order of effects is according to the order of causes, which must be because of the likeness of effect and cause. Nor can a second cause [influence] an effect of the first cause through its proper power, even though it be an instrument of the first cause with respect to this effect. For an instrument is in a certain way a cause of the effect of the principal cause, not through its form or proper power, but inasmuch as it participates somewhat in the power of the principle cause through being moved by it, as for example the axe is the cause of the thing made not through its form or proper power but through the power of the art[36] by which it is moved and which it in a certain way participates. And so a fourth

35. *et hoc non cessat quosque perveniatur ad Deum.*
36. *artis.* The Marietti edition has "artificis."

way one thing is a cause of another's action is as the principal agent is the cause of the instrument's action. And in this way also we must say God is the cause of every action of a natural thing. For the higher a cause, the more common and efficacious it is. And the more efficacious it is the more profoundly it enters into the effect and the more remote the potency from which it draws that effect into act. Now in every natural thing we find that it is a being, that it is a natural thing, and that it is of this or that nature. The first of these is common to all beings, the second to all natural things, the third to one species, and a fourth, if we add accidents, is proper to this individual. Therefore a particular individual cannot by its action make <another thing> of the same species except as an instrument of that cause which is over[37] the whole species and, beyond that, the whole being of the lower nature. And because of this, these lower beings do not effect species[38] except through the power of the heavenly body. Neither does anything effect being except through the power of God. For being itself is the most common and first effect and more profound than all other effects, and so this effect belongs to the proper power of God alone. This is why an intelligence gives being only to the extent that the divine power is in it, as the Book of Causes maintains.[39] God is, therefore, the cause of every action inasmuch as every agent is the instrument of the operation of divine power.

Therefore, if we consider subsistent[40] agency, any particular agent is immediate to its effect. But if we consider the power by which it does the act, in this way the power of the higher cause will be more immediate to the effect than the power of the lower, for the inferior power is not connected with its effect except through the power <of the superior cause>. And so the Book of Causes says that the

37. *respicit.*

38. *agit ad speciem*; compare *agit ad esse* ("effect being") in the next sentence. See Blanchette's discussion of the universal mode of causality vs. the particular, *The Perfection of the Universe*, 161–73. He discusses this text from the *De potentia* on pp. 168 and 170.

39. *Book of Causes*, Prop. 9. The *Book of Causes* does not, however, say that intelligence gives being, *"dat esse,"* as Thomas says here. The text Thomas is referring to says *"Intelligentia est regens omnes res quae sunt sub ea per virtutem divinam quae est in ea et per eam retinet res, quia per ipsam est causa rerum"* (*Super librum de causis expositio* [*ed. Saffrey*], 57).

40. *supposita.*

power of the first cause acts first in the caused thing and enters more profoundly into it.[41] And so it is therefore necessary that the divine power be present to every acting thing, just as the power of the heavenly body must be present to every acting elemental body. But these do differ in that the divine essence is wherever the divine power is, while the essence of the heavenly body is not wherever its power is. And further, God is his own power, while the heavenly body is not. And so we can say that God operates in everything insofar as everything needs his power to act, but we cannot properly say that the heaven always acts in an elemental body, although the elemental body acts by [the heaven's] power.

Therefore God is the cause of the action of all things inasmuch as he gives them power to act and preserves them and applies them to action and inasmuch as by his power every other power acts. And when we add that God is his own power and that he is within each thing, not as a part of its essence, but as holding the thing in being, it follows that he operates immediately in every operation, without excluding the operation of the will and nature.

AD 1. The active and passive powers of a natural thing suffice for [its] action in its own order. Divine power is nevertheless required, for the reason just given.

AD 2. The relation of natural power to God and [that] of an elemental body to a heavenly body are similar in some respects but not in all.

AD 3. In an operation which God effects by moving nature, nature does not operate but the very operation of nature is an operation of the divine power, just as the operation of an instrument is through the power of the principal agent. Nor does this prevent nature and God from operating to the same [effect] because of the order between God and nature.

AD 4. Both God and nature operate immediately, although they are ordered as prior and posterior, as is clear from what has been said.

AD 5. It is essential[42] to a lower power that it be a principle of op-

41. *Book of Causes*, Prop. 1.
42. *de ratione*.

eration in its order in a certain way, that is, by acting as the instrument of a higher power. And so, apart from the higher power the lower power has no operation.

AD 6. God is the cause of nature's operation not only as preserving natural power in being but [also] in other ways, as has been said.

AD 7. The natural power which is given to natural things at their formation[43] is in them as certain forms which are fixed and constant in nature. But what God does in a natural thing to allow it to actually act is as a mere intention which is not complete in being, in the way that colors are in the air and the power of art is in the craftsman's instrument. Therefore just as an axe can through art be given an edge as a permanent form in it but it could not be given the power of act as a permanent form in it unless it had intelligence, so can proper power be given to a natural thing as a permanent form in the thing itself, but not the power to cause being[44] as an instrument of the first cause unless it were given to it that it be the universal principle of being. Nor could it be given to a natural power that it move itself or preserve itself in being. And so, just as it clearly cannot be given to a craftsman's instrument that it operate without being moved by him, neither can it be given to a natural thing that it operate without the divine operation.

AD 8. Natural necessity, through which heat does act, is constituted by the order of all the preceding causes, and so the power of the first cause is not excluded.

AD 9. Although nature and will are distinct in themselves,[45] nevertheless they have a certain order in action. For, just as the action of nature precedes the act of our will (which is why operations of art, which are voluntary, require the operation of nature), so does the will of God, which is the origin of all natural motion, precede the operation of nature. And so its operation is required in every operation of nature.

AD 10. A creature has a certain likeness to God by participating in his goodness insofar as it is and acts, but not in such a way that it could attain equality [with God] by perfection of that likeness. And

43. *institutione.*

44. *vis qua agit ad esse.*

45. *secundum esse.*

so, just as the imperfect requires the perfect, so does the power of nature require the divine operation in [its] action.

AD 11. With respect to degrees of nature, two angels are less distant than God and created nature. Nevertheless, God and nature come together in the order of cause and effect, while two angels do not. And so God operates in nature but one angel does not operate in another.

AD 12. God is said to have left man in the hand of his own counsel not as though he does not operate in the will but because he gave the human will dominion over its acts so that it is not bound to a particular alternative. Such dominion he did not give to nature, since by its form it is determined to one [course].

AD 13. The will is said to have dominion over its own act not to the exclusion of the first cause, but because the first cause does not act in the will in such a way that it determines it of necessity to [follow] one [course], in the way that it does determine nature.[46] And so determination of an act is left in the power of reason and will.

AD 14. Not every cause excludes freedom, but only a cause which compels. But God is not a cause of our operation in this way.

AD 15. Since the first cause has more power[47] over the effect than the second, whatever there is of perfection in the effect is to be traced principally to the first cause. But what there is of defect is to be traced to the second cause, which does not operate as efficaciously as the first cause.

AD 16. God operates perfectly as the first cause. Nevertheless the operation of nature is required as a second cause. On the other hand, God could make the natural effect even without nature, but he wants to act through the mediation of nature in order to preserve the order in things.

46. On this point, cf. *ST* I-II Q. 10, a. 4.
47. *magis influit.* See note 15.

ARTICLE 8

The eighth thing to be asked is whether God operates in nature by creating, which is to ask whether creation is mingled with the work of nature. And it seems that it is.[1]

OBJ. 1. In On the Trinity III, Augustine says, *The apostle Paul, distinguishing God creating and forming things inwardly from the operations of nature which are conducted outwardly, takes a metaphor from agriculture and says, I planted, Apollo watered, but God gave the increase.*[2]

OBJ. 2. But one might reply that creation here is meant loosely as any kind of making. On the contrary, Augustine on the authority of the Apostle intends in these words to distinguish the operation of the creature from the operation of God. But this distinction will not be made if creation is taken in the general sense of any kind of making (since in this sense even nature creates, for it makes something, as was shown above),[3] but only if creation is taken in the proper sense. Therefore the words must be understood with creation taken properly.

OBJ. 3. In the same passage Augustine adds, *Just as in our life only God can form the mind for justification, while even men can proclaim the gospel outwardly ..., so in the creation of visible things God operates inwardly,* [*unlike*] *the outward operations of good or evil angels and men* or *any animals whatsoever ... thus he makes use of the nature of things in which he creates all things just as a farmer cultivates the earth.*[4] But he forms our

1. For a parallel discussion of this question, see *ST* I, Q. 45, a. 8.

2. Augustine, *The Trinity,* III 8.

3. In article 7.

4. *Sicut in ipsa vita nostra mentem justificando formare non potest nisi Deus, predicare autem extrinsecus evangelium* etiam *homines possunt ..., ita creationem rerum visibilium Deus interius operatur, exteriores autem operationes bonorum sive malorum angelorum vel hominum* vel *quorumcunque animalium ... ita rerum nature adhibet in qua creat omnia quemadmodum terre agriculturam.* Augustine, *The Trinity,* III 8. I am following Stephen McKenna's translation of Augustine in taking *justificando* as a dative and in reading *quemadmodum terre agriculturam* as "as a farmer cultivates the earth." In *The Trinity,* the complete passage reads, "Sicut ergo in ipsa vita nostram mentem justificando formare non potest nisi Deus, predicare autem evangelium extrinsecus et homines possunt, non solum boni per veritatem, sed etiam mali per occasionem: ita creationem rerum visibilium Deus

minds through justification by creation in the proper sense, for grace is said to be through creation. Therefore he also creates natural forms by creation properly speaking.

OBJ. 4. It may be replied that natural forms have a cause in the subject while grace does not, and so grace is created in the proper sense while natural forms are not. On the contrary, as the gloss on Genesis I says, *To create is to make something from nothing.*[5] Now this preposition "from" sometimes connotes a relation to an efficient cause, as in Romans XI: *From whom all things* [are], *through whom all things* [are];[6] but sometimes [it connotes] a relation to a material cause, as we find in Tobit XIII, *All its surrounding walls* [*made*] *from stone brilliant and fine.*[7] And so when something is said to be made from nothing, relation to an efficient cause is not negated, for thus God would not be the efficient cause of created things, but relation to a material cause is negated. Now natural forms have efficient causes in their subjects, and in this they differ from grace. But they also have matter in which they are, which also is true of grace. Therefore the nature[8] of creation does not belong more to grace than to natural forms because of having a cause in the subject.

OBJ. 5. Artificial forms do not have a cause in the subject, but they are totally from without. Therefore, if grace is said to be created because it does not have a cause in the subject, it stands to reason that artificial forms are created.

OBJ. 6. That which has no matter on its part[9] cannot be made from matter. But forms do not have matter on their part, since form is distinct from both matter and the composite, as is clear in the beginning of On the Soul II.[10] Therefore since forms are made, for they have a beginning of existence, it seems that they are not made from matter, and thus they are made from nothing, and so it follows that they are created.

---

interius operatur, exteriores autem operations sive bonorum sive malorum, vel angelorum vel hominum, sive etiam quorumcunque animalium, secundum imperium suum et a se impertitas distributions potestatum et appetitiones commoditatm, ita rerum nature adhibet in qua creat omnia, quemadmodum terre agriculturam."

5. Bede, *In Genesim*, I 1.
6. Romans 11:36.
7. Tobit 13:21.
8. *ratio.*
9. *non habet materiam partem sui.* Fr. Shapcote translates this as, "has no matter as a constituent part."
10. Aristotle, *On the Soul*, II 1, 412a6–10.

OBJ. 7. One might say that although natural forms have no matter on their part from which they are, they do have matter in which they are, and as such they are not created. On the contrary, like other natural forms, the rational soul is a form in matter. But it is granted that the rational soul is created. Therefore this must likewise be granted for other natural forms.

OBJ. 8. One might reply that the rational soul is not educed from matter as other natural forms are. On the contrary, nothing is educed from something which it is not in.[11] But before the completion of generation, form, which is the term of generation, was not in the matter. Otherwise contrary forms would be in the matter simultaneously. Therefore natural forms are not educed from matter.

OBJ. 9. Form, which is the term of generation, does not appear before generation is complete. Therefore, if it was there, it was latent and so it would follow that all sorts [of forms] are latent in all sorts [of matter], which Anaxagoras claims and Aristotle rejects in Physics I.[12]

OBJ. 10. But one might say that before generation is complete the natural form does not exist in matter completely, as Anaxagoras held,[13] but incompletely. On the contrary, if form is in any way in matter before the term of generation, it is there with respect to something of itself. But if it is not there completely, then something of itself does not pre-exist. Therefore the form has several parts,[14] and thus is not simple, which is contrary to what is maintained at the beginning of the Six Principles.[15]

OBJ. 11. If [form] does pre-exist incompletely in matter and later is completed, it must be that this complement accrues to it through generation. But this complement did not pre-exist in matter, since if it had form would be there completely. Therefore at least this complement will be created.

OBJ. 12. But one might reply that [form] pre-existed in matter incompletely, not with respect to parts, but in the sense that [form]

11. *quod non est in eo.*

12. Anaxagoras, Diels-Kranz, 59B4. Aristotle, *Physics,* I 4, 187b7–188a18.

13. Anaxagoras, Diels-Kranz, 59B4.

14. *habet ergo forma aliquid et aliquid.*

15. Gilbert de la Porrée, *Liber Sex Principiorum.* This work is not currently in print and is available only in manuscript form.

exists in one way before and in another after, that it was first in potency and later it is in act. On the contrary, when something is first one way and then another, it is altered[16] not generated. If therefore something comes to be through the work of nature only if a form which first was in potency later comes to be in act, it follows that the operation of nature produces not generation but only alteration.

OBJ. 13. The only active principles found in a lower nature are accidents. For fire acts through heat, which is an accident, and likewise the rest. But an accident cannot be the active cause of substantial form, since *nothing acts beyond its own species.*[17] For an effect does not surpass the cause, while substantial form does surpass an accident. Therefore substantial form is not produced through the action of a lower nature. And so it must be that it is created.

OBJ. 14. The imperfect cannot be the cause of the perfect. But the power of soul is in the semen of the brute animal only imperfectly. Therefore the soul of the brute is not produced through natural action of the seminal power.[18] And so it must be that it is created, and likewise all other natural forms.

OBJ. 15. That which is neither ensouled nor living cannot be the cause of any ensouled living thing. But animals which are generated from putrid matter are ensouled living things, and no living things are found in nature which give them life.[19] Therefore it must be that their souls are created by the first living being, and for the same reason other natural forms as well.

OBJ. 16. Nature produces only its like. But some natural things are generated which have no preceding likeness in the generator. For the mule is like neither the horse nor the ass in species. Therefore

16. *alteratio.*

17. This is a more particular formulation of the "law of similarity." See article 1, note 10 above. On the perpetuation of species as an instance of this law in Aristotle, see Rosemann, *Omne Agens Agit Sibi Simile,* 43–44. Cf. Aquinas, *Commentary on Aristotle's Physics* II, lect. 11, where Thomas distinguishes between "univocal" agents, for which this principle holds true, and "non-univocal" agents, for which it does not.

18. For a full discussion of the power of soul present in semen, see article 9 (especially ad 9) and articles 10–12. See also *ST* I, Q. 118, aa. 1–2, Q. 119, aa. 1–2, and *SCG* II 89.

19. On Thomas' understanding of spontaneous generation, see Blanchette, *The Perfection of the Universe,* 169.

the form of the mule is not [made] through the action of nature but through creation, and so the same conclusion follows.

OBJ. 17. In his book Of True Religion, Augustine says that natural things would not be informed by their forms if there were not some first thing by which they were informed.[20] But this [first thing] is God himself. Therefore all forms are created by God.

OBJ. 18. In his book On the Trinity, Boethius says that *from forms which are* without matter *come forms which are in matter.*[21] Now the forms which are without matter [referred to] in this proposition can only be understood to be the ideas of things existing in the divine mind. For angels, who can be called forms without matter, are not the cause of natural forms, as Augustine makes clear in his On the Trinity III.[22] Therefore natural forms are produced not by the action of nature but by a creating giver.

OBJ. 19. In the Book of Causes it is said that being is created.[23] But this cannot be unless forms are created, for form is the principle of being. Therefore forms are created and God operates in nature by creating something, namely the forms themselves.

OBJ. 20. That which is self-subsistent is the cause of that which is not self-subsistent.[24] The forms of natural things, however, are not self-subsistent, but subsist in matter. Therefore their cause is a form which subsists on its own, and thus it must be that natural forms are created by an extrinsic agent. And so it seems that God operates in nature by creating forms.

On the contrary (1), the work of creation is distinct from that of governance and propagation. Now that which is done by the action of nature pertains to the work of governance and to the propagation of things. Therefore creation is not mingled with the work of nature.

Further (2), only God can create. Therefore, if forms are created, they will only be from God, and so all natural action, the goal of which is form, will be in vain.

Further (3), just as substantial form has no matter on its part,[25]

20. Augustine, *Of True Religion*, xviii, 35. See also xi, 21.
21. Boethius, *On the Trinity*, II.
22. Augustine, *The Trinity*, III 8.
23. *Book of Causes*, Prop. 18. See also Prop. 4.
24. *Illud quod per se est, est causa eius quod non per se est.*
25. *non habet materiam partem sui.*

neither does accidental form. Therefore, if substantial form must be created because it has no matter, then by the same reasoning the same is true of accidental form. Now just as a generated thing is perfected by the substantial form, so is it disposed by[26] the accidental form. Therefore no natural thing would take part in generation, either as perfecting or as disposing, and so all natural action would be empty.

Further (4), nature procreates like from like. But the generated thing is like the generator in species and form. Therefore the very form of the generated thing comes to be by the action of the generator and not by creation.

Further (5), actions of diverse agents do not terminate in a single effect. But from matter and form comes something absolutely one. Therefore it cannot be that there is one agent which disposes the matter and another which induces the form. Now the natural agent disposes the matter. Therefore it also induces form and so forms are not created, and creation is not mingled with the works of nature.

I answer that there have been different opinions concerning this question, all of which seem to be rooted in one and the same principle, namely that nature cannot make something from nothing.

Based on this, some believed that nothing was made by another except in that it was drawn from another thing in which it was latent. In Physics I, Aristotle reports that this view was held by Anaxagoras,[27] who seems to have been deceived because he did not distinguish between potency and act, for he thought it was necessary for that which is generated already to exist actually. But it must pre-exist in potency not in act, for if it did not pre-exist in potency it would be made from nothing, while if it pre-existed in act it would not be made [at all], for what [already] exists does not come to be.

But since the thing generated is in potency through matter and in act through its own form, some maintained that a thing comes to be with respect to its form [although its] matter already exists. And since the operation of nature cannot be from nothing and consequently must presuppose something, according to them nature op-

26. I.e., so does it receive a disposition from.
27. Aristotle, *Physics*, I 4, 187a36–37.

erates only to dispose matter to its form. On the other hand, form, which must come to be and not be presupposed, must be from an agent which presupposes nothing, but can make [something] from nothing. And this is the supernatural agent which Plato held to be the giver of forms,[28] and which Avicenna called the lowest intelligence among the separated substances.[29] Certain modern followers say this is God.

But this seems unreasonable since, because every natural thing[30] produces its like (for everything acts insofar as it is in act, namely by making actual what was in potency),[31] there would be no need of a likeness of substantial form in the natural agent, unless the substantial form of the thing generated were produced by the agent's action. Because of this, that which is to be acquired in the thing generated is found in the natural generator actually and everything acts insofar as it is in act. And so it seems unreasonable to overlook this generator and inquire beyond it into some other.

And so we should note that these opinions seem to arise from ignorance of the nature of form, just as the first [opinion mentioned] arose from ignorance of the nature of matter. For being is not univocally predicated of natural form and of the thing generated. The natural generated thing is said to be *per se* and properly, as having being and subsisting in that being. But form is not said to be in this way, since it neither subsists nor has being *per se,* but is called being or a being because by it something is, just as accidents also are called beings because a substance is qualified by them, not because it is absolutely by them, as it is through the substantial form. And so accidents are more properly said of something than called beings, as is clear in Metaphysics XI.[32] Now everything which is made is said to come to be in the [same] way that it is said to be, for being is the

28. Fr. Henle cites Averroës' *Commentarium in Aristotelis Metaphysicorum libri XIV,* VII, com. 31, and XII, com. 18. See his *Saint Thomas and Platonism,* 25.

29. Avicenna, *Liber de Philosophia Prima sive Scientia Divina,* IX 4.

30. *unumquodque natum,* literally "every born thing."

31. Here Thomas is explicitly deducing the "law of similarity" among natural things from the principle that "everything acts insofar as it is in act," using Aristotle's understanding of the relationship between act and potency as the "middle term" in the argument. See article 1, notes 10 and 14.

32. This seems actually to be a reference to Aristotle, *Metaphysics,* VII 7, 1033a12.

term of coming to be. And so that which is made properly and *per se* is the composite, whereas the form is not properly made, but is that whereby [the composite] is made. That is, it is through the acquisition of form that something is said to be made. Therefore nothing here opposes the position that in nature nothing comes from nothing. Rather we say that substantial forms are by the operation of nature: for that which is made is not the form but the composite, which is made from matter and not from nothing. Indeed, it is made from matter insofar as matter is in potency to that composite in that it is in potency to this form. And so it is not properly said that form comes to be in matter, but more that it is educed from the potency of the matter. Because the composite, not the form, is made, the Philosopher shows in Metaphysics VII that forms are from natural agents. Since a made thing must be like the maker, and that which is made is composite, that which makes must be a composite and not a form existing *per se,* as Plato claimed.[33] And so, just as the thing made is composite, even as that whereby it is made is a form reduced to actuality in matter, so is the generator composite, not form alone. But form is that whereby it generates; a form, that is, existing in particular matter, as *in this flesh and in these bones*[34] and so on.

AD 1. In these words of Augustine, creation is attributed to God in the operation of nature because of the natural powers which he implanted in matter from the beginning through the work of creation, not as though something were created in every work of nature.

AD 2. Creation is meant properly in Augustine's words; however, it is referred not to the effects of nature but to the powers by which nature operates, which were implanted in nature by the work of creation.

AD 3. Since grace is not a subsistent form, neither being nor being made properly belongs to it in itself. And so neither is it created properly, in the way that substances which subsist in themselves are created. Nevertheless the infusion of grace belongs to the nature[35] of creation insofar as grace has no cause in the subject, neither an effi-

33. Aristotle, *Metaphysics,* VII 8, 1033b24–1034a7.
34. Aristotle, *Metaphysics,* VII 8, 1034a5.
35. *rationem.*

cient nor a material cause in which it might be in potency in such a way that it could be educed into act through a natural agent, as other natural forms are.

And so the solution to the fourth objection is clear, for when something is said to be made from nothing, the material cause is negated. Surely this pertains in some way to the poverty[36] of matter, that a form cannot be educed from the natural potency of matter.

AD 5. Although an efficient principal with respect to artificial forms is not found in nature, nevertheless forms of this sort do not exceed the order of nature as grace does. In fact they are beneath it,[37] since natural being is more noble than artificial being.

AD 6. From the fact that form has no matter on its part[38] it would follow that to be created belonged to it if it could properly [be said] to be made, as a self-subsisting thing is.

AD 7. Although the rational soul has matter in which it is, it is nonetheless not educed from the potency of matter, since its nature is elevated above the entire material order, as its intellectual operation demonstrates. Moreover this form is a self-subsisting thing, since it remains when the body corrupts.

AD 8. Before generation was complete, the form which is the term of generation was not actually in the matter, but [only] potentially. And it is possible for one of two contraries to be in act while the other is in potency.

And so the response to the ninth objection is clear. For Anaxagoras holds that forms actually pre-exist in matter, but latently.[39]

AD 10. Form pre-exists in matter imperfectly, which does not mean that some part of it is there actually and another is absent but that the whole pre-exists in potency and later the whole is produced in act.

And so the response to the eleventh objection is also clear. For it is clear that the being of the form is not perfected in matter by some added extraneous thing which was not in the potency of the matter.

36. *carenciam.*

37. *immo infra subsistunt.*

38. *forma non habet materiam partem sui.*

39. Anaxagoras, Diels-Kranz 59B4. For Aristotle's presentation of Anaxagoras on this point, see *Physics,* I 4, 187a28–b6.

AD 12. Being in potency and being in act are diverse not accidentally,[40] which would give rise to alteration, but substantially. For indeed, substance is divided by potency and act like any other genus.

AD 13. Accidental form acts in virtue of substantial form in that it is in a way its instrument, as for example in On the Soul II the heat of fire is said to be the instrument of the nutritive power. And so it is not unreasonable for the action of an accidental form to terminate in substantial form.

AD 14. Again, the heat of the semen acts as an instrument of the power of soul which is in the semen. Although this power is imperfect, it is nevertheless a kind of impression of a perfect soul, for it is left in the semen by the generator's soul. Moreover it acts by virtue of a heavenly body, whose instrument it is in a way. And because of this we do not say that semen generates but that an animal and the sun do.[41]

AD 15. Animals generated from putrid matter are less perfect than other animals, and so in generating them the power of the heavenly body impressed on lower matter accomplishes what the same heavenly power does in generation of perfect animals with the power of semen.

AD 16. Although the mule is not of the same species as the horse or the ass, it is nevertheless of the same proximate genus, by reason of which likeness a sort of intermediate species is generated from different species.

AD 17. Just as the divine power does not exclude the action of natural power, even though it is the first agent, neither does the first exemplar form, which is God, exclude the derivation of forms from other lower forms, which produce forms like themselves.

AD 18. And so the response to the eighteenth objection is clear, for Boethius understands the forms which are in matter to come from forms which are without matter as from first exemplars, not proximate causes.

40. In Latin, Thomas' words here have the poetry of those he is echoing from Aristotle. The text is: "esse in potencia et esse in actu non dicunt diversos modos accidentales." Unfortunately it is difficult to render Aristotle's formula, "X is said in many ways" in a way that sounds sensible to the modern ear.

41. *Physics* II 2, 194b14. See article 7, note 19.

AD 19. We say that to be <being> is through creation[42] in the sense that every secondary cause which gives being does so in virtue of the first creating cause, because being is the first effect and presupposes nothing else.

AD 20. A natural form which subsists in matter cannot be reduced to a self-subsisting form of the same species, since a natural form has matter in its very nature.[43] But it can be reduced to a self-subsistent form in the way that has been noted.[44]

42. *dicendum quod esse <esse> per creationem.*
43. *sui ratione.*
44. See ad 18, above.

ARTICLE 9

The ninth thing to be asked is whether the rational soul is brought into being by creation or by the transmission of semen. And it seems that it is propagated with semen.[1]

OBJ. 1. For Genesis XLVI says, *All the souls that went into Egypt with Jacob and came out of his thigh, except his sons' wives, sixty-six.*[2] But nothing comes out of the thigh of a father except by the transmission of semen. Therefore the rational soul is transmitted with the semen.

OBJ. 2. But one might reply that the part stands for the whole there, that is, the soul for the man. On the contrary, a human being is composed of soul and body. If, therefore, the whole man came from his father's thigh, not only the body but also the soul will be transmitted, as before.

OBJ. 3. An accident cannot be transmitted unless the subject is transmitted, because an accident does not pass from subject to subject. But the rational soul is the subject of original sin. Therefore since original sin is transmitted from parent to child, it seems that the rational soul of the child is also transmitted by the parent.

OBJ. 4. But one might reply that although original sin is in the soul as its subject, it is nevertheless in the flesh as its cause, and so it is transmitted through the transmission of the flesh. On the contrary, according to Romans V, sin came into this world through one man, and through sin death, and so death passed to all, in which all have sinned.[3] Now a Gloss points out that "in which" could mean in which sinner or in which sin.[4] But all would not have sinned in that sin had that same sin not been transmitted to all. Therefore that

1. For parallel discussions of how the rational soul comes to be and comes to be the form of a particular human body, see *ST* I QQ. 90, 91, and 118, and *SCG* II 83–90. On the particular question of whether the rational soul of a new human being is transmitted via his or her father's semen, see *ST* I Q. 118, a. 2, and *SCG* II 86–89.

2. Genesis 46:26.

3. *Peccatum per unum hominem in hunc mundum intravit et per peccatum mors, et ita mors in omnes pertransiit, in quo omnes peccauerunt* (Romans 5:12).

4. Fr. Shapcote notes that Augustine makes this observation in his *De Peccatorum Meritis et Remissione et de Baptismo Parvulorum ad Marcellinum*, I 10.

same sin which was in Adam is transmitted to all, and so the soul which was the subject of that sin is transmitted to all.

OBJ. 5. *Every agent produces its like,*[5] but *every agent acts by virtue of form.*[6] Therefore what an agent produces is the form of the thing made. But to generate is to produce. Therefore the form of the generated thing is [made] by the action of the generator. Therefore, since man generates man and the rational soul is the form of man, it seems that the rational soul is generated and not created.

OBJ. 6. According to the Philosopher in Physics II, an efficient cause is of the same species as its effect.[7] But man receives his species through the rational soul.[8] Therefore it seems that what the generator makes in the generated is the rational soul.

OBJ. 7. Children are like their parents because they are propagated by their parents. And they are like their parents not only in corporeal dispositions but also in dispositions of the soul. Therefore, just as body is from body, so is soul transmitted by soul.

OBJ. 8. In Leviticus XVII, Moses says, *The soul of* all *flesh is in the blood.*[9] But blood is transmitted with semen, especially since *sperm* is nothing other than *concentrated blood.*[10] Therefore the soul also is transmitted with semen.

OBJ. 9. Before it is perfected by the rational soul, an embryo has some operations of soul, since it grows and takes in nutrition and feels. But there can be no operation of soul without life. Therefore it lives. But the principle of corporeal life is the soul, and so it has soul. But we cannot say that it receives another soul, since there would be two souls in one body. Therefore the very soul which was in the semen at the beginning and was propagated with the semen, <is> the rational soul.

OBJ. 10. Souls of different species constitute animals of different

5. See article 1, note 10 above.

6. Cf. Aristotle, *Physics* III 2, 202a9–12. In his commentary on this text, Thomas says, "omne agens moveat secundum formam" (lect. 4, no. 593).

7. Aristotle, *Physics*, II 7, 198a26.

8. *animam*.

9. Leviticus 17:14.

10. *sanguis decoctus*, literally "boiled down blood." See Aristotle, *Generation of Animals*, I 19, 726b2–11 and I 20, 728a16–21. For a summary explanation of Aristotle's understanding of the nature of male seed, see Prudence Allen, R.S.M., *The Concept of Woman*, vol. 1, p. 96.

species. If therefore there was a non-rational soul in the semen before a rational soul, then there was an animal of a different species than the human. And so that should not become a human being, because animals of different species do not change into each other.[11]

OBJ. 11. But one may reply that operations of this sort belong to the embryo not through a soul but through some power of soul which is called the formative power. On the contrary, power is rooted in substance, and so it is placed intermediate between substance and operation, as Dionysius maintains in the eleventh chapter of The Celestial Hierarchy.[12] If therefore a power of soul is present, the substance of soul will be present.

OBJ. 12. In On Animals XVI, the Philosopher says that the embryo is a living thing before it is an animal and an animal before a human being.[13] But every animal has a soul. Therefore some soul is present before the rational soul, through which man is man, is present.

OBJ. 13. According to the Philosopher in On the Soul II, *soul is the act of a* living *body* insofar as it is [a body] of this sort.[14] But if the embryo lives and employs operations of soul through a formative power of this sort, then this power itself will be its act insofar as it is living. Therefore it will be a soul.

OBJ. 14. According to On the Soul I, *life is in all living things* through the vegetative soul.[15] But it is manifest that the embryo lives before the infusion of the rational soul, since the operations of life are found in it. Therefore the vegetative soul is there before the rational soul is.

OBJ. 15. In On the Soul II, the Philosopher proves that the principle agent of growth is not fire but the vegetative soul.[16] But the em-

11. For a contemporary treatment of evolution from within the framework of Thomistic metaphysics, see W. Norris Clarke's chapter "The Metaphysics of Evolution" in his *The One and the Many,* 245–59. He also offers a helpfully annotated bibliography on the subject on p. 259. See also Wojciech Grygiel, F.S.S.P, "The Metaphysics of Chaos: A Thomistic View of Entropy and Evolution," *The Thomist* 66 (2002): 251–66.

12. Pseudo-Dionysius, *The Celestial Hierarchy,* 11, no. 2.

13. Aristotle, *On the Generation of Animals,* II 3, 736a34–b6.

14. Aristotle, *On the Soul,* II 1, 412a21.

15. Aristotle, *On the Soul,* II 2, 413a31–b1 and II 4, 415a25.

16. Aristotle, *On the Soul,* II 4, 416a9–18.

bryo grows before the advent of the rational soul. Therefore it has a vegetative soul.

OBJ. 16. If there is no vegetative soul present before the advent of the rational soul, but [only] a formative power, then at the advent of the soul, that power will cease its operation, since the operation which that power performed in the embryo will then be sufficiently performed in the animal through the soul. Therefore it will be superfluous, which seems unreasonable, since *nothing in nature is superfluous.*[17]

OBJ. 17. But one might say that this power is destroyed at the advent of the soul. On the contrary, dispositions are not destroyed with the advent of form, but they remain and in some way maintain the form in matter. But that power was a certain disposition to soul. Therefore at the advent of soul, that power is not destroyed.

OBJ. 18. By its action this power attains[18] the introduction of soul. Therefore, if that power is destroyed with the advent of soul, it seems that something effects its own destruction, which is impossible.

OBJ. 19. Man is man through the rational soul. Therefore, if the soul does not come into being through generation, we will have to say that man is not generated, which is clearly false.

OBJ. 20. The human body comes into being through the generator's action. Therefore if the soul does not come into being from the generator, there will be a twofold being in man: one of the body, which the generator makes, and the other of the soul, which he does not make. And thus soul and body will not become one simply, since they differ in being.

OBJ. 21. It is impossible that the action of one agent terminate in matter and [the action] of another in form (otherwise from form and matter there could not be one thing simply, for one thing is made by one action). But the generative action of nature terminates in the body. Therefore it also terminates in the soul which is its form.

OBJ. 22. According to the Philosopher in On Animals XVI, *principles* whose actions are not *independent of the body* are produced with

17. Aristotle, *Parts of Animals,* IV 2, 691b5.
18. *ex actione illius virtutis pervenitur.*

the body.[19] But the action of the rational soul is not independent of the body, for to understand would most of all be independent of the body, which is clearly false, for we cannot understand *without phantasms,* as is said in On the Soul I and III.[20] But a phantasm cannot be independent of a body. Therefore the rational soul is transmitted with the body.

OBJ. 23. But one might reply that, in order to understand, the rational soul needs phantasms for the acquisition of intelligible species but not after it has acquired them. On the contrary, after he has acquired knowledge man is impeded in the action of his intellect if the organ of the imagination[21] is injured. But this would not be the case if the intellect did not need the phantasms after the acquisition of knowledge. Therefore it needs them not only for acquiring knowledge but also for using acquired knowledge.

OBJ. 24. But one might say that injury to the organ of the imagination impedes the intellect's operation not because the intellect needs phantasms for using acquired knowledge but because the imagination and the intellect are in one essence of the soul, and so whatever impedes the imagination accidentally impedes the intellect as well. On the contrary, the conjunction of powers in one essence of the soul is the reason that when one of the powers increases its activity another decreases its activity, just as when someone looks attentively, he hears less attentively. This is also why when one power ceases its action, the other is strengthened in its activity, and so the blind often hear more acutely. Therefore a conjunction of this sort is not the reason that an impediment to the imaginative power impedes the action of the intellect, but rather it should be strengthened [by such impediment, given this conjunction].

OBJ. 25. Whoever gives the final complement to an operation, cooperates to the greatest degree with the operator. But if all human souls are created by God and infused into bodies by him, then he gives the final complement to the generation that results from adultery. Therefore he would cooperate in adultery, which seems absurd.

OBJ. 26. According to the Philosopher in Meteorology IV, a per-

19. Aristotle, *On the Generation of Animals,* II 3, 736b22–26.
20. Aristotle, *On the Soul,* I 1, 403a8; III 7, 431a16; and III 8, 432a7.
21. *fantasie.*

fect thing is one that can make its like.[22] Therefore the more perfect something is the more able it is to make its like. But rational souls are more perfect than the material forms of the elements which produce forms like themselves. Therefore a rational soul can also be produced by the power of a rational soul by way of generation.

OBJ. 27. The rational soul is situated between God and corporeal things, whence in the Book of Causes it is said that it is created *on the horizon of eternity* and time.[23] But we find generation in God and likewise in corporeal things. Therefore the soul, which is between them, is produced by generation.

OBJ. 28. In On Animals XVI,[24] the Philosopher says that *the spirit which comes forth with the sperm is a power of the generating soul*[25] *and is a thing divine, and such a thing is called intellect.* And so it seems that the intellect is propagated with the semen.

OBJ. 29. In the same book the Philosopher says that in generation *the female gives the body* and *the soul is from the male.*[26] And so it seems that the soul is produced through the propagation of the semen and not by creation.

On the contrary, it is said in Isaiah, *Every breath I have made.*[27] And by breath we are to understand the soul. Therefore it seems that the soul is created by God.

(2) Further, in the Psalm it is said, [*He*] *Who formed one by one the heart of each.*[28] Therefore one soul is not propagated from another, but all are created separately by God.

I answer that in times past different people have said various things concerning this question.[29] Some said the soul of the child

22. Aristotle, *Meteorology*, IV 3, 380a15. See also *De Anima*, II 4, 415a27. This is another specification of the law of similarity. See article 1, note 10.

23. *"in orizonte eternitatis et temporis."* This is a reference to *Book of Causes*, Prop. 2, but it is not quite accurate. The text says, "Esse autem quod est post aeternitatem et supra tempus est anima, quoniam est in horizonte aeternitatis inferius et supra tempus" (*Super librum de causis expositio* [*ed. Saffrey*], 10).

24. This seems to be a reference to Aristotle, *On the Generation of Animals*, II 3, 736b13–29.

25. *virtus principii anime.*

26. Aristotle, *On the Generation of Animals*, II 3, 737a9–11, 23–24 and II 4, 738b22–23.

27. Isaiah 57:16.

28. Psalm 33:15.

29. For an overview of various views of the human embryo and the source

is propagated from the soul of the parent, just as the body is propagated from the body [of the parent]. Others said all souls were created separately, but they held that [souls] were created all together at the beginning, apart from bodies, and later they were united to begotten bodies either by a proper motion of [each soul's] will, according to some, or by God's command and action, according to others. Others said that souls are simultaneously created and infused into bodies. As Augustine makes clear in On the Literal Interpretation of Genesis X and in the books he wrote On the Origin of the Soul,[30] [all of] these opinions were held at one time and which of them was more true was in doubt. Nevertheless the first two were later condemned by the church and the third approved. And so it is said in On Church Dogma, *we do not* believe *that human souls were from the beginning among other intellectual natures, neither created simultaneously with them, as Origen contrived, nor* begotten *with bodies through coition, as the Luciferians and Cyril and some presumptuous Latin writers affirm. Rather we say ... the body alone is begotten by sexual intercourse ... and once the body is informed, the soul is created and infused.*[31]

When carefully considered, it is apparent that it was reasonable to condemn the opinion that the rational soul is propagated with the semen. And at present this can be shown with three arguments.

The first is that the rational soul differs from other forms in that other forms have, not being in which they themselves subsist, but being by which the things they inform subsist. But the rational soul has being in such a way that it subsists in itself. And this is demonstrated by the different modes of acting, for since only what exists can act, a thing is related to operation and action in the way that it is related to being. And so, since the body necessarily shares in the operation of other forms but not in the operation of the rational soul, which is to think and to will, being must be attributed to the ratio-

and timing of its ensoulment, see D. A. Jones, *The Soul of the Embryo: An Enquiry into the Status of the Human Embryo in the Christian Tradition* (London: Continuum, 2004). Jones begins by looking at ancient Hebrew and Greek views and then traces historical development of opinions and teaching on the status of the human embryo to the present day. For the views Thomas is responding to here in the respondeo and in ad 9, see Jones, chs. 7 and 8.

30. Augustine, *De Genesi ad litteram libri XII,* X 21 and 22; Augustine, *On the Soul and Its Origin.*

31. Gennadius Massiliensis, *De Ecclesiasticis Dogmatibus,* XIV.

nal soul itself as a subsistent thing, but not to the other forms. And it is because of this that, of all the forms, only the rational soul is separated from matter. From this therefore it is clear that the rational soul does not come into being in the way that other forms do, which are not themselves made but which are said to be made in the made thing [which they inform]. Now a thing is made which is properly and *per se* made. But what is thus made, is made either from matter or from nothing. Now that which is made from matter must be made from matter subject to contrariety, for generations are *from contraries,* according to the Philosopher.[32] And so, since a soul either has no matter at all or at least has no matter subject to contrariety, it cannot be made from anything. Thus it follows that it comes into being through creation, as being made from nothing. But to hold that it is made through the generation of the body is to hold that it is not itself subsistent and consequently is corrupted with the body.

The second argument is that it is impossible for the action of a corporeal power to be elevated to the point that it could cause a wholly spiritual and incorporeal power. For *nothing acts beyond its own species;*[33] in fact, the agent must be superior to the patient, according to Augustine's On the Literal Interpretation of Genesis.[34] Now human generation is effected through the generative power, which has a bodily organ. Indeed, the power which is in the semen can act only by means of heat, as is said in On Animals XVI.[35] And so, since the rational soul is a wholly spiritual form, independent of the body, not sharing in operation with the body, there is no way it can be propagated through the generation of the body or produced in being through some power which is in the semen.

The third argument is that every form which comes into being by generation or by the power of nature, is educed from the potency of matter, as is proved in Metaphysics VII.[36] But the rational soul cannot be educed from the potency of matter, for forms which operate independent of the body cannot be educed from corporeal matter.

32. Aristotle, *On the Generation of Animals,* I 18, 724b9.
33. See article 8, note 17.
34. Augustine, *De Genesi ad litteram libri XII,* XII 16.
35. Aristotle, *On the Generation of Animals,* II 3, 736b35.
36. Aristotle, *Metaphysics,* VII 7, 1032a15–17 and 1032b17–22.

And so it follows that the rational soul is not propagated through the power of the generator. And this is Aristotle's argument in On Animals XVI.[37]

AD 1. The passage quoted is using a synecdoche, in which the part stands for the whole. That is, the soul stands for the whole human being, because the soul is the more fundamental part of a man, and every whole is considered to be that [part] which is more fundamental. And so the whole man is considered to be the soul or the intellect, as is said in Book IX of the Ethics.[38]

AD 2. The whole man comes from the generator's thigh in that the power of the semen coming from the thigh effects the union of body and soul by giving matter its final disposition, which is necessary to the form. And from this union a man is a man, but not as though each part of the man is caused by the power of the semen.

AD 3. Original sin is called the sin of the entire nature, just as actual sin is called personal sin. And so the comparison of actual sin to one single person is the same as the comparison of original sin to the whole human nature transmitted by the first parent, in whom was the beginning of sin and through whose will original sin is imputed to all as voluntary. Therefore in this way original sin is in the soul insofar as it pertains to human nature. But human nature is transmitted from parent to child through the transmission of the flesh, into which the soul is subsequently[39] infused, and [the soul] incurs the infection because it becomes one nature with the transmitted flesh. For if it were united to [the flesh] in a way that did not form one nature, as an angel is united to an assumed body, it would not contract the infection.

AD 4. Just as the nature of all of us was originally in Adam's nature, so also the original sin which is in us was originally in his original sin. For as was said above, original sin *per se* concerns[40] nature, and consequently concerns the soul.

AD 5. A man generates his like in species by virtue of his form,

37. Aristotle, *On the Generation of Animals,* II 3, 736b22–29.

38. Aristotle, *Nicomachean Ethics,* IX 4, 1166a16 and 23.

39. *postmodum.* The chronological sequence implied by this term is obviously problematic.

40. *respicit.*

namely the rational soul; not that this is the immediate principle acting in human generation, but because it is only to the extent that they act as instruments of a rational soul that the generative power and that which acts in the semen dispose matter to become a body perfectible by a rational soul. Nevertheless, this action cannot extend to making the rational soul, for the reasons discussed above.

AD 6. The generator generates his like in species insofar as the generated is produced by the generator's action in order to share in his species. And this comes about because the generated arises from a form like the generator's. Therefore, if this form were not subsistent, but its being consisted merely in being united to that whose form it is, it would be necessary that the generator be the cause of this form, just as is the case in all material forms. But if the form is one which has subsistence and its being does not depend entirely on its union with matter, as is the case in the rational soul, then it suffices that the generator be the cause of the union of such a form with matter by disposing the matter to the form. Nor must it be the cause of this form.

AD 7. The disposition of the rational soul is in accord with the disposition of the body, both because the rational soul is received by the body and because forms are diversified according to the diversity of matter. And it is because of this that children are like their parents even in those things which pertain to the soul, not because souls are transmitted by souls.

AD 8. Since the soul is properly the act of a living body, and life is made possible by[41] heat and humidity, which are maintained in the animal by the blood, thus it may be said that the soul is in the blood in order to designate the proper disposition of the body inasmuch as it is matter perfected by soul.

AD 9. There are several different opinions about the life of the embryo.

1. Some compared the progress of the rational soul in human generation to the progress of the human body, claiming that the human body is in the semen virtually,[42] without actually having the perfec-

41. *est per.*
42. *uirtualiter.*

tion of the human body (which consists in the distinction of the organs), but reaching this perfection gradually through the power of the semen.[43] In the same way, they say, the soul is present from the beginning of generation, but, since activities of the soul are not apparent [at the beginning], [the soul] has virtually,[44] but not actually, all the perfection which later appears in the complete human being. But gradually over time it acquires [that perfection], so that first activities of the vegetative soul appear in it and later those of the sensitive soul, and finally those of the rational soul. And Gregory of Nyssa touches on this opinion in his book, On Man.[45]

But this opinion cannot stand, because it means either that the soul itself according to its species exists in the semen from the beginning, not yet having perfect operation because of the lack of organs, or that from the beginning there is in the semen some power or form which does not yet have the species of the soul (just as the semen does not have the species of the human body), but gradually through the action of nature it is transformed[46] into a soul which is at first vegetative, next sensitive, and finally rational.

Now the first alternative is rebutted first on the authority of the Philosopher, for in On the Soul II he says that the potency for life which is in a physical organic body, of which the soul is the act, is *not* [properly ascribed to that which is] *without soul, as in the case of the semen and the fruit.*[47] By this he means that the semen is in potency to the soul which it lacks. Secondly, since the semen is not yet assimilated by final assimilation to the members (for thus its resolution would be a kind of corruption), but it is *the residue of the final digestion,* as is said in On Animals XV,[48] [while] existing in the body of

43. *uirtutem seminis.*

44. *uirtute.*

45. Gregory of Nyssa, *On the Making of Man,* XXIX.

46. *producatur.*

47. *dicitur enim in II De anima quod potencia vite que est in corpore phisico organico, cuius actus est anima,* non *est* abciens animam sicut semen et fructus .... Thomas is citing Aristotle, *On the Soul,* II 1, 412b25–26. The text of Aristotle from Aquinas' commentary (i.e. the Latin as Thomas had it) is as follows: "Est autem non abjiciens animam, potentia ens, ut vivat; sed quod habens. Semen autem et fructus, potentia tale corpus est" (*In Aristotelis Librum de Anima,* ed. A. M. Pirotta, O.P. [Turin: Marietti, 1925], Bk II, lect. II, p. 85). See article 12, sed contra 1 below, for another use of this text.

48. Aristotle, *On the Generation of Animals,* I 18, 725a11–28 and 726a26–28.

the generator it was not yet perfected by the soul, and so it can not be that the soul is in it from the beginning of its separation. Thirdly, granted that the soul was separated with it, nevertheless this cannot refer to the rational soul which, since it is not the act of a part of the body, cannot be separated when the body is separated.

The second alternative is also clearly false. For since substantial form is not produced in act continuously or gradually but instantaneously (otherwise motion would necessarily be in the genus of substance as well as in the genus of quality), it cannot be that that power which is in semen from the beginning gradually progresses to different stages of the soul. For the form of fire is not induced in the air in such a way that it continuously proceeds from imperfection to perfection, since no substantial form admits of more or less, but only matter is changed by earlier alteration so that it is more or less disposed to form. But form does not begin to be in matter until the final instant of the alteration.

2. But others say that in the semen at first there is a vegetative soul and later, while this soul remains, a sensible soul is induced by the power of the generator, and finally a rational soul is induced by creation. Thus they hold that in man there are three souls through different essences.

But against this is what is said in the book On Church Dogma: *Nor do we say there are two souls in one man, as James and other Syrians write, one animal by which the body* is ensouled *and which is mixed with the blood, and another spiritual, which serves reason.*[49] Moreover, it is impossible that there be multiple substantial forms of one and the same thing. For, since substantial form makes something be not merely this or that, but be absolutely, and establishes it in the genus of substance, if the first form does this, the one which comes second finds a subject already constituted in substantial being and accrues to it accidentally. And so it will follow that in man the sensitive and rational souls would be united to the body accidentally. Nor can it be said that the vegetative soul, which is the substantial form in plants, is not the substantial form in man but a disposition to form, since that

---

For Thomas' understanding of semen as a product of digestion, see article 12 below and *ST* I Q. 119, a. 2.

49. Gennadius Massiliensis, *De Ecclesiasticis Dogmatibus,* XV.

which is in the genus of substance cannot be an accident, as is said in Physics I.[50]

3. And so others say that the vegetative soul is in potency to the sensitive soul and the sensitive is its act, whence the vegetative soul which is first in the semen is brought to perfection in the sensitive soul by the action of nature, and moreover the rational soul is the act and perfection of the sensitive soul. Whence the sensitive soul is brought to its perfection, namely the rational soul, not by the generator's action, but by the creator's. And thus they say that in man the rational soul is partly from without, namely in terms of its intellectual nature, and partly from within, in terms of its vegetative and sensitive nature.

But there is no way this can stand. For this means either that intellectual nature is a soul distinct from the vegetative and sensitive, and thus it returns to the second opinion, or that these three natures constitute the substance of a soul in which the intellectual nature will be the formal aspect and the sensitive and vegetative natures will be the material. From the latter it follows that, since sensitive and vegetative natures are corruptible inasmuch as they are educed from matter, the substance of the human soul could not be perpetual. It also leads to the same absurdity cited against the first opinion, namely that the substantial form is educed into actuality by degrees.

4. Others say that the embryo has no soul until it is perfected by the rational soul, and the vital operations which are displayed in it are from the soul of the mother.

But this cannot be. For living and non-living things differ in that living things move themselves with respect to vital operations, which cannot be said of non-living things. And so it cannot be that nutrition and growth, which are operations proper to living things, are in the embryo from an extrinsic principle, namely from the soul of the mother. And further, the mother's nutritive power would assimilate nutrients to the mother's body and not to the embryo's, because the nutritive [power] serves the individual just as the generative serves the species. And further sensation cannot be in the embryo from the mother's soul.

50. Aristotle, *Physics,* I 2, 185a31, and I 3, 186b32.

5. And so others say that there is no soul in the embryo before the infusion of the rational soul, but there is a formative power in it which carries out these vital operations in the embryo.

But this also cannot be. For, since different vital operations appear in the embryo before its final perfection, these cannot be from one power. And so a soul, having various powers, must be in it.

6. And so we must take another position, namely that from the beginning of its separation there is in the semen not a soul but a power of soul which is based on the spirit contained in the semen, which by its nature is foamy[51] and consequently contains corporeal spirit. Now this power acts by disposing matter and forming it for reception of the soul.[52] And we should note the difference between the generation of human beings or animals and the generation of air or water. For the generation of air is simple, since in that entire generation only two substantial forms appear, one which is corrupted[53] and one which is induced, which all happens simultaneously in one instant. And so before the introduction of the form of air, the form of water is always present, and there are no dispositions to the form of air present. But in the generation of animals different substantial forms appear, since first sperm appears and later blood and so on until the human or animal form [appears]. And so generation of this sort cannot be simple, but contains within it many generations and corruptions. For it cannot be that one and the same substantial form is gradually educed into act, as has been shown. And so it must be that through the formative power which is in the sperm from the beginning, the sperm form is set aside and another form is induced, which in turn being set aside, another is induced. And in this way the vegetative soul is first induced; then, it being set aside, a soul which is at once sensitive and vegetative is induced; and, this being set aside, another soul which is at once rational, sensitive, and vegetative is induced, not through the [formative] power but by a creator.[54]

51. *spumosum est.*

52. For parallel discussions of this "formative power" in the semen, see *ST* I QQ. 118 and 119, and *SCG* II 89 (8).

53. *abicitur.*

54. For Thomas' arguments that a soul with rational power must be creat-

And so according to this opinion, before it has a rational soul, the embryo lives and has a soul, which is set aside and a rational soul induced.[55] And so it does not follow that there are two souls in the same body or that the rational soul is transmitted with the semen.

AD 10. Before the embryo has a rational soul it is not a perfected being but on the way to perfection. And so it has neither genus nor species except through reduction, just as the incomplete is reduced to the genus or species of the complete.

AD 11. Although there is no soul in the semen at the beginning, a power of soul is nevertheless there, as has been said, and this power is based on the spirit which is contained in the sperm. It is called a power of soul because it is from the soul of the generator.

AD 12. Before the [infusion of the] rational soul the embryo lives and has a soul, as was said above. And so we concede this argument.

And likewise for the thirteenth, fourteenth, and fifteenth objections.

AD 16. The formative power which is in the semen from the be-

---

ed, see the respondeo for this article, above. See also *ST* I Q. 118, a. 2 and *SCG* II 86 (7) and 87.

55. The idea that there is succession of souls in the developing human embryo is called "delayed hominization." The best work I have seen that applies Thomas' thinking on this issue to the contemporary science of which Thomas did not have benefit is John Haldane and Patrick Lee's "Aquinas on Human Ensoulment, Abortion and the Value of Life," *Philosophy* 78 (2003): 255–78. Haldane and Lee give a comprehensive bibliography of 33 works in English on the timing of ensoulment on pp. 259–60, n. 5. For an up-to-date account of what science has established regarding embryogenesis, see Maureen L. Condic, "When Does Human Life Begin? A Scientific Perspective," *National Catholic Bioethics Quarterly* 9 (2009): 131–49. See also John Meyer, "Embryonic Personhood, Human Nature, and Rational Ensoulment," *Heythrop Journal* 47 (2006): 206–25; Jason Eberl, "Aquinas's Account of Human Embryogenesis and Recent Interpretations," *Journal of Medicine and Philosophy* 30 (2005): 379–94; David Hershenov and Rose Koch, "How a Hylomorphic Metaphysics Constrains the Abortion Debate," *National Catholic Bioethics Quarterly* 5 (2005): 751–64; D. A. Jones, *The Soul of the Embryo*, ch. 8; Denis Bradley, "'To Be or Not to Be': Pasnau on Aquinas's Immortal Human Soul," *The Thomist* 68 (2004): 1–39; Kevin L. Flannery, S.J., "Applying Aristotle in Contemporary Embryology," *The Thomist* 67 (2003): 249–78; Pascal Ide, "Le zygote: est-il une personne humaine?" *Nova et Vetera* 76 (2001.1): 45–88 and (2001.2): 53–88; Angelo Serra and Roberto Colombo, "Identity and Status of the Human Embryo: The Contribution of Biology," in *Identity and Statute of Human Embryo: Proceedings of the 3rd Assembly of the Pontifical Academy for Life*, ed. J. Correa and E. Sgreccia (Rome: Libreria Editrice Vaticana, 1998), 128–77.

ginning remains even with the advent of the rational soul, just as the [animal] spirits, into which nearly the whole substance of the sperm is converted, remain. This force, which at first formed the body, later regulates the body, just as heat which was a disposition to the form of fire remains at the advent of the form of fire as an instrument of that form's activity.

And through this the solution to the seventeenth and eighteenth objections is clear.

AD 19. Although the rational soul is not from the generator, nevertheless its union with the body is in a way from the generator, as has been said, and in this way man is said to be generated.

AD 20. There is no twofold being in man, for we are not to understand the body to be from the generator and the soul from the creator, as though the being acquired by the body from the generator is distinct from that which the soul acquires from the creator. Rather, the creator gives being to the soul in the body and the generator disposes the body to be a sharer[56] in this being through the soul united to it.

AD 21. Two wholly disparate agents cannot be related in such a way that the action of one terminates in matter and [the action] of the other in form. Nevertheless, this does occur in two ordered agents, where one is the instrument of the other, for the action of the principal agent sometimes extends itself to something to which the action of the instrument cannot extend itself. Now nature is a kind of instrument of the divine power, as was shown above.[57] And so it is not unreasonable if the divine power alone make the rational soul, with the action of nature extending itself only to the disposition of the body.

AD 22. In order to understand, the intellect existing in a body does not need something corporeal which would be a co-principle of intellectual operation with the intellect. This is unlike what happens in vision, for the principle of vision is not the sense of sight alone, but the eye consisting of the sense of sight and the pupil. But [the intellect] does need the body as an object, as it were, just as vision re-

56. *particeps*.
57. In article 7.

quires the wall on which the color is, for *phantasms are compared to the intellect as colors to the sense of sight,* as is said in On the Soul III.[58] And it is because of this that the intellect is impeded in understanding when the organ of the imagination[59] is injured, for, when it is in the body, it needs phantasms not only as receiving from the phantasms when it acquires knowledge, but also for relating intelligible species to phantasms when it uses the knowledge it has acquired. And because of this examples are necessary in science.

And through this the response to the twenty-third and twenty-fourth objections is clear.

AD 25. According to Gregory of Nyssa, this is the argument of Apollinaris.[60] He was deceived through failing to distinguish the operation of nature (which is the generation of the child, to which God gives the complement) from the voluntary act of the adulterer (in which the sin consists).

AD 26. Since the soul is more perfect than material forms, it could produce its like if a rational soul could be produced in any way other than through creation. But it cannot be, and this is because of its perfection, as should be clear from what has been said.

AD 27. Only in God can there be one nature in several supposits, and so in him alone can there be generation without the imperfection of change and division. Hence the more noble creatures, which are indivisible and substantially unchangeable, such as the rational soul and the angel, are not generated, unlike inferior creatures, which are divisible and corruptible.

AD 28. As the Commentator says in Metaphysics VII, the Philosopher calls the power which is in the semen intellect by analogy, because, just as the intellect operates without an organ, so does this power.[61]

AD 29. In that passage the Philosopher is referring to the sensitive soul, not the rational.

58. This seems to be an inference from Aristotle, *On the Soul,* III 5, 430a16.
59. *fantasie.*
60. Gregory of Nyssa, *De Anima,* col. 206.
61. Averroës, *Metaphysicorum libri XIV,* VII 9, com. 31.

ARTICLE 10

The tenth thing to be asked is whether the rational soul is created in the body or apart from the body. And it seems that it is created apart from the body.[1]

OBJ. 1. Things which are of the same species come into being in the same way. But our souls are of the same species as the soul of Adam, and his soul was created apart from the body when the angels were created, as Augustine says in On the Literal Interpretation of Genesis VII.[2] Therefore other human souls are also created apart from the body.

OBJ. 2. Any whole which lacks a part pertaining to its perfection is imperfect. But the rational soul pertains to the perfection of the universe more than corporeal substance does, since intellectual substance is more noble than corporeal substance. Therefore, if rational souls were not all created from the beginning, but are created day by day when bodies are generated, it would follow that the universe is imperfect because it lacks its most noble parts. But this seems unreasonable. Therefore rational souls are created from the beginning apart from the body.

OBJ. 3. It seems like theatrics to say that the universe is to be destroyed when it attains its ultimate perfection. But the world will come to an end when the generation of men ceases, and at that point the universe will be most completely perfect, if souls are created simultaneously with the generation of bodies. Therefore, according to this view, the divine governance which rules the world will be like a play, which seems absurd.

OBJ. 4. But one might reply that the perfection of the universe does not require each individual, since it is nevertheless complete in that it has all of its species. On the contrary, species of things, having in themselves a certain perpetuity, pertain to the essential perfection

1. For parallel discussions of this question, see *ST* I Q. 90, a. 4, and *SCG* II 83.

2. Augustine, *De Genesi ad litteram libri XII,* VII 24.

of the universe, inasmuch as they are themselves intended by the author of the universe. But individuals, which do not have perpetual being, pertain to a certain accidental perfection of the universe, inasmuch as they are not intended in themselves but for the preservation of their species. Now rational souls have perpetuity not only in species but also as single individuals. Therefore, if not all rational souls existed from the beginning, then the universe was as imperfect as if some species were absent from it.

OBJ. 5. In his Commentary on the Dream of Scipio, Macrobius placed two gates in heaven: one for the gods and the other for souls, in Cancer and Capricorn, through one of which souls descended to bodies.[3] But this could not be unless souls were created in heaven apart from the body. Therefore souls are created apart from the body.

OBJ. 6. The efficient cause precedes its effect in time. But the soul is the efficient cause of the body, as is said in On the Soul II.[4] Therefore it exists before the body, and thus is not created in the body.

OBJ. 7. In the book On Spirit and Soul, it is said that *before* it is united *to the body,* soul *has* irascibility and concupiscence.[5] But these cannot be in the soul before the soul exists. Therefore the soul exists before it is united with the body and thus is not created in the body.

OBJ. 8. The substance of rational souls is not measured by time because, as is said in the Book of Causes, it is *above time.*[6] Neither again is it measured by eternity, since this belongs to God alone. Indeed, in the Book of Causes the soul is said to be beneath eternity.[7] Therefore it is measured by eviternity,[8] as angels are, and thus angels and souls have the same measure of duration. Therefore, since angels were created at the beginning of the world, it seems that souls also were created then and not in bodies.

OBJ. 9. There is no before and after in eviternity; otherwise it would not differ from time, as some think. But if angels were cre-

3. Macrobius, *Commentary on the Dream of Scipio,* I 12.

4. Aristotle, *On the Soul,* II 4, 415b11, 22–27.

5. Augustine, *De Spiritu et Anima,* 13.

6. *Book of Causes,* Prop. 2.

7. *Book of Causes,* Prop. 2. See article 9, note 23 above.

8. *evo.* On eviternity, see article 14, ad contrary 9 and article 17, ad 23 below, and *ST* I, Q. 10, aa. 5–6. Also, see J. Collins, *The Thomistic Philosophy of the Angels,* 346–61 and Dario Schioppetto, "L'Ombra dell'Eterno: Note sul Tempo degli Angeli," in *Il Tempo in Questione: Paradigmi della Temporalità nel Pensiero Occidentale,* ed. L. Ruggiu (Milan: Guerini, 1997), 155–81.

ated before souls or if one soul is created after another, then before and after would be in eviternity, since the measure of the soul is eviternity, as has been shown. Therefore all souls must be created at the same time as the angels.

OBJ. 10. Unity of place attests to unity of nature, and so bodies of different natures are in different places. But the angel and the soul agree in nature, since they are spiritual and intellectual substances. Therefore souls are created in the empyrean heaven just as the angels were and not in bodies.

OBJ. 11. The more subtle a substance is, the higher the place that is due to it; thus the place of fire is higher than that of air or water. But the soul is a much simpler substance than a body. Therefore it seems that it was created above all bodies and thus not in the body.

OBJ. 12. The ultimate perfection of any thing is [achieved] insofar as it is in its proper place, since it is outside of this place only by some violence. But the ultimate perfection of the soul is in [its] heavenly abode. Therefore that is the place fitting to its nature and thus it seems that it was created there.

OBJ. 13. According to Genesis I, *On the seventh day,* God *rested from* all *the work he had done,*[9] from which we are given to understand that God then ceased creating new creatures. But this would not be if souls are now being created daily. Therefore souls are not created in the body but are created from the beginning apart from the body.

OBJ. 14. The work of creation precedes the work of propagation. But this would not be if souls are created at the same time bodies are propagated. Therefore souls were created before bodies.

OBJ. 15. God does all things justly. But diverse and unequal [gifts] are not justly given except to those in whom some inequality of merit pre-exists. But men have many spiritual inequalities from birth, as for example when some are united to bodies well suited to the operations of the soul while others are not well suited, and when some are born of non-believers while others are born of believers and are saved through receiving the sacraments. Therefore it seems that inequality of merit already exists in souls, and thus that souls existed before bodies.

OBJ. 16. It seems that things which are one in inception are de-

9. Genesis 2:2.

pendent on each other in being. But the soul does not depend on the body in its being, which is clear from the fact that it remains when the body corrupts. Therefore neither does it begin to exist at the same time as the body.

OBJ. 17. When one thing impedes another they are not naturally united. But the soul is impeded by the body in its operation, *for the body which is corrupted burdens the soul,* as is said in Wisdom IX.[10] Therefore the soul is not naturally united to the body and thus it seems that it previously existed apart from the body and then was united to it.

On the contrary (1) according to the book On Church Dogma, *souls* are not created *from the beginning at the same time as other intellectual creatures.*[11]

Further (2) Gregory of Nyssa says that *the assertion of either opinion does not escape*[12] *censure, either that of those who* talk *of souls living previously in a certain state and order unto themselves, or of those who think they are created after bodies.*[13]

Further (3) in his On the Symbol of Faith, Jerome says, *We condemn the error of those who* say that souls *sinned or lived in heaven before they were dispatched into bodies.*[14]

Further (4) *the proper act comes to be in the proper matter.*[15] But the soul is the proper act of the body. Therefore the soul is created in the body.

I answer that, as has been said above, it was the opinion of some that all souls were created at the same time apart from bodies. The falsity of this opinion can be shown at present with four arguments.

The first is that things were created by God in their [state of] natural perfection. For *the naturally perfect precedes the imperfect,* according to the Philosopher, and Boethius says *nature* takes its *start* from perfect things.[16] But the soul does not have the perfection of its nature

10. Wisdom 9:15.

11. Gennadius Massiliensis, *De Ecclesiasticis Dogmatibus,* XIV.

12. *non caret.*

13. Gregory of Nyssa, *On the Making of Man,* XXVIII.

14. The title Thomas cites is *Symbolo Fidei.* I have been unable to trace this reference. For a sample of Jerome on Origen's view of the pre-existence of human souls, see Jerome's Letter 124, "To Avitus."

15. Aristotle, *De Anima* II 2, 414a25–26.

16. Aristotle, *On the Heavens,* I 2, 269a20; Boethius, *The Consolation of Philosophy,* III, Prose 10.

apart from the body, because in itself it is not a complete species of a nature; rather, it is part of human nature (otherwise it would follow that soul and body become one only accidentally). And so the human soul was not created apart from the body. Now those who held that souls existed apart from the body before they were united with bodies thought them to be natures in a way perfected in themselves, and that the natural perfection of the soul is not in being united to the body, but it is united to it accidentally, as a man to his clothes, just as Plato said that man is not [made] of body and soul but is a soul using a body.[17] And because of this, all who held the soul to be created apart from the body, [also] held the transmigration of souls, or that the soul having laid aside one body is united with another, just as a man having laid aside one set of clothes puts on another.

The second argument is Avicenna's. Since the soul is not composed of matter and form (for it is distinguished from both matter and the composite in On the Soul II),[18] souls could be distinguished from each other only in terms of formal difference if they are distinguished only in themselves. But difference of form induces diversity of species, while the diversity of individuals in the same species proceeds from material differences.[19] But the latter cannot apply to the soul with respect to matter from which it is made, but only with respect to matter in which it is made. Therefore we can maintain that there are many human souls of the same species but numerically distinct only if they are united to bodies from their beginning. Thus their distinction in a certain way arises from union with the body as from a material principle, although such distinction is from God as efficient principle. But if human souls were created apart from bodies, and thereby lacked a principle of material distinction, it would be necessary that they be of different species, just as philosophers maintain that all separated substances are of different species.

The third argument is that the rational human soul does not differ in substance from the sensitive and vegetative, as was shown above.[20] But the vegetative and the sensitive soul can originate only

17. I am following Henle in tracing this to Nemesius, *On the Nature of Man* I. See his *Saint Thomas and Platonism*, 26.

18. Aristotle, *On the Soul*, II 1, 412a6–10.

19. Avicenna, *Liber de Philosophia Prima sive Scientia Divina*, IX 4.

20. In article 9, ad 9, nos. 2, 3, and 6.

in the body, since they are the acts of certain parts of the body. And so with respect to what is fitting to its nature, neither can the rational soul be created except in the body; without prejudice, however, to the divine power.[21]

The fourth argument is that if the rational soul were created apart from the body and had there the perfection of its natural being, then it is impossible to give a fit cause for its union with the body. For it cannot be said that it joined itself to the body by its own proper motion, since we see that it is not in the soul's power to abandon the body, which it could if it were voluntarily united with the body. And further, if they are by nature entirely distinct, we cannot say why union with the body was attractive to the will of the separated soul. Nor can it be said that after passage of years it acquired a natural appetite for union with a body and that this union was caused by a natural operation. For things that occur at fixed intervals of time are traced to the motion of the heavens as the cause through which intervals of time are measured. But separated souls cannot be subject to the motion of heavenly bodies. Likewise it cannot be said that they were bound to bodies by God if they were created earlier without bodies. For if it be said that he did this for their perfection, there was no reason they were created without bodies. But if this was done to punish them for their sins, so that they are shut up in bodies as in prisons, as Origen said,[22] it would follow that the establishment of natures composed of spiritual and corporeal substances was accidental and not according to God's first intention. And this is contrary to what we read in Genesis 1: *God saw all* the things *he had made and they were very good,*[23] where it is made manifestly clear that the goodness of God, not the wickedness of any creature, was the cause of the good works [later] to be condemned.

AD 1. In his book On the Literal Interpretation of Genesis and especially when inquiring into the origin of the soul, Augustine speaks more inquisitively than assertively, as he himself says.

21. I.e., this is not a constraint on God's freedom to create human beings. But if God does freely choose to create human beings, then because of human nature the human soul must be created in the human body. See article 16 below on Thomas' view of this "necessity of the end" or "necessity of supposition" as it bears on God's act of creation.

22. Cf. Origen, *On First Principles,* I 7, no. 5.

23. Genesis 1:31.

AD 2. In its beginning, the universe was perfect with respect to species rather than with respect to every individual, or with respect to the causes of natural things from which other things can later be propagated rather than with respect to every effect. Now although the rational soul is not made by a natural cause, nevertheless the bodies into which they are infused by God as connatural to them are made through the operation of nature.

AD 3. In a play, nothing is sought beyond the play itself. But the motion by which God moves corporeal creatures is for the sake of something beyond the motion itself, namely the complete number of the elect, at which point that motion, but not the substance of the world, will cease.[24]

AD 4. The multitude of souls pertains to the final essential perfection of the universe, but not to its initial [perfection], since the entire transformation of worldly bodies is ordered in a certain way to the multiplication of souls, for which the multiplication of bodies is required, as we have shown.

AD 5. The Platonists maintained that the nature of the soul is complete in itself and accidentally united to a body,[25] and so they even maintained the migration of souls from body to body.[26] They were especially drawn to this position because they held that human souls are immortal and that generation never fails. And so in order to avoid an infinity of souls, they posited a kind of circle such that souls after leaving [bodies] are again united [with them]. And it is in terms of this erroneous opinion that Macrobius speaks, whence his authority is not accepted in this matter.

AD 6. In On the Soul II the Philosopher does not say that the soul is the efficient cause of the body, but the cause whence its motion originates, inasmuch as it is the source of local motion, growth, and other motions of that sort in the body, as he himself explains there.[27]

AD 7. That authority means that irascibility and concupiscence

24. Here and in his next reply, Thomas makes explicit his position that the purpose of the material creation is the generation of a certain number of rational incarnate beings. See also *De potentia* Q. 5, aa. 5 and 9; *SCG* III 22; and *SCG* IV 97. For a discussion of this position, see Blanchette, *The Perfection of the Universe,* 258–66 and 280–85.

25. Nemesius, *On the Nature of Man,* 3.

26. Augustine, *On the City of God,* X 30.

27. Aristotle, *On the Soul,* II 4, 415b11, 22–27.

are in the soul before it is united with the body, not with respect to time but with respect to nature, because the soul does not derive them from the body but rather the body from the soul.

AD 8. The soul is measured by time with respect to the being in accordance with which it is united to the body, although when it is considered as a spiritual substance it is measured by eviternity. Nevertheless it need not be that it began to be measured by eviternity when the angels did.

AD 9. Although the things measured by eviternity have no before and after, nothing prevents one thing from partaking in eviternity before another.

AD 10. Although the soul and angel agree in intellectual nature, they differ in that the angel is a nature complete in itself, whence it could be created in itself. But since the soul's nature is perfected in its union with the body, it must be created not in heaven but in the body whose perfection it is.

AD 11. Although the soul is in itself simpler than any body, nevertheless it is the form and perfection of a body composed of the elements, the place of which is intermediate, and it must be created here at the same time as [the body].

AD 12. The first perfection of the soul is in its natural being, and this perfection consists in its union with the body. Thus from the beginning it must be created in the place of the body. Its eternal perfection, however, is in that which it shares with other intellectual substances, and thus that perfection will be given to it in heaven.

AD 13. Although the souls which are created now are new creatures as individuals, nevertheless they are ancient with respect to their species. For they already existed in the work of the six days in those like them in species, that is in the souls of [our] first parents.[28]

AD 14. The sort of creation whereby the principles of nature were established necessarily preceded the work of propagation. But the creation of souls is not this kind of work.

AD 15. It is just to render what is due, and so it is contrary to justice if unequal things are given to equal people when they are given what is owed them, but not when they are given something

28. See article 9, note 11.

gratuitously,[29] which is the case in the creation of souls. Or we can reply that such diversity proceeds not from differing merit in souls but from different dispositions of bodies, whence Plato also says that forms are infused by God according to the merit of matter.[30]

AD 16. Although the soul does depend on the body in a certain way for its beginning, in order that it begin to be in the perfection of its nature, nevertheless it does not depend on the body for its end, because it exists in the body as a subsisting thing. And so, at the destruction of the body it nevertheless remains in its being, though not in the completion of its nature, which it has in union with the body.

AD 17. It is not the nature of the body but its corruption that burdens the soul, as the text itself shows.

29. *gratis.*

30. Henle cites a "challenged interpretation" of the *Timaeus* as the source for this reference (*Saint Thomas and Platonism,* 26), but the Marietti edition cites the *Laws* X. It seems to me that the source is a misreading of *Laws* X 904c–d.

ARTICLE 11

The eleventh thing to be asked is whether the sensitive or vegetative souls are created or transmitted through the semen. And it seems that they are created.[1]

OBJ. 1. For things which are of the same kind[2] have the same way of coming into being. But sensitive and vegetative souls are of the same kind in men, brute animals, and plants. Now in men they are created, since they are of one substance with the rational soul which is created, as has been shown.[3] Therefore the sensitive and vegetative [souls] in brute animals and plants are also created.[4]

OBJ. 2. Someone might say that sensitive and vegetative souls are in plants and brutes as [their] form and perfection, but they are in men as a disposition. On the contrary, the more noble something is, the more noble is its way of coming into being. But it is more noble to be form and perfection than to be a disposition. Therefore, if the sensitive and vegetative soul which is in man as a disposition comes into being by creation, the most noble way of coming into being, then since the most noble creatures come to be in this way, it seems that much more are these souls [which are in plants and animals as forms, not as mere dispositions] in plants and brutes by creation.

OBJ. 3. In Physics I, the Philosopher says, *That which truly is,* that is, substance, *is accidental to nothing.*[5] Therefore, if sensitive and veg-

1. For a parallel discussion of this question, see *ST* I Q. 118, a. 1.
2. *rationis.*
3. In article 9, ad 9, nos. 2, 3, and 6.
4. In this objection and several that follow, we find this rather awkward reference to "the sensitive and vegetative souls in brute animals and plants." This formula is "shorthand" for the Aristotelian doctrine that, although all living things are ensouled, the soul of a plant is merely vegetative, whereas the soul of a brute animal is both vegetative and sensitive and the human soul is simultaneously vegetative, sensitive, and rational. See Thomas' reply to obj. 2 below for a discussion of this. In his reply to obj. 1, Thomas points out that the souls of plants, brute animals, and human beings are similar according to genus (i.e., the souls of all three are the source of life and activity) and this generic similarity is the basis for the difficulties raised in several of these objections. But, he shows, these difficulties are resolved by noting the specific differences among these souls.
5. Aristotle, *Physics,* I 2, 185a31, and I 3, 186b32.

etative souls are in brutes and plants as substantial forms, then they cannot be in men as accidental dispositions.

OBJ. 4. In living things, a thing is produced in being by the power of the generator through the power which is in the semen. But sensitive and vegetative souls are not actually in the semen. Therefore, since *nothing acts except insofar as it is in act,*[6] it seems that sensitive and vegetative souls cannot be produced by the power of the semen and thus [they are produced] not by generation but by creation.

OBJ. 5. But one might reply that although the power which is in the semen is not actually a sensitive soul, it nevertheless acts in virtue of the sensitive soul which was in the father from whom the semen came. On the contrary, that which acts in virtue of another, acts as its instrument. Now an instrument does not move unless it is moved, *but mover and moved must be together,* as is proved in Physics VII.[7] Therefore, since the power which is in the semen is not conjoined with the sensitive soul of the generator, it seems that it could act neither as its instrument nor in virtue of it.

OBJ. 6. An instrument is related to the principal agent as a commanded motive power to a commanding motive power, which is an appetitive power. But a commanded motive power does not move if it is separated from the commanding motive [power], as is clear in the severed limbs of an animal. Therefore neither can the power which is in the separated semen operate in virtue of the generator's soul.

OBJ. 7. When an effect lacks the perfection of [its] cause, it cannot extend itself to the proper operation of the cause, for diversity of action indicates diversity of nature. But while the power in the semen is the effect of the generator's sensitive soul, it nevertheless lacks its perfection. Therefore it cannot accomplish what properly belongs to the sensitive soul, namely to produce a soul like itself in species.

OBJ. 8. Corruption of the subject entails corruption of [its] form and power. But in the process of generation the sperm is corrupted and receives another form, as Avicenna says.[8] Therefore any power that was in the semen is corrupted, and so a sensitive soul cannot be produced in being through it.

6. See article 1, note 14 above.
7. Aristotle, *Physics,* VII 2, 243a3–4.
8. Avicenna, *Liber de Philosophia Prima sive Scientia Divina,* VI 4.

OBJ. 9. Lower nature acts only by means of heat and other active and passive qualities. But heat cannot bring the sensible soul into being, because *nothing acts outside its own species,*[9] nor can a made thing be more noble than the maker. Therefore the sensitive or vegetative soul cannot be brought into being by a natural agent, and so it is created.

OBJ. 10. A natural agent acts not by informing[10] but by transmuting matter. But the transmutation of matter leads only to accidental form. Therefore sensitive and vegetative souls, which are substantial forms, cannot be produced by a natural agent.

OBJ. 11. Sensitive or vegetative souls have a certain quiddity which is made by something else. Now this quiddity did not exist before generation, except insofar as matter could have it. Therefore it must be produced by an agent which operates without drawing on matter,[11] and only God creating is this sort [of agent].

OBJ. 12. Animals generated from semen are more noble than animals generated from putrid matter, inasmuch as they are more perfect and generate their like. But the souls of animals generated from putrid matter are created, for there is no agent of like species by which they are brought into being. Therefore it seems all the more that souls of animals generated from semen are created.

OBJ. 13. But one might reply that the sensitive soul is produced in animals generated from putrid matter by the power of the heavenly body, just as [it is produced] in others by the formative power in the semen. On the contrary, as Augustine says in his book Of True Religion, living substance surpasses any non-living substance.[12] But the heavenly body is not a living substance, since it is not ensouled. Therefore the sensitive soul which is the principle of life, cannot be produced by its power.

OBJ. 14. But one might reply that the heavenly body can be the cause of the sensitive soul insofar as it acts by virtue of the intellectual substance which moves it. On the contrary, that which is received in another is in it according to the mode of the recipient and not according to its own mode.[13] Therefore, if the power of an intel-

9. See article 8, note 17.

10. *influendo.*

11. *quod operetur non ex materia.*

12. Augustine, *Of True Religion,* XXIX, 52.

13. *Book of Causes,* especially Prop. 10. See article 3, note 2.

lectual substance is received in a non-living heavenly body, it will not be there as a vital power capable of being a principle of life.

OBJ. 15. An intellectual substance is not only living but also intelligent. Therefore, if through its power a heavenly body moved by it can confer life, it follows that [the heavenly body] will [also] be able to confer intellect.[14] Thus the rational soul will be from the generator, which is false.

OBJ. 16. If the sensitive soul is from some natural agent and not created, then it is produced either by the body or by the soul. But it is not [produced] by the body, for thus a body would act *outside its own species*.[15] Neither is it [produced] by the soul, since it would follow that either the whole soul of the father is transfused into the child, and thus the father would be left without a soul, or part of it is transfused, and thus the whole soul would not remain in the father. Both of these are false. Therefore the sensitive soul is not from the generator but from the creator.

OBJ. 17. In On the Soul III, the Commentator says that no cognitive power comes from the action of mixed elements.[16] But the sensitive soul is a cognitive power. Therefore [cognitive power] is not from the action of the elements, and so neither is it from the action of nature, since no action of nature among lower things is independent of the action of the elements.

OBJ. 18. Only a subsistent form can be a mover and so according to the Philosopher in Physics VIII the forms of the elements are not movers. Rather, only a generator or something which removes an obstacle is a mover.[17] But the sensitive soul is a mover, since every animal is moved by its soul. Therefore the sensitive soul is not merely a form, but a self-subsistent substance. It is also evident that it is not composed of matter and form. But every substance of this sort is brought into being by creation and in no other way. Therefore the sensitive soul is brought into being by creation.

OBJ. 19. But one might say that the sensitive soul does not move the body by itself but that the ensouled body moves itself. On the

14. See *SCG* III 24. Also see Blanchette, *The Perfection of the Universe*, 166–67.
15. See article 8, note 17 above.
16. Averroës, *De Anima libri tres*, III no. 4.
17. Aristotle, *Physics*, VIII 4, 255b35–256a2.

contrary, in Physics VIII the Philosopher proves that in anything which moves itself there must be one part which is only a mover and another which is moved.[18] But the body cannot be only a mover, since *no body moves unless it is moved.*[19] Therefore the soul must be only a mover, and thus the sensitive soul will have an operation in which its body does not share, and so it will be a subsistent substance.

OBJ. 20. But one might say that the sensitive soul moves under the command of the appetitive power, whose motion is shared by the soul and the body. On the contrary, in the animal there is not only a power which commands motion but also a power performing motion, the operation of which cannot be shared by soul and body, for the reasons already given. And so it must be that the sensitive soul has some operation in itself. Therefore it is a self-subsistent substance, and thus brought into being by creation and not by natural generation.

On the contrary (1) Genesis I says, *Let the waters produce a creeping thing*[20] *with a living soul.*[21] And so it seems that the sensitive souls of creeping things and other animals are from the action of corporeal elements.

Further (2) just as the father's body is related to his soul, so is the son's body related to his soul. Therefore reciprocally, as the son's body is to the father's body, so is the son's soul to the father's soul. But the son's body is traced to the father's body. Therefore the son's soul is traced to the father's soul.

I answer that we should note that philosophers' opinions concerning the production of substantial forms have varied. Some have said that the natural agent only disposes matter, whereas the form, which is the highest perfection, arises from supernatural principles. This opinion is shown to be false chiefly on two counts. The first is that, since the being of natural and corporeal forms consists solely in union with matter, it seems the same agent would produce them in being that transmutes matter. The second is that, since forms of this sort do not exceed the order and faculty of the active principles in nature, there seems to be no necessity to trace their origin to higher principles.

And so in Metaphysics VII the Philosopher says that flesh and

18. Aristotle, *Physics,* VIII 5, 258a18–25.
19. Aristotle, *Physics,* VIII 4, 256a2.
20. *reptile.*
21. Genesis 1:20.

bone are generated by a form which is *in this flesh and* in these *bones.*[22] In his opinion the natural agent not only disposes matter but also educes form into act, contrary to the first opinion [noted above].

But we must exclude the rational soul from this generality of forms. For it is a self-subsisting substance, and so its being does not consist merely in its being united with matter; otherwise it could not be separated [from it]. This indeed is manifested in its operation, which the soul has insofar as it is independent of communion with the body. Nor can it operate otherwise than it exists, for that which does not exist *per se* does not operate *per se.*

And again the intellectual nature exceeds the entire order and faculty of material and corporeal principles, since in understanding[23] the intellect can transcend all corporeal nature, which would not be the case if its nature were contained within the limits of corporeal nature.

Now neither of these can be said about the sensitive or vegetative soul. For the being of such souls consists only in union with the body. This is shown by their operations, which require a corporeal organ. And so neither do they have being absolutely without dependence on a body. Because of this they cannot be separated from the body, nor can they be produced in being except insofar as the body is produced in being. And so, just as the body is produced by an act of the generator's nature, so are these souls. To hold that they are created separately seems to lead to the opinion of those who held that souls of this sort remain after [the death of] the body, and so these positions are condemned together in the book On Church Dogma.[24]

Again, [vegetative and sensitive] souls do not exceed the order of material principles. And this is clear through consideration of their operations, for the order of action is according to the order of nature. Now we find certain forms which do not extend themselves beyond what can be done by material principles, as for example, elementary forms and forms of mixed bodies, which do not go beyond the action of heat and cold and so are wholly immersed in matter. But although the vegetative soul acts only by means of the qualities mentioned above, nevertheless its operation attains to something to which

22. Aristotle, *Metaphysics,* VII 8, 1034a5.
23. *intelligendo.*
24. Gennadius Massiliensis, *De Ecclesiasticis Dogmatibus,* XVII.

these qualities do not extend, namely to the production of flesh and bone and the determination of the term of growth and things of this sort. And so [the vegetative soul] is kept within the order of material principles to this extent, but not to the extent that [elementary forms and forms of mixed bodies] are. But the sensitive soul does not act by virtue of heat and cold of necessity, as is clear in the activity of vision and imagination and the like, although operations of this sort require a fixed measure of heat and cold in the constitution of the organ, without which these actions cannot be performed. And so it does not entirely transcend the order of material principles, although it is not lowered to their level as much as [elementary forms and forms of mixed bodies] are. But the rational soul also performs[25] an action which is beyond the power of heat and cold, and it does not perform[26] it by virtue of heat or cold, or use a corporeal organ. And so it alone transcends the order of material principles, while the sensitive soul in brutes and the vegetative soul in plants do not.

AD 1. Although the sensitive soul in men and in brute animals is of the same kind according to genus, it is not of the same kind according to species, just as man and the brute are not of the same animal species. And so the operations of the sensitive soul are much more noble in men than in brutes, as is clear in touch and in interior apprehension. Neither is it necessary that things which agree in genus but differ in species come into being in the same way, as is clear in animals generated from semen and from putrid matter which agree in genus but not in species.[27]

AD 2. The sensitive soul is not said to be in man as a disposition in the sense that it differs in substance from the rational soul and is a disposition to it, but in the sense that in man the sensitive soul is distinguished from the rational only as one power from another. But the sensitive soul in the brute is distinguished from the rational soul in man as one substantial form from another. Nevertheless, as sensitive and vegetative power in man flow from the essence of the soul, the same is true in brutes and plants, but with this difference: in plants, only vegetative powers flow from the essence of the soul, and from them their soul is denominated; in brutes, on the other hand,

25. *agit.*

26. *exercet.*

27. See article 8, note 19 above.

there are not only vegetative but sensitive powers, from which their soul is denominated; and finally in man there are intellectual powers, from which he is denominated.

AD 3. The substance from which sensitive power flows in both brutes and men is the substantial form, while the power in both cases is an accident.

AD 4. The sensitive soul is actually in the semen not according to its proper species but as in an active power, just as a house is actually in the mind of the builder as in an active power and as corporeal forms are in heavenly powers.

AD 5. An instrument is understood to be moved by a principal agent as long as it retains the power impressed on it by the principal agent. Thus a javelin is moved by the one who throws it as long as it retains the power of the thrower's thrust. So also in heavy and light things, the generated is moved by the generator as long as it retains the form transmitted to it by the generator. And so also the semen is understood to be moved by the generating soul as long as the power impressed in it by the soul remains, even though they are distinct corporeally. And the mover and moved must be together at the beginning of the motion but not for the entirety of the motion, as is plain in things which are thrown.

AD 6. The appetitive power of the soul has command of only the body united to it, and so a severed limb does not obey the wish of the appetitive soul. But the semen is moved not by the command of the generator's soul but by the transfusion of a certain power which remains in the semen even after it issues forth.

AD 7. Sensitive and vegetative souls are educed from the potency of matter as are other material forms whose production requires the power of transforming matter. Now the power in the semen has this power even though it lacks other functions of the soul. For just as in nutritive action the soul wholly transforms and converts matter, so also is matter transformed through the power [in the semen] so that the embryo[28] is generated. Whence nothing prohibits that same power from acting as the sensitive soul acts through its own power.[29]

28. *conceptum.*

29. I.e., through the sensitive soul's own power. The Latin is "unde nichil prohibet quin virtus predicta operetur, quantum ad hoc, actionem anime sensibilis in virtute ipsius."

AD 8. The power mentioned is rooted in the [animal] spirit which is included in the semen as in a subject. But Avicenna says that nearly all the semen is converted into [animal] spirit.[30] And so, although the corpulent matter from which the embryo[31] is formed undergoes many changes in the course of generation, the subject of the power mentioned is nevertheless not destroyed.

AD 9. Just as heat acts as the instrument of the substantial form of fire, so can it act as the instrument of the sensitive soul in bringing a sensitive soul into actuality, though it cannot do this by its own power.

AD 10. Matter is transmuted not only by accidental but also by substantial change, for both forms pre-exist in the potency of matter. And so the natural agent which transmutes matter is the cause not only of the accidental but also of the substantial form.

AD 11. Since it is not a subsisting thing, the sensible soul, like other material forms, is not a quiddity but part of a quiddity, and its being is in its union[32] with matter. And so the production of sensitive soul is nothing other than the transmutation of matter from potency to act.

AD 12. The less perfect something is, the fewer things are required for making it. And so, since animals generated from putrid matter are less perfect than those generated from semen, in animals generated from putrid matter the power of the heavenly body alone suffices. That power also operates in the semen, but it does not suffice for the production of the animal generated from semen without the power of soul. For the power of the heavenly body remains in lower bodies insofar as they are transmuted by it as by the first cause of alteration. And because of this, in his book On Animals the Philosopher says that all lower bodies are full of the soul's powers.[33] Now although the heaven is not of the same species as the kinds of animals generated from putrid matter, nevertheless it is like them insofar as an effect pre-exists virtually in the active cause.

AD 13. Although the heavenly body is not alive, nevertheless it acts in virtue of a living substance by which it is moved, whether this be an angel or God. According to [some] philosophers, however, the heavenly body is ensouled and alive.[34]

30. Cf. Avicenna, *Liber de Philosophia Prima sive Scientia Divina,* VI 4 and VIII 2.
31. *conceptum.*
32. *concretione.*
33. Aristotle, *On the Generation of Animals,* III 11, 762a21.
34. Cf. *On the Heavens,* II 12, 292a18–22.

AD 14. The power of a moving spiritual substance remains in a heavenly body and its motion, not as a form which has being complete in nature, but in the mode of an intention, as the power of art is in the artist's instrument.

AD 15. The rational soul exceeds the entire order of corporeal principles, as has been said.[35] Wherefore no body can act even as an instrument in its production.

AD 16. The sensitive soul is produced in the embryo[36] neither by the action of the body nor by transmission[37] of the soul, but by the action of the informing power, which is in the semen from the generator's soul, as has been said.[38]

AD 17. We deny that cognitive power is from the action of the elements in the sense that the power of the elements suffices to cause it, as it suffices to cause hardness and softness. But we do not deny that it can operate instrumentally in some way.

AD 18. The sensitive soul causes motion through the appetite. But the activity of the sensitive appetite is not only in the soul but in the composite, since this power has a prescribed organ. And so it is not necessary to hold that the sensitive soul has some operation independent of communion with the body.

AD 19. A body can cause motion and not be moved with the same kind of motion that it causes, even though it cannot cause motion unless it is in some way moved. For a heavenly body causes alteration without being altered, but it is moved locally. And likewise the organ of the appetitive power causes local movement without being moved locally, but it is in some way altered, for the sensitive appetite does not operate without alteration of the body, as is clear in anger and passions of that sort.

AD 20. The motive power performing a motion is more a disposition of the mobile thing (because of which it is apt to be moved by a certain mover) than a cause of motion itself.

35. In article 10.
36. *concepto.*
37. *decisionem.*
38. In article 9, ad 9, no. 6, ad 11, ad 16; article 11, ad 4–7.

ARTICLE 12

The twelfth thing to be asked is whether the sensitive or vegetative soul is in the semen from the beginning, when it issues forth. And it seems that it is.[1]

OBJ. 1. For, as Gregory of Nyssa says, *The assertion of either opinion does not escape*[2] *censure, either that of those who* talk *of souls living previously in a certain state and order unto themselves or of those who think they are created after bodies.*[3] But if the soul was not in the semen from the beginning, it must be that it comes to be after the body. Therefore the soul was in the semen from the beginning.

OBJ. 2. If the sensitive soul was not in the semen from the beginning just as the rational soul was not, the same rule[4] will apply to the sensitive and to the rational soul. But the rational soul is created. Therefore the sensitive soul will also be created. But we have shown the contrary to be the case.

OBJ. 3. In On Animals XVI, the Philosopher says that the power which is in the semen is *like the son* going forth from *his father's house.*[5] But the son going forth from his father's house is of the same species as his father. Therefore that power which is in the semen is also of the same species as the sensitive soul from which it is derived.

OBJ. 4. In On Animals XVI, the Philosopher says that that power is like art which, were it in matter, would perfect the artwork.[6] But the species of the artwork is in the art. Therefore the species of the sensitive soul which is produced through the semen is in that power of the semen as well.

OBJ. 5. The sundering[7] of semen is natural, while the sundering of an annulose animal is contrary to nature. But the soul is in

1. For a parallel discussion of this question, see *ST* I, Q. 119, a. 1.
2. *non caret.*
3. Gregory of Nyssa, *On the Making of Man,* XXVIII.
4. *ratio.*
5. Aristotle, *On the Generation of Animals,* II 4, 740a5–7.
6. Aristotle, *On the Generation of Animals,* II 4, 740b26–31.
7. *decisio.* The semen is divided ("sundered") from the father's body when it is emitted. An annulose animal is divided when part of it is cut off and the part cut off becomes a new individual (as, for example, in some species of starfish).

the sundered part of the annulose animal, as the Philosopher says.[8] Therefore much more is it in the sundered semen.

OBJ. 6. In On Animals XVI, Aristotle says that in the generation of an animal the male provides the soul.[9] But nothing issues from the father except the semen. Therefore the soul is in the semen.

OBJ. 7. An accident is transmitted only through the transmission of its subject. But some diseases are transmitted from parents to children, such as leprosy, gout, and the like. Therefore the substance of these [diseases] is also transmitted. But this [substance] cannot be without a soul. Therefore the soul is in the semen from the beginning.

OBJ. 8. Hippocrates says that generation is impeded by severing a vein which is near the ear.[10] But this would not be unless the semen were severed from the whole body as an actual part already existing [in it]. Therefore, since that which is already part of an animal has soul, it seems that the semen has soul from the beginning.

OBJ. 9. He also says that a certain horse was found to have no brain because of excessive coition.[11] But this would not be unless semen were removed from an actual part of the body. Therefore the same conclusion follows.

OBJ. 10. Whatever is superfluous is not of a thing's substance. Therefore, if semen were superfluous it would not be of the generator's substance, and so the son, who is from semen, would not be of the father's substance, which is unreasonable. Therefore semen is of the generator's substance and thus the soul is in it actually.

OBJ. 11. Everything which lacks a soul is inanimate. Therefore, if semen lacks a soul, it will be inanimate, and thus an inanimate body will be transformed and become animate, which seems absurd. Therefore the soul is in semen from the beginning.

On the contrary, in On the Soul II the Philosopher says that the *semen and fruit,* which are *without soul,* are potentially ensouled.[12]

Further (2) if semen has soul from the beginning, this seems to be

8. This seems to be a reference to Aristotle, *On the Soul,* I 5, 411b19–25.

9. Aristotle, *On the Generation of Animals,* II 4, 738b20.

10. Hippocrates, *Places in Man,* 3.

11. I have not been able to trace this reference.

12. *semen et fructus* est in tali potencia ad animam quae est *abiciens animam.* Thomas is citing Aristotle, *On the Soul,* II 1, 412b25–26.

possible only in two ways: either the generator's whole soul is transmitted[13] in the semen or part of it is. But both of these seem unreasonable, for from the first it follows that the soul would not remain in the father, and from the second it follows that not the whole soul remains. Therefore the soul is not in the semen from the beginning.

I answer that some held the opinion that from the beginning of its emission [from the body] the soul is in the semen, meaning that, just as body is divided from body, at the same time soul is propagated by soul, so the soul would be immediately present [in the emitted semen].[14]

But this opinion seems to be false for, as the Philosopher proves in On Animals XV, the semen is not severed from an actual part but from the residue *of final digestion*[15] which has not yet been finally assimilated. Now no part of the body is actually perfected by the soul unless it is finally assimilated. And so before it issues forth the semen has not yet been perfected by the soul in such a way that the soul would be its form. Nevertheless there was present in it some power of soul through which [the semen] was altered by the soul's action and brought to the disposition suitable for final assimilation. And so even after it issues forth, soul is not present in it but some power of soul. And because of this, in On Animals XVI the Philosopher says that *the power of the soul's beginning is* in the semen.[16]

Moreover, if soul were in the semen from the beginning, the semen would either have the species of soul actually or it would actually have not this species but a certain power later to be converted into soul. Now the first cannot be because, since the soul is the *act of an organized body,*[17] the body cannot receive the soul[18] before it is in any way organized. And further it would follow that all it does in the semen is give a certain disposition to the matter, and as a result this would not be generation, since generation does not follow but precedes substantial form (unless perhaps it were said that the body has

13. *transeat.*

14. *ut statim cum corporis particula esset etiam ibi anima.*

15. Aristotle, *On the Generation of Animals,* I 18, 725a11–28 and 726a26–28. See article 9, note 48 above.

16. Aristotle, *On the Generation of Animals,* II 3, 736b9–12, 736b35, and 737a30–34.

17. Aristotle, *On the Soul,* II 1, 412b5.

18. *corpus susceptiuum anime esse non potest.*

another substantial form besides the soul, from which it would follow that the soul is not substantially united with the body, since it comes to the body after it is already constituted as a particular thing by another form). Moreover, it would also follow that the generation of a living thing would be not generation but a kind of separation, just as a piece of wood cut from wood is actually wood.

The second alternative cited above also cannot be because, if it were, it would follow that substantial form arises in matter not all at once but by degrees, and so there would be movement in substance just as in quantity and quality, which is contrary to what the Philosopher says in Physics V.[19] It would also follow that substantial forms increase and decrease, which is impossible.

And so it remains that no soul is in the semen but a certain power of soul which effects the soul and is derived from soul.

AD 1. The living body of an ox or an olive, for example, does not exist before the soul, but the seed[20] of the body does exist before the soul. It does not, however, exist before the power which makes the soul, for the seed bears the same relation to that power as the body to the soul.

AD 2. It is important to note regarding the rational soul and other souls that the rational soul is not by virtue of the semen as other souls are, although no soul is in the semen from the beginning.

AD 3. That power is not compared to a son going forth from his father's house with respect to the completion of the species but with respect to the acquisition of a certain complement which is lacking. For a first perfection is often manifested through a likeness to a second perfection.

AD 4. There will be a likeness between art and this power insofar as it is the case that, just as the artwork pre-exists in the art as in an active power, so also does a living thing [which is] to be generated [pre-exist] in the formative power. And there is no other likeness between them.

AD 5. The sundering of an annulose animal is violent and contrary to nature because the sundered part was actually part [of the animal] and perfected by its soul. And so through the sundering of

19. Aristotle, *Physics,* V 2, 225b10 and 226a24–32.
20. *semen.*

the matter the soul, which previously in the whole body was actually one and potentially many, remains in each part. This occurs because animals of this kind are homogeneous[21] in whole and in part, for their souls, which are less perfect than those of other animals, require little diversity of organs. And this is why a sundered part can harbor the soul, inasmuch as it has organs which suffice to harbor the soul,[22] as occurs also in other similar bodies, as for example in wood and stone, air and water. And from this the Philosopher proves in On Animals XV that the sperm was not actually a part before its separation, since its separation would have been not natural but a kind of corruption.[23] And so it is not necessary that the soul remain in the semen through its separation.

AD 6. The male is said to provide the soul inasmuch as the power which effects[24] the soul is contained in the semen of the male.

AD 7. The diseases the objection refers to are not transmitted with the semen as though they were actually in the semen, but because their beginning is there through an indisposition of the semen.

AD 8. Since sperm is a kind of superfluity, it has certain proper outlets, like other superfluities. It is the severing of this outlet which impedes generation rather than the destruction of some thing which was actually part of [the body].

AD 9. Just as the immoderate discharge of other superfluities violently and unnaturally destroys something of that which was already transformed,[25] so also does immoderate emission of semen. But that which occurs contrary to nature ought not to be considered as following from nature.

AD 10. Semen is superfluous in the sense that, although it is not actually part of the father's substance, it is potentially the whole [of that substance], and because of this a son is said to be of [his] father's substance.

AD 11. Although semen is not actually animate it is nevertheless virtually animate. And so it is not simply inanimate.

21. *similia.*

22. Aristotle, *On the Soul,* I 5, 19–27.

23. Aristotle, *On the Generation of Animals,* I 18, 724b30.

24. *agit.*

25. *resolvit aliquid de eo quod erat iam conversum.* Fr. Shapcote translates this as: "destroys that which has already been converted into bodily tissue."

ARTICLE 13

The thirteenth thing to ask is whether something which is from another can be eternal. And it seems that it cannot.[1]

OBJ. 1. For nothing which always is needs something in order that it be. But everything which is from another needs that by which it is in being. Therefore nothing which is from another always is.

OBJ. 2. *Nothing receives that which it already has.*[2] But that which always is, always has being. Therefore that which always is does not receive being. But everything which is from another receives being from that from which it is. Therefore nothing which is from another always is.

OBJ. 3. That which [already] is, is not generated or made or in any way produced in being, since something [to be] made does not [yet] exist. But everything which is generated or made or produced must at some time not exist, and everything which is from another is of this sort. Therefore everything which is from another at some time does not exist. But that which at some time does not exist, is not always. Therefore nothing which is from another is sempiternal.[3]

OBJ. 4. That which has being only from another, considered in itself is not. But a thing of this sort must at some time not be. Therefore everything which is from another must at some time not be and consequently is not sempiternal.

1. As the replies to the objections and the respondeo make clear, the question here is whether the second person of the Trinity (the Son) can be both from another (*ab alio*, i.e., from the Father) and also eternal. For parallel discussions of issues raised here, see *ST* I Q. 27, a. 1; *ST* III Q. 16, a. 9 and Q. 17, a. 2; and *SCG* IV 14, especially par. 3. The next article here in Q. 3 of the *De potentia* deals with the question whether a creature (which is not from the Father in the way the Son is, but is from God as its efficient cause) can be both from God and eternal.

2. I have been unable to trace a reference for this text.

3. *est sempiternum*. As I read Thomas, he uses *"sempiternus"* interchangeably with *"aeternus."* In the *De potentia* he uses the former only here in article 13 and in article 14, and then only in response to objections which use this term. For an examination of sempiternity as a distinct concept, see Dario Schioppetto, "L'Ombra dell'Eterno: Note sul Tempo degli Angeli," cited above in article 10, note 8.

OBJ. 5. Every effect is posterior to its cause. But that which is from another is the effect of that which it is from. Therefore it is posterior to that from which it is and thus cannot be sempiternal.

On the contrary, Hilary says, *That which* is born of the Father *from eternity, is born from eternity.*[4] But the Son of God is born of the eternal Father. Therefore he is born from eternity. Therefore he is eternal.

I answer that, since we hold that the Son of God proceeds from the Father naturally, we must say that he is from the Father in such a way as to be nevertheless coeternal with him.

This may be shown as follows.

For the will and nature differ, in that nature is determined to one thing both with respect to what is produced by the power of nature and with respect to producing or not producing. But the will is found to be determined in neither respect. For by the will someone is able to make this or that, as for example a craftsman is able to make a bench or a box, and again to make or to stop making. Fire, on the other hand, cannot fail to heat if the subject of its action is present, nor can it induce in matter an effect other than its like. And so, although it may be said of creatures which proceed from God by the divine will that he could make this or that creature at this or that time, this cannot be said of the Son, who proceeds naturally. For in his nature the Son could be in no other way than that he has in himself the nature of the Father. Nor could the Son be sooner or later in relation to the Father's nature. For it cannot be said that the perfection of the divine nature failed at some time, at which point the Son was generated by the power of nature, since the divine nature is simple and immutable. Nor can it be said that this generation was delayed because of the absence or indisposition of matter, since this generation is wholly immutable. And so it remains that, since the nature of the Father is from eternity, and the Son is eternally generated of the Father, it follows that the Son is co-eternal.

Now because the Arians held that the Son did not proceed from the Father naturally, they held that the Son is neither co-equal nor co-eternal with the Father, as is the case in other things which proceed from God according to his will's decree.

4. *Quod ab aterno* Patre natum, *aternum esse habet quod natum est.* Hilary of Poitiers, *The Trinity,* XII 21.

It was difficult to consider the generation of the Son from the Father co-eternal because of the familiarity of human understanding with the production of natural things, in which one thing is produced by another through motion. A thing produced in being through motion first begins to be at the term of the motion. But since the beginning of motion necessarily precedes the term of motion in time, which is necessary because of the successive nature of motion, and there cannot be a beginning or commencement of motion without a moving cause to produce it, it is necessary that the moving cause in the production of a thing precedes in time that which is produced by it. And so that which proceeds from something without motion is simultaneous with that from which it proceeds, as for example light [is simultaneous] with fire or the sun: for light proceeds from the illuminating body not gradually but all at once, since illumination is not a motion, but a term of motion.

It follows, therefore, that in the divine, which is wholly without local motion, that which proceeds is simultaneous with that from which it proceeds, and thus, since the Father is eternal, the Son and holy Spirit which proceed from him are co-eternal with him.

AD 1. If need implies defect or lack of what is needed, then that which always is does not need anything in order that it be. But if it implies only order of origin in relation to that from which it is, then nothing prevents that which always is from needing something in order that it be, inasmuch as it has being not from itself but from another.

AD 2. That which receives something does not have it before receiving it, but has [it] at the time it receives it. And so, if it receives [it] from eternity, it has [it] from eternity.

AD 3. That argument applies to generation effected through motion, since that which is moved to being does not [yet] exist. And this is said inasmuch as that which is generated does not [yet] exist, but that which has been generated [already] is. And so where being generated and having been generated are not distinct, it is not necessary that what is generated not exist at some time.

AD 4. That which has being from another considered in itself is not if it is itself distinct from that being which it receives from another. But if it itself is the being which it receives from another, then it cannot be considered non-being in itself. For non-being cannot be considered in being, although that which is distinct from being can be considered in it. For *that which is can* have something else mixed with it but not *being itself*, as Boethius says in his book On the Hebdomads.[5] Now the first is the situation of the creature, but the second is the situation of the Son of God.

AD 5. The Son of God cannot be called an effect, since he is not made but generated. For that whose being is distinct from its maker is made. And so neither can the Father properly speaking be called the cause of the Son, but rather the principle. Nor must every cause precede its effect in time but only in nature, as is clear in the case of the sun and its shining.

5. Boethius, *De Hebdomadibus*, Axiom 4.

ARTICLE 14

The fourteenth thing to be asked is whether that which is from God, differing in essence from him, can have always been. And it seems that it can.[1]

OBJ. 1. The cause which produces the whole substance of a thing has no less power over its effect than a cause which produces form alone. But a cause which produces form alone can produce it from eternity if it be from eternity, for *the light which is produced and diffused by fire is united with it and would be co-eternal if the fire were eternal,* as Augustine says in On the Trinity VI.[2] Therefore much more can God, who produces the whole substance of a thing, produce an effect co-eternal with himself.

OBJ. 2. But someone might say that this is impossible since it leads to an absurdity, namely that it equates the creature and the creator in duration. On the contrary, duration which is not all at once but successive cannot be compared to duration which is all at once. But if the world had always been, its duration would not have been all at once, since it would have been measured by time, as Boethius also says at the end of the Consolation.[3] Therefore God is not equated with the creature in duration.

OBJ. 3. Just as a divine person proceeds from God without motion, so also does a creature. But a divine person can be co-eternal with God, from whom he proceeds. Therefore a creature can likewise.

OBJ. 4. That which always exists in the same way, can always act in the same way. But God exists in the same way from eternity. Therefore he can always act the same way from eternity. Therefore, if he

1. Thomas' definitive treatment of the question whether the universe can be both created and eternal is his *De aeternitate mundi (On the Eternity of the World).* See also *ST* I Q. 46, aa. 1–2 and *SCG* II 31–38. For a recent contemporary discussion of Thomas' view, see Brian Shanley's "Eternity and Duration in Aquinas," *The Thomist* 61 (1997): 525–48, the footnotes of which lead to many other treatments. See also John F. Wippel, "Did Thomas Aquinas Defend the Possibility of an Eternally Created World?" *Journal of the History of Philosophy* 19 (1981): 21–38; reprinted in *Metaphysical Themes in Thomas Aquinas* (Washington, D.C.: The Catholic University of America Press, 1984), pp. 191–214.

2. Augustine, *The Trinity,* VI 1.

3. Boethius, *The Consolation of Philosophy,* V, Prose 6.

produced a creature at some time, he could produce it from eternity.

OBJ. 5. But someone might say that this argument applies to the natural agent but not to the voluntary agent. On the contrary, God's will does not diminish his power. But if he did not act voluntarily, it follows that the creature was produced from eternity. Therefore, granting that he acts voluntarily, it remains the case that he was able to produce [a creature] from eternity.

OBJ. 6. If God produced a creature at a certain time and his power does not increase, then he was also able to produce the creature before that time or instant, and by the same reasoning also before that time and so on to infinity. Therefore he was able to produce it from eternity.

OBJ. 7. God can do more than the human intellect can understand, wherefore it is said in Luke 1, *No word will be impossible with God.*[4] But the Platonists understood there to be something made by God which nevertheless always was, and so in On the City of God X, Augustine says, *Plato writes concerning the world and those gods that God made in the world* [and] *clearly* says *that they began to be and have a starting point, yet they will have no end, but,* he says, *by the all-powerful will of their maker they will be eternally. But in explaining this* the Platonists *found this beginning clearly is not a temporal one but a beginning* of institution. *For, they say, just as if a foot had always been in the dust from eternity, the footprint would always be beneath it, which no one would doubt was made by the walker . . . , thus the one who made it always existed, and yet* it is made.[5] Therefore God could make something which always was.

OBJ. 8. Whatever is not contrary to the notion[6] of a creature, God can do in a creature; otherwise he would not be omnipotent. But to have always been is not contrary to the notion of a creature, inasmuch as it is made; otherwise it would be the same thing to say that a creature had always been and that it was not made, which is clearly false. For in On the City of God XI, Augustine distinguishes two opinions, one that the world always was in such a way that it was not made by God and the other that the world always was but nevertheless was made by God.[7] Therefore God is able to act so that something he makes is always.

4. Luke 1:37.
5. Augustine, *City of God,* X 31.
6. *rationem.*
7. Augustine, *City of God,* XI 4. See also *City of God* X 31.

OBJ. 9. Just as nature is able to produce its effect immediately, so also can the unimpeded voluntary agent. But God is a voluntary agent who cannot be impeded. Therefore creatures which are produced in being by his will could be produced from eternity, just as the Son is, who proceeds from the Father naturally.

On the contrary (1) in On the Literal Interpretation of Genesis, Augustine says, *Since the nature of the Trinity is wholly unchangeable ..., thus it is eternal in such a way that nothing can be co-eternal with it.*[8]

(2) In Book I, Damascene says *That which is drawn from non-being to being is naturally unfit*[9] *to be co-eternal with that* which *is always and without beginning.*[10] But a creature is produced in being from non-being. Therefore it cannot have always been.

(3) Every eternal thing is invariable. But the creature cannot be invariable because if it were left alone it would fall back into nothingness. Therefore it cannot be eternal.

(4) Nothing which depends on another is necessary, and consequently neither is it eternal, since every eternal thing is necessary. But everything which is made depends on another. Therefore no made thing can be eternal.

(5) If God was able to produce creatures from eternity, he did produce them from eternity, because, according to the Philosopher in Physics III, *In sempiternal things, there is no difference between what is and what can be.*[11] But to hold that creatures were produced from eternity is contrary to faith. Therefore to hold that they could have been produced [from eternity] is as well.

(6) If it can, the will of the wise person does not delay doing what it intends, unless there is some reason. But no reason can be given why God made the world at a certain time and not earlier or from eternity, if it could be made from eternity. Therefore it seems that it could not be made from eternity.

(7) If a creature is made, then it is either from something or from nothing. But it is not from something, since it would be either from the divine essence, which is impossible, or from something else. And

8. Augustine, *De Genesi ad litteram libri XII,* VIII 23.

9. *non est aptum natum.*

10. John Damascene, *Exposition of the Orthodox Faith,* I 8.

11. I cannot find a text to correspond to this reference in *Physics* III. It may be a reference to Aristotle, *Metaphysics,* IX 8, 1050b7–27.

if this [other thing] were not made, there would be something other than God not created by him, which was disproved above.[12] But if it were made by something else, either this would proceed to infinity, which is impossible, or we would arrive at something which is made from nothing. But it is impossible that something made from nothing always existed. Therefore it is impossible for a creature always to have been.

(8) It is essential[13] to the eternal to have no beginning, whereas it is essential to the creature that it have a beginning. Therefore no creature can be eternal.

(9) A creature is measured either by time or by eviternity.[14] But eviternity and time differ from eternity. Therefore no creature can be eternal.

(10) If something is created, it is necessary to grant some instant in which it was created. But before that [instant] it was not. Therefore we must say that no creature has always been.

I answer that, according to the Philosopher in Metaphysics V, a thing is said to be possible sometimes in reference to some potency and sometimes in reference to no potency.[15] In reference to a potency, this may be active or passive: in reference to an active [potency], as we might say that it was possible for the builder to build; and in reference to a passive [potency], as we might say it was possible for wood to burn. Sometimes, however, a thing is said to be possible not in reference to some potency but either metaphorically, as in geometry a line is said to be potentially rational (which we may let pass for the moment), or absolutely, that is when the terms stated do not contradict each other. On the other hand, [a thing is] impossible when [the terms stated] do contradict each other, for it is impossible simultaneously to affirm and to deny that something is, not because it is impossible for some agent or patient, but because it is impossible in itself, since it is self-contradictory.

Therefore if we consider the statement: "Something differing in substance, [which] God causes to exist, has always existed," this cannot be said to be impossible in itself, as though it were self-

12. In article 5.

13. *de ratione.*

14. *evo.* See article 10, note 8, above.

15. Aristotle, *Metaphysics,* V 12, 1020a1–4.

contradictory. For, as was shown above, being caused by another is not inconsistent with being always, except when something proceeds from another through motion, which does not occur in the procession of things from God. When "differing in substance" is added, likewise there is no contradiction, absolutely speaking, with the notion that it "has always existed." Now if we take possible to refer to an active potency, [in this sense] also God does not lack the power to produce an essence other than himself from eternity.

But if we take it to refer to a passive potency, then, given the truth of the Catholic faith, it cannot be said that something differing in essence and proceeding from God could always have existed. For, the Catholic faith supposes that everything other than God once was not. But just as it is impossible to hold that something which once was, never was, so is it impossible to hold that something which once was not, always was.

And so some say that this is indeed possible on the part of God creating, but not on the part of an essence proceeding from God, because faith holds the contrary.

AD 1. This argument considers the power of the maker but it does not consider the made thing, which is supposed not to have existed at some time.

AD 2. Even if the creature had always been, nevertheless it would not be equated with God absolutely, but in the sense that it imitates him, which is not absurd. And so this objection has little force.

AD 3. In a divine person there is nothing which is supposed not to have been at some time, as there is in every essence other than God.

AD 4. That objection considers the power of the maker, which indeed is not diminished by his will, except insofar as it was because of the decree of the divine will that the creature did not always exist.

And so the response to the fifth objection is clear.

AD 6. If one holds that a creature existed before a certain time, the position of faith which holds that nothing besides God always existed is preserved. But it is not preserved if one holds that [a creature] always existed. And so [these positions] are not the same. We should also note that the form of the argument is flawed. For God can make any creature better, but he cannot make a creature of infinite goodness; for infinite goodness is incompatible with the very notion[16] of a creature, while determinate goodness is not, however great it might be.

Further it should be noted that if God is said to have been able to make the world before he did make it, this is undoubtedly true if this priority is referred to the potency of the maker, since he has the power to do this from eternity and eternity precedes the time of creation. But if it be referred to the being of the made thing, meaning that before the instant of the creation of the world there was a real time during which the world could have been made, this is clearly entirely false, since before the world there was no motion, and so no time. We can however imagine a time before the world, just as [we can imagine] an altitude or certain dimensions beyond the heaven, in terms of which we can say that he could raise the heaven higher and that he could have made [it] sooner, since he could have made the time longer and altitude higher.

AD 7. The Platonists did understand this, but this was not based on the truth of faith, which was unknown to them.

AD 8. This argument proves only that, considered in themselves, to be made and to be always are not mutually exclusive. And so it considers what is possible absolutely.

AD 9. This argument proceeds from what is possible on the part of an active power.

But since the opposing arguments seem to conclude that there is no sense in which it is possible [for a creature to have always been], we must also respond to them.

AD CONTRARY 1. According to Boethius, at the end of The Consolation of Philosophy, even if the world had always been it would not be coeternal with God, because its duration would not be wholly simultaneous, which is required by the very notion[17] of eternity. For *eternity* is *unending life wholly simultaneous and perfectly possessed,* as he says there.[18] Now the succession of time is caused by motion, as the Philosopher makes clear in Physics IV.[19] And so that which is subject to change cannot be eternal even if it always is. And because of this

16. *rationi.*
17. *rationem.*
18. Boethius, *The Consolation of Philosophy,* V, Prose 6.
19. Aristotle, *Physics,* IV 11, 220a24.

Augustine says that no creature can be coeternal with the invariable essence of the Trinity.[20]

AD CONTRARY 2. Damascene speaks on the supposition of the truth of faith, which is clear when he says, *That which* was drawn *from non-being to being* etc.

AD CONTRARY 3. The notion[21] of variability excludes eternity but not infinity of duration.

AD CONTRARY 4. That which depends on another is able to be only through the infusion[22] of that by which it is. And if the latter is always, the former will be always as well.

AD CONTRARY 5. Because he acts voluntarily, not out of natural necessity, it does not follow that if God could do something he did do it. And when it is said that *In sempiternal things there is no difference between what is and what can be,* this refers to passive but not to active potency. For a passive potency not united with its act is a principle of corruption and thus incompatible with sempeternity. On the other hand, no damage is done to the perfection of an acting cause whose effect does not exist in act, especially in the case of a voluntary cause. For the effect is not the perfection of active power in the way that form is of passive power.

AD CONTRARY 6. Our intellect cannot inquire into the production of the first creatures because it cannot comprehend that art which alone is the reason these creatures were as they were. And so just as no human being can say why the heaven is so great and not greater, no one can say why the world was not made earlier, although both were subject to the divine power.

AD CONTRARY 7. The first creatures were produced not from something but from nothing. However it follows not from the nature[23] of their production but from the truth of faith that they once were not and later were brought into being. For, according to Anselm in the Monologion, one sense of the statement that a creature is made from nothing is that it is not made from something, so that

20. Augustine, *De Genesi ad litteram libri XII,* VIII 23.

21. *de sui ratione.*

22. *influxum.* I am following the translation of this word in Guagliardo's translation of Thomas' *Commentary on the Book of Causes* (cf, xxxiv). The *Liber de causis* is certainly the work Thomas has in mind here.

23. *ratione.*

the negation includes the preposition but is not included in it and thus the negation denies the order implied by the preposition, but the preposition does not imply an order to nothing. On the other hand, if an order to nothing were affirmed, with the preposition including the negation, it still does not follow that the creature was at one time nothing. For it can be said, as indeed Avicenna says, that non-being precedes the being of a thing, not in duration but in nature,[24] because this thing would be nothing if it were left on its own, and it has being only from another. For that which something is able of itself to have, naturally belongs to it prior <to that> which can be in it only from another.

AD CONTRARY 8. It is essential to the eternal to have no beginning of duration, while it is essential to creation to have a beginning of origin but not of duration, unless we consider creation as the faith considers it.[25]

AD CONTRARY 9. Eviternity and time differ from eternity not only with respect to beginning of duration but also with respect to succession. For the notion[26] of succession is contained in time, whereas it is joined[27] to eviternity inasmuch as eviternal substances are changeable in some way, although they are unchanged inasmuch as they are measured by eviternity. But eviternity does not contain succession, nor is succession joined to it.

AD CONTRARY 10. The operation by which God produces things in being should not be understood to be like the operation of the craftsman who makes a box and later leaves it. Rather God continually infuses being,[28] as Augustine says in On the Literal Interpretation of Genesis.[29] And so it is not necessary to assign some instant of the production of things before which they were not, unless one presupposes the faith.

24. Avicenna, *Liber de Philosophia Prima sive Scientia Divina,* IV 1.

25. "Beginning of origin" means that a thing is dependent on another for its being. "Beginning of duration" means that a thing has a particular starting point in time and then endures from that time. Thomas' point here is that the very fact of creaturehood entails beginning of origin, but there is no intrinsic contradiction between the claims "X is a creature" and "X has no beginning of duration." The ontological order does not specify a chronological order.

26. *ratio.*

27. *adiungitur.*

28. *influat esse.*

29. Augustine, *De Genesi ad litteram libri XII,* IV 12 and VIII 12. Augustine does not, however, use the phrase *"influat esse"* in his discussion.

ARTICLE 15

The fifteenth thing to be asked is whether things proceeded from God by natural necessity or by the decree of his will. And it seems that it was by natural necessity.[1]

OBJ. 1. For in the fourth chapter of The Divine Names, Dionysius says, *Just as our sun, without reasoning or choosing, but by* its *very being, illuminates all those things that can participate in its light, so does* the divine goodness ... *by* its own *essence cast the rays of* [its] *goodness* on all existing *things proportionately.*[2] But the sun, illuminating things without choice or reason, does so out of natural necessity. Therefore God also produces creatures by communicating his goodness by natural necessity.

OBJ. 2. Every perfection of lower nature is derived from the perfection of the divine nature. But it pertains to the perfection of lower nature that by its own power it make something like itself, producing an effect. Therefore much more does God communicate a likeness of his goodness to creatures naturally and not voluntarily.

OBJ. 3. *Every agent produces its like;*[3] therefore, insofar as a certain effect is produced by an acting cause, it bears a likeness to it. But the creature bears a likeness to God in things which pertain to God's nature, namely being and goodness and unity and the like, not only in that which is in the will or intellect. On the other hand, works of art are like their maker [only] in terms of the form of art, not in terms of the maker's nature, because they proceed from their maker voluntarily and not naturally. Therefore creatures proceed from God by virtue of the divine nature and not by will.

OBJ. 4. But one might reply that the likeness of natural attributes is communicated to creatures by the divine will. On the contrary, a likeness of nature can be communicated only by a natural power.

1. For parallel discussions of whether God's creation of things is voluntary or necessary, see *ST* I Q. 19, a. 3 and *SCG* I 81–83. For a recent discussion of these texts and this topic, see Msgr. Wippel's "Thomas Aquinas on God's Freedom to Create or Not," in *Metaphysical Themes in Thomas Aquinas II*, 218–39.

2. Pseudo-Dionysius, *The Divine Names*, 4, nos. 1 and 4.

3. See article 1, note 10.

But there is no thing in which natural power is subject to the will, and so even in God the generation of the Son from the Father, which is natural, does not come about by a command of the will; and in human beings the powers of the vegetative soul, which are called natural, are not subject to the will. Therefore it cannot be that the likeness of natural attributes is communicated to creatures by the divine will.

OBJ. 5. In the book On Christian Doctrine, Augustine says that *Because* God *is good, we are.*[4] And thus the goodness of God seems to be the cause of the production of creatures. But goodness is natural to God. Therefore the emanation[5] of things from God is natural as well.

OBJ. 6. In God, will and nature are one and the same. Therefore, if God did produce things voluntarily, it would follow that he produced them naturally.

OBJ. 7. Natural necessity results from the fact that nature invariably operates in the same way unless it is impeded. But God is more immutable than lower nature. Therefore God produces his effects of greater necessity than lower nature does.

OBJ. 8. God's operation is his essence. But his essence is natural to him. Therefore whatever he does, he does naturally.

OBJ. 9. According to the Philosopher in Ethics III, *will is of the end, choice of those things which are means to the end.*[6] But God has no end, since he is infinite. Therefore he does not act voluntarily but rather from natural necessity.

OBJ. 10. God operates inasmuch as he is good, as Augustine says.[7] But he is necessarily good. Therefore he operates out of necessity.

OBJ. 11. Everything that exists is either contingent or necessary. Now a thing is necessary in three ways, namely by coercion, by supposition, or absolutely.[8] Now it cannot be said that anything in God is possible or contingent, for this would indicate mutability, as the Philosopher makes clear in Metaphysics XI, since *what is contingent,*

4. Augustine, *On Christian Doctrine,* I 32.
5. *fluxus.*
6. Aristotle, *Nicomachean Ethics,* III 2, 1111b26.
7. Augustine, *On Christian Doctrine,* I 32.
8. Cf. *ST* I Q. 82, a. 1.

may happen not to be.[9] Likewise nothing in God is necessary through coercion, since there is nothing violent or contrary to nature in him, as is said in Metaphysics V.[10] Likewise nothing is necessary through supposition, since such necessity is caused by presupposed causes and God has no cause. Therefore what remains is that whatever is in God is necessary absolutely and thus it seems that things are produced in being out of necessity.

OBJ. 12. The second letter to Timothy says, God *remains faithful, he cannot deny himself.*[11] But, since God is his own goodness, he would deny himself if he were to deny his own goodness. But he would deny his goodness if he did not pour it out by communicating it, since this is proper to goodness.[12] Therefore God cannot but produce creatures by communicating his own goodness [to them]. Therefore he produces [them] out of necessity, since what "cannot but be" and what "necessarily is" are convertible, as is made clear in On Interpretation II.[13]

OBJ. 13. According to Augustine, for the Father to generate the Son is for the Father to express his own word.[14] But Anselm says that the Father speaks himself and the creature by the same word.[15] Therefore, since the generation of the Son by the Father is natural and not by command of the will, it seems that the production of creatures is as well, for in God to speak and to make are not distinct, as it is written: *He spoke and they were made.*[16]

OBJ. 14. Every voluntary agent necessarily wills its ultimate end, as man for example necessarily wills to be happy.[17] But the ultimate end of the divine will is communication of its own goodness, for he produced creatures in order that he might communicate his good-

9. *quod contingit esse, contingit non esse.* This seems to be a corollary of Aristotle, *Metaphysics,* XI 5, 1062a20.

10. Aristotle, *Metaphysics,* V 5, 1015a26–b5.

11. Timothy 2:13.

12. Pseudo-Dionysius, *The Divine Names,* 4, no. 1. On the principle that the good is self-diffusive and the challenge this seems to pose to God's freedom, see Fran O'Rourke, *Pseudo-Dionysius and the Metaphysics of Aquinas* (Leiden: E. J. Brill, 1992; reissued by University of Notre Dame Press, 2005), esp. 250–54.

13. Aristotle, *On Interpretation* 13, 22a21.

14. Augustine, *On the Trinity,* XV 14.

15. Anselm, *Monologion,* 33.

16. Psalms 33:9 and 148:5.

17. Cf. *ST* I Q. 82, a. 1.

ness [to them]. Therefore God necessarily wills this and therefore he also produces them necessarily.

OBJ. 15. Just as God is good in himself, so is he necessary in himself. But since God is good in himself, in him there is nothing but what is good. Therefore there is in him likewise nothing but what is necessary. And thus he produces things out of necessity.

OBJ. 16. The will of God is determined to one thing, namely the good. But nature operates necessarily, because it is determined to one thing. Therefore the divine will also produces[18] creatures necessarily.

OBJ. 17. The Father is the principle of the Son and the holy Spirit by virtue of his nature, as Hilary says.[19] But the same nature which is in the Father and the Son is in the holy Spirit. Therefore for the same reason the holy Spirit is naturally a principle. But he is a principle only of creatures. Therefore creatures naturally proceed from God.

OBJ. 18. An effect proceeds from an acting cause <by means of its action>. Therefore an agent is not related to its effect except by being related to its action or operation. But God is naturally related to his operation or action, since his action is his essence. Therefore he is related to his effect in the same way, producing it naturally.

OBJ. 19. Nothing comes from a *per se* good except what is good and well made. Therefore nothing comes from something necessary *per se* except what is necessary and necessarily made. But God is of this sort. Therefore everything proceeds from him by necessity.

OBJ. 20. Since that which is *per se* is prior to that which is through another, the first agent must act through his own essence. But his essence and his nature are one and the same. Therefore he acts through his own nature and thus creatures proceed from him naturally.

On the contrary, in his book On the Synods, Hilary says, *The will of God gives substance to all creatures.* And in the same book [he says], creatures are as *God willed* them *to be.*[20] Therefore God produces creatures voluntarily and not by natural necessity.

Further (2) in Confessions XII, Augustine speaks to God saying,

18. *operator.*
19. Hilary of Poitiers, *Liber de Synodis,* XII 33.
20. Hilary of Poitiers, *Liber de Synodis,* XXIV 58.

You made two things, Lord, one near to you, namely the angel, and the other *near to nothing,* namely matter.[21] Nevertheless, neither of these is of your nature, since neither is what you are. But the Son proceeds from the Father naturally, because he has the same nature as the Father, as Augustine says.[22] Therefore creatures do not proceed from God naturally.

I answer that without any doubt we are to hold that God produced creatures in being by the free decree of his will with no natural necessity. And this can be shown now with four arguments.

The first is that the universe must be said to have some end. Otherwise everything in the universe happens by chance, unless it were perhaps said that the first creatures have no end but are by natural necessity, while later creatures do have an end. Democritus, for example, held the heavenly bodies to be made by chance and lower bodies to be from determinate causes.[23] This is disproved in Physics II because things which are more noble cannot be less ordered than things of lower dignity.[24] Therefore it is necessary to say that there is an intended end in God's production of creatures. Now both will and nature act for an end, but not in the same way. For since nature does not know its end or have any notion[25] of an end or the relation of means to an end, it cannot determine an end for itself or move or order or direct itself toward an end. But a voluntary agent, who understands both the end and all the rest of these, can do this. And so a voluntary agent acts for an end in such a way that it determines an end for itself and moves itself in some way to the end, by ordering its actions to it. Nature, on the other hand, tends to its end as moved and directed by another which knows and wills, just as an arrow tends to a determinate mark because of the archer's aim. And in this sense philosophers say that *the work of nature is the work of an intelligence.*[26] Now that which is through another is always preceded by that which is *per se.* And so the first orderer to an end must do so

21. Augustine, *Confessions,* XII 7.
22. Augustine, *The Trinity,* XV 14.
23. I cannot see a source for this in Democritus.
24. This seems to be a reference to Aristotle, *Physics,* II 4, 196a25–b4.
25. *rationem.*
26. Aristotle, *Generation of Animals* I 23, 731a24, and *On Breath* (*De spiritu,* generally considered spurious) 9, 485b8.

voluntarily, and thus God produced creatures in being voluntarily, not naturally. Nor can it be objected that the generation of the Son, who proceeds from the Father naturally, precedes creation, because the Son proceeds not as one ordered to an end but [as] the end of all.

The second argument is that *nature is determined to one thing.*[27] Since every agent produces its like, it follows that nature must tend to produce this likeness which is determined to one thing. Now since equality is caused by unity, while inequality is from a multitude which is various (which is why one thing is equal to another in only one way, while inequality has many degrees), nature always makes its equal unless there is a defect in either the active or the receptive or passive power. But there can be no defect of passive potency in God, since he requires no matter. Nor is his power deficient, but rather infinite. And so only that which is his equal, namely the Son, proceeds from him naturally. On the other hand, creatures, which are unequal, proceed not naturally but voluntarily, for there are many degrees of inequality. Nor can it be said that the divine power is determined to only one, since it is infinite. And so, since the divine power extends itself to different degrees of inequality in making creatures, the fact that a creature is fashioned in a particular determinate degree is by decree of [God's] will, not by natural necessity.

The third argument is that since *every agent produces its like*[28] in some way, it must be that an effect somehow pre-exists in its cause. Now everything which is in something is in it according to the mode of that in which it is.[29] And so, since God himself is intellect, creatures pre-exist in him intelligibly, which is why John 1 says, *What was made, was life in him.*[30] Now that which is in the intellect is produced only by means of the will, for the will is the executor of the intellect and the intelligible moves the will. And so it follows that created things proceeded from God voluntarily.

The fourth argument is that, according to the Philosopher in Metaphysics IX, action is twofold: one which remains in the agent it-

27. I have been unable to trace a source for this reference.

28. See article 1, note 10 above.

29. This is an instance of the Book of Causes' "recipitur" principle. See article 3, note 2 above.

30. John 1:3–4.

self, and is the perfection and act of the agent, as for example to understand, to will, and the like; and another which issues from the agent into an extrinsic patient, and is the perfection and act of the patient, as for example, to heat, to move, and the like.[31] Now God's action cannot be understood to be of the second kind of action because, since his action is his potency,[32] it does not issue forth from him. And so [his action] must be understood to be of the first kind, which is [found] only in intelligent and voluntary agents (or also in sensitive agents, which also does not apply to God, because although sensory action does not tend to something extrinsic, it is [caused] by an extrinsic action). Therefore whatever God does outside himself, he understands and wills. Nor does this deny the natural generation of the Son, since generation of this sort is not understood to terminate in something outside the divine essence. Therefore it is necessary to say that every creature proceeded from God voluntarily and not by natural necessity.

AD 1. The comparison Dionysius makes should be understood in terms of universality of diffusion. For the sun sheds rays on all bodies, not distinguishing one from another, and so does the divine goodness. But this [comparison] does not extend to the absence of will.

AD 2. It is because of the perfection of the divine nature that, by virtue of the divine nature, a likeness of that very nature is communicated to creatures. Nevertheless, this communication comes about not by natural necessity but by will.

And through this the response to the third objection is clear.

AD 4. Nature is not subject to the will in those things which are within something, but in those things which are external to something nothing prevents nature being subject to the will. And so in the local motion of animals, nature, in their muscles and sinews, is

31. Aristotle, *Metaphysics* IX 8, 1050a30–b1. The terms "immanent" and "transitive action" are often used to refer to this distinction. Here in the *De potentia,* Thomas argues that God's act of creation is an immanent act. We should note that this contradicts what he says in *SCG* II 1 (par. 3), which was completed prior to the *De potentia.* On the meaning of creation as an immanent act, see Susan Selner-Wright, "Aquinas on Acts of Creation and Procreation," *National Catholic Bioethics Quarterly* 3 (2003): 710–14.

32. *cum actio sua sit eius potencia.* Fr. Shapcote translates *"potencia"* as "essence."

subject to the command of appetite. And so it is not unreasonable if creatures are produced in being by virtue of the divine nature according to the decree of the divine will.

AD 5. The good is the proper object of the will. And so the goodness of God, inasmuch as it is desired and loved by God, causes creatures through his will.

AD 6. Although will and nature are one and the same thing in God, nevertheless they differ logically[33] in that they designate different things in relation to creatures.[34] For nature connotes a relation to one determinate thing, but will does not.

AD 7. Nature produces something of necessity not only because of its invariability but also because of its determination to one thing, which [latter] does not belong to the divine will, although it is supremely immutable.

AD 8. God's operation does belong to him naturally, since it is his nature or essence. But, according to our mode of understanding, the principle of the operation from which the created effect follows is the [divine] will, [and so the effect follows from it according to the mode of the will,] just as the effect of heating follows according to the mode of heat.[35]

AD 9. Although God is infinite, he is nevertheless the end to which all things are ordered. For he is not infinite in a privative sense, in the way that quantity, which naturally has an end, is deprived of something if it is infinite.[36] For in this sense of end he is neither infinite nor finite. But he is said to be infinite in a negative sense, since he is entirely unbounded.

AD 10. Although God operates inasmuch as he is good and goodness is in him of necessity, nevertheless it does not follow that he operates out of necessity. For goodness operates through the will, insofar as it is the will's object and end. But the will is not of necessity inclined to the means to the end, although it is necessitated with respect to the ultimate end.

33. *ratione.*

34. *per ea diversimode designatur respectus ad creaturam.*

35. *effectus tamen creature operationem consequitur cuius per modum intelligendi consideratur ut principium voluntas, sicut et effectus calefactionis sequitur secundum modum caloris.* This argument is clarified below in ad 18.

36. *sicut infinitum est passio quantitatis que nata est habere finem.*

AD 11. Insofar as something is in God himself, it cannot be considered possible, but only naturally and absolutely necessary. But with respect to creatures, something in God can be considered possible, not in terms of passive potency but in terms of active potency, which is not limited to one [effect].

AD 12. Were God to deny his own goodness by doing something contrary to his goodness or something in which his goodness was not expressed, then the impossible conclusion would follow that he denied himself. But this would not follow if he did not communicate his goodness, for nothing of his goodness would be lost if it were not communicated.

AD 13. Although the word of God itself comes forth from the Father naturally, it nevertheless does not follow that creatures proceed from God naturally. For the Father speaks his creatures in the way that they are in the Father himself, and they are in him as one who produces not out of necessity, but voluntarily.

AD 14. The ultimate end is not communication of goodness, but rather the divine goodness itself, from love of which God wills to communicate it. For he acts because of his goodness not as though he desires something he does not have, but because he desires to communicate what he does have: for he acts not from desire, but from love of the end.

AD 15. Just as in God there is nothing but what is good, so in him there is nothing but what is necessary. Nevertheless it does not follow that whatever is from him proceeds necessarily.

AD 16. As has been said, God's will is naturally inclined to his goodness, and so he can will only that which is fitting to it, namely the good. Nevertheless, he is not determined to this or that good, and it does not follow that the good things which are from him proceed necessarily.

AD 17. Although the same nature is in the Father, Son, and holy Spirit, nevertheless it does not have the same mode of existence in each of the three. I refer to mode of existence in terms of relation: for in the Father [nature] is not considered as from another, while in the Son it is considered as from the Father. And so it does not follow that whatever belongs to the Father by virtue of his nature belongs [also] to the Son and holy Spirit.

AD 18. An effect follows from an action according to the mode of the principle of the action. But in [our] mode of thinking, the principle of divine action with regard to creatures is considered to be the divine will, which has no necessary relation to creatures. And so it does not follow that creatures proceed from God by natural necessity, although God's action is his essence or nature.

AD 19. Creatures are likened to God with respect to general conditions but not with respect to the mode of participation. For God and creatures have different modes of being and likewise of goodness. And so, although every good is from the first good and every being is from the first being, those goods which are from the supreme good are not all supreme, nor are those beings from the necessary being all by necessity.

AD 20. God's will is his essence, and so his acting voluntarily does not prevent him from acting by his own essence. For the will of God is not something added to the divine essence, but that essence itself.

ARTICLE 16

The sixteenth thing to be asked is whether a multitude can proceed from one first thing. And it seems that it cannot.[1]

OBJ. 1. For just as God is good *per se* and consequently is the supreme good, so is he the *per se* and supreme one. But insofar as he is good nothing can proceed from him except what is good. Therefore neither can anything proceed from him except what is one.

OBJ. 2. As good is convertible with being, so also is one. But those things which are common must be considered a likeness of the creature to God, as was said above.[2] Therefore, just as in goodness so also in unity is the creature to be likened to God, as namely being one thing from one thing.

OBJ. 3. Just as good and evil are mutually exclusive if taken together (although they are contraries considered as differentiating habits), so one and many are mutually exclusive, as is made clear in Metaphysics X.[3] But wickedness can in no way be said to proceed from God, but rather it occurs because of deficiency in second causes. Therefore, neither should we hold that God is the cause of a multitude.

OBJ. 4. We must understand cause and effect to be proportionate, for it is clear that *single things* cause *single things* and universal things cause universal things, as the Philosopher makes plain in Physics II.[4] But God is the supremely universal cause. Therefore his proper effect is the most universal effect, namely being. But multitude does not result from things having being, since diversity and difference are the cause of multitude, while all things agree in being. Therefore multitude comes not from God but from second causes which cause the particular conditions of things in terms of which beings differ.

OBJ. 5. Every effect is understood to have a proper cause. But it is

1. For parallel discussion of this question and the issues raised in response to it, see *ST* I Q. 47, a. 1, and *SCG* II 39–45 and III 97.

2. In article 1, ad 12.

3. Aristotle, *Metaphysics,* X 3, 1054a23–27.

4. Aristotle, *Physics,* II 3, 195b25–27.

impossible that one be proper to many. Therefore it is impossible that one be the cause of a multitude.

OBJ. 6. But one might say that this holds for natural causes but not for voluntary causes. On the contrary, a craftsman is the voluntary cause of his work, but his work proceeds from him according to the proper form of that work which is in the [mind of the] craftsman. Therefore even in voluntary effects, each one requires a proper cause.

OBJ. 7. There must be conformity between cause and effect. But God is entirely one and simple. Therefore neither multitude nor composition ought to be found in the creature which is his effect.

OBJ. 8. One effect cannot proceed immediately from different agents. But just as cause is appropriated to effect, so is effect to cause. Therefore neither can one cause immediately produce many effects. And so the same conclusion follows.

OBJ. 9. In God the same power generates, spirates,[5] and creates. But the generative power terminates in only one, and likewise the spirating power, since there can be only one Son and one holy Spirit in the Trinity. Therefore the creative power also terminates in only one thing.

OBJ. 10. But one might say that the universe of creatures is in a certain way one, namely by order. On the contrary, an effect must be like its cause. But God's unity is not a unity of order, since in God there is neither prior and posterior nor higher and lower. Therefore a unity of order does not suffice to make it possible that many things be educed from one God.

OBJ. 11. One simple thing has only one action. But only one effect comes from one action. Therefore only one effect can proceed from one simple thing.

OBJ. 12. A creature proceeds from God not only as an effect from an efficient cause, but also as exemplate from exemplar. But one exemplar has only one proper exemplate. Therefore only one creature can proceed from God.

OBJ. 13. God causes things through his intellect. But intellectual agents act through the form of their intellects. Therefore, since there

5. I am following Fr. Shapcote's translation of *spirandi*.

is only one form in the divine intellect, it seems that only one creature can proceed from it.

OBJ. 14. But one might reply that although the form of the divine intellect is one in reality, which is its essence, it may nevertheless be considered to have a kind of plurality in terms of its different relations[6] to different creatures, and thus to have a logical plurality. On the contrary, these multiple relations are either in the divine intellect or they are only in our minds. If it were the first, then it would follow that in the divine intellect there would be plurality and not supreme simplicity. If it were the second, then it would follow that God produced different creatures only by means of our reason, from which it follows that he produces different creatures through different relations to creatures which exist only in our intellect. And thus the proposed position is reached: namely that a multitude does not proceed from God immediately.

OBJ. 15. God produces things in being by the apprehension of his intellect. But there is only one apprehension in him, since his understanding[7] is his essence, which is one. Therefore he produces only one creature.

OBJ. 16. That which exists only in the mind is not created by God, since such things, like chimeras and things of that sort, seem to be delusive. But multitude exists only in the mind, for it indicates an abstraction from many things which is not found in reality. Therefore God is not the cause of multitude.

OBJ. 17. According to Plato, the best brings the best.[8] But the best can be only one. Therefore, since God is the best, only one thing can be produced by him.

OBJ. 18. Every agent acting for an end makes its effect as close to the end as it can. But in producing creatures God ordains them for an end. Therefore he makes them as close to the end as he can. But this can be done in only one way. Therefore God produces only one creature.

OBJ. 19. It is unjust to bestow unequal [gifts] on things, except

6. *diversos respectus.*

7. *intelligere.*

8. Henle cites Pseudo-Dionysius, *On the Divine Names* 4, no. 19. For his explanation, see *Saint Thomas and Platonism,* 9.

because of some pre-existing inequality of merit or some other differing condition among them. But no difference precedes the divine operation, otherwise it would not be the first cause of all things. Therefore in the first creation of things he did not give creatures unequal gifts. But the diversity and multitude of creatures occur insofar as things receive more or less of the divine gifts, as is clear in the fourth chapter of The Celestial Hierarchy.[9] Therefore in the first creation of things God did not produce a multitude.

OBJ. 20. God communicates his goodness to creatures according to their capacity.[10] But the nature of higher creatures was capable of the kind of perfection and dignity which could be proper to the cause of lower creatures. For that which is more perfect can act on that which is less perfect and communicate its own perfection to it. Therefore it seems that God produced lower creatures by means of higher creatures.[11] And thus he immediately produced only one creature, higher than the others, whatever that be.

OBJ. 21. The more immaterial a form is, the more active it is, since it is more separated from potency. *For each thing acts insofar as it is in act,*[12] not insofar as it is in potency. But the forms of things which are in an angel's mind are more immaterial than the forms which are in natural things. Therefore, since natural forms cause forms like themselves, it seems all the more that the forms in an angel's mind produce forms of natural things like themselves. But the diversity, and consequently the multitude, of things is from the form. Therefore it seems multitude proceeds from God only by the mediation of higher creatures.

OBJ. 22. Whatever God makes is one. Therefore only one thing can be from him, and thus he is not the cause of multitude.

OBJ. 23. God understands only one, since he understands nothing beyond himself, as is proved in Metaphysics XI.[13] But he causes things by his intellect. Therefore he causes only one thing.

OBJ. 24. Anselm says that in God the creature is the creative es-

9. Pseudo-Dionysius, *The Celestial Hierarchy,* 4, no. 2.

10. This another example of the "recipitur principle." See article 3, note 2, above.

11. *Book of Causes,* see Props. 3 and 9.

12. See article 1, note 14.

13. This is a reference to Aristotle, *Metaphysics,* XII 9, 1074b15–1075a4.

sence.[14] But the creative essence is only one. Therefore in God the creature also is only one. But the creature is created by God in the same way that it pre-existed in him. Therefore only one creature comes from God, and thus a multitude does not proceed from him.

On the contrary (1) according to Wisdom XI, Lord, *you disposed all in number and weight and measure.*[15] But there is no number without multitude. Therefore a multitude does proceed from God.

(2) The power of God exceeds the power of anything else. But one point can be the beginning of many lines.[16] Therefore although God is one he can be the principle of many creatures.

(3) That which is proper to one thing insofar as it is one belongs in the highest degree to that which is supremely one. But it is proper to unity to be the principle of multitude. Therefore it belongs in the highest degree to God, who is supremely one, that a multitude proceed from him.

(4) At the beginning of his Arithmetic, Boethius says that God produced things in being according to the exemplar of number.[17] But the exemplate conforms to the exemplar. Therefore he produced things in multitude and number.

(5) The Psalm says, *You have done all things in wisdom.*[18] But since it belongs to a wise man to order things, those things which are done through wisdom have order, and consequently multitude. Therefore the multitude of things proceeds from God.

I answer that the impossibility of many proceeding from one immediate and proper principle seems to result from the determination of cause to effect, from which it seems due and necessary that if there is a certain cause, a certain effect should follow. Now of the four causes, the material and the efficient for some time precede the effect in being, whereas the end [precedes it] if not in being at least in intention. The form, however, [precedes the effect] in neither way, inasmuch as it is form, because, since the effect has being through it, its being is simultaneous with the being of the effect; but

14. Anselm, *Monologion,* 9, 10, and 12.
15. Wisdom 11:21.
16. Cf. Pseudo-Dionysius, *On the Divine Names,* V, no. 6.
17. Boethius, *De Arithmetica,* I 2.
18. Psalm 104:24.

insofar as the form is the end, it precedes [the effect] in the intention of the agent. And although the form is the end of operation, in that the agent's operation terminates in it, not every end is a form, for there is an end of intention beyond the end of operation, as is clear in a house: for its form is the end that terminates the operation of the builder, but his intention does not terminate there, but in a further end, which is a dwelling place. And thus it may be said that the end of operation is the form of house, while that of intention is a dwelling place. Therefore the necessity of the existence of a certain effect[19] cannot be from the form insofar as it is form, since it is thus concomitant with the effect. Rather it is from either the power of the efficient cause or the matter or the end, whether that be the end of intention or of operation.

But it cannot be said that God's effect is necessitated by matter,[20] for, since he is the author of all being, nothing having being in any way is presupposed in his action in such a way that it would be necessary to say that this or that effect of God was because of the disposition of matter.

Likewise [God's effect] cannot [be necessitated] by an effective potency. For, since his active potency is infinite, it does not terminate in one except that one which is his equal, which cannot be the case with any effect. And so, if it be necessary that he produce an effect beneath himself, his potency, insofar as it is in him, is not determined to this or that degree of distance, so that it would be necessary that a certain effect be produced by his active power.

Likewise it cannot [be necessitated] by the end of intention. For this end is the divine goodness itself, which gains nothing from the production of effects. Neither indeed can it be totally represented by its effects nor entirely communicated to them, so that it could be said that a certain effect of God had to be, in order that it participate totally in the divine goodness. Rather it is possible for the effect to participate in [the divine goodness] in many ways, and so no one [of these ways] is made necessary by the end. For necessity arises from the end when the intention of the end cannot be completed, either entirely or suitably, unless this or that exists.

19. *debitum igitur existendi tale causatum.*
20. *non potest autem dici in Deo quod effectus eius habeat debitum essendi ex materia.*

It remains therefore that [any] necessity in divine works can arise only from the form which is the end of operation. For since [the form] is not infinite, it has determinate principles without which it cannot be and a determinate mode of being. So for example we might say that if God intends to make a human being, it is necessary and due that he confer a rational soul and organic body on him, without which a human being cannot be.

And likewise we can say concerning the universe, that the fact that God willed to establish such a universe was not made necessary or due, either by the end or by the <nature>[21] of the efficient potency or of the matter, as has been shown. But rather, supposing that he willed to produce such a universe, it was necessary that he produce certain creatures, from which a certain form of universe would arise. And because the very perfection of the universe requires both the multitude and the diversity of things, since it cannot be found in [any] one of them because of its distance[22] from the perfection of the first good, given the intended form it was necessary that God produce many and diverse creatures, some simple, some composite, some corruptible, and some incorruptible.

But some philosophers, failing to consider these things, strayed from the truth in various ways. Some who did not understand God to be the author of the universe, held that matter is self-existent and the diversity of things is produced because of [matter's] necessity. Some of these held that diversity of things was according to the rarity or density of matter, like the ancient natural philosophers who perceived only the material cause.[23] Others maintained this diversity was according to the action of an efficient cause which produced different effects according to the diversity of matter. In this way, Anaxagoras held that the divine intellect produced different things by separating them from commixture with matter.[24] And thus Empedocles held that different effects were distinguished and conjoined in various ways through friendship and strife according to the diversity of matter.[25] The falsity of these positions is apparent in two ways. First,

21. *ratione.* 22. *recessum.*

23. This may be a reference to Anaximenes. See Diels-Kranz, 13A5 and 13A7.

24. Anaxagoras, Diels-Kranz, 59B12–13.

25. Empedocles, Diels-Kranz, 31B17, 21, 22, 26, 35.

they did not hold that all being came from one first and highest being, which has been proved in another question.[26] Second, according to [these positions] it would follow that the distinction and order of the parts of the universe would be by chance, because they were necessitated by the necessity of matter.

Others like Avicenna and his followers held that the plurality and diversity of things arose from the necessity arising from an efficient cause. For he maintained that the first being, insofar as it understands itself, produces only one effect, which is the first intelligence. [The first intelligence] necessarily lacks the simplicity of the first being, since in it potentiality begins to be mixed with act inasmuch as it receives being from another and is not its own being, but is in a certain way in potency to that [being]. And so, insofar as it understands the first being, another intelligence inferior to it proceeds from it; and insofar as it understands its own potency, the heavenly body which it moves proceeds from it; and insofar as it understands its own act, the soul of the first heaven proceeds from it. And thus follows the multiplication of different things through many intermediates.[27] But this position also is not fit to stand. First, because it holds that the divine power is determined to one effect, the first intelligence. Second, because it holds that substances other than God create other things, which has been shown to be impossible in another question.[28] In addition, like the first position, this one leads to the view that the beauty of the order of the universe is a matter of chance, since it ascribes the diversity of things not to the intention of an end but to the determination of active potencies to their effects.

Others like Plato and his followers erred concerning the necessity arising from the final cause. For he maintained that this sort of universe had to be produced because of the divine goodness as understood and loved by God, so that the best produced the best.[29] This can indeed be true if we consider only what is, but not if we consider what could be. For this universe is the best of what is, and it has this

26. In article 5.

27. Avicenna, *Liber de Philosophia Prima sive Scientia Divina,* IX 4.

28. In article 4.

29. Again, Henle cites Pseudo-Dionysius, *On the Divine Names* 4, no. 19. For his explanation, see *Saint Thomas and Platonism,* 9.

status because of God's supreme goodness. But God's goodness is not bound to this universe in such a way that he could not have made another universe that was more or less good.

Others erred by considering not the necessity arising from the formal cause, but only the necessity due to the divine goodness. Thus since they understood God to be the supreme good, the Manicheans believed that only the best of creatures, namely spiritual and incorruptible creatures, were from God, while corporeal and corruptible things were attributed to another principle.[30]

Although it is contrary to this, Origen's error has the same source. For he considered God to be supremely good and just, and so he believed that at the very beginning he made only the best creatures and [all] equal [to each other], namely rational creatures, whose free choice to act in different ways for good or evil led, he said, to the different degrees of things established in the universe. He said that those rational creatures who turned to God were elevated to the dignity of angels, and to different ranks insofar as they merited more or less. On the other hand, he said that rational creatures who sinned by their free will, fell to the lower world and were bound to bodies: some who sinned less were bound to the sun, the moon, and the stars, while some were bound to human bodies, and some were turned into demons.[31]

Both of these errors seem to disregard the order of the universe and consider only single parts of it. For the very order of the universe makes it apparent to reason that from one principle, without any previous difference of merits, different degrees of creatures were established in order that the universe be complete. And the universe, through multiple and various creatures, represents what pre-exists in the divine goodness simply and without distinction. In the same way, the perfection of a house or of the human body requires diversity of parts, and neither of them would be complete if all their parts were of one condition, as if for example every part of the human body were an eye, since the functions of the other parts would be missing. Likewise if every part of a house were the roof, the house

30. Cf. Augustine, *De Duabus Animabus contra Manichaeos*, 1.
31. Origen, *On First Principles*, I 7, no. 5; I 8, nos. 2, 4.

would be imperfect and fail in its goal, namely to ward off *rain and cold*.[32]

Therefore we must say that the multitude and diversity of creatures proceeds from one first thing, not out of material necessity or the limitation of potency or the obligation of goodness, but from the order of wisdom, in order that the perfection of the universe would be in the diversity of creatures.

AD 1. As God is one, so also did he produce something one, not only because each thing is one in itself but also because all things [taken together] are in a certain way one perfect thing, with a unity which requires a diversity of parts, as has been shown.

AD 2. Creatures are likened to God in unity inasmuch as each thing is one in itself and insofar as all things are one by unity of order, as has been said.

AD 3. Wickedness consists entirely in non-being, while multitude is caused by being. For the very difference through which beings are distinguished from each other is a being. And so God, who *is not the source of tendency to non-being*,[33] but is rather the source of all being, is not the principle of wickedness but is the principle of multitude. But we should note that [the word] "one" has two senses. There is [the sense in which] one is convertible with being, which adds nothing to being except indivision, and this [sense of] one excludes multitude insofar as multitude is caused by division. [This does] not [exclude] extrinsic multitude, which has unities as parts, but [only] intrinsic multitude, which is opposed to unity, for something is said to be one, not because there is nothing else with which it may constitute a multitude, but because there is no division of the thing itself into many. The other [sense of] one is the principle of number, which adds the notion of measure to the notion of being. And multitude does exclude this [sense of] one, since number comes from division of continuity. Multitude does not entirely exclude unity, since division of the whole leaves parts undivided, but it does exclude unity of the whole. But wickedness, considered in itself, [absolutely] excludes

32. *imbribus et caumatibus.* Cf. Aquinas, *De Physico Auditu sive Physicorum Aristotelis* II, lect. 15, no. 525. where Thomas clarifies his use of *"caumate"* by adding, *"idest a caliditate et pluviis."*

33. I have been unable to trace a reference for this text.

goodness, in no way constituting or being constituted by goodness.

AD 4. Being is related to those things which are included under being in a way that is different from the way animal or any other genus is related to its species. For species add some difference which is beyond the essence of the genus, as for example human being [adds] to animal. For animal designates only the sensitive nature, which does not include rationality. But those things which are included under being do not add anything to being which is beyond its essence. And so it does not follow that that which is the cause of animal as such is the cause of the rational being as such, but it does follow that that which is the cause of being as such is the cause of all the diversity of being, and consequently of the whole multitude of being.

AD 5. The appropriation of cause to effect is considered in terms of the likeness of the effect to the cause. Now the likeness of a creature to God is considered in terms of whether the creature fulfills what is in God's intellect and will concerning it, just as a craftsman's works are like him insofar as the form of art is expressed in them and what the craftsman intends in their production is shown in them. For, just as a natural thing acts by its form, so does a craftsman act by his intellect and will. Therefore God is the proper cause of each creature, inasmuch as he knows and wills each creature to be. The claim that "the same cannot be proper to many" applies when appropriation is made through adequation, which is not the case here.

The solution to the sixth objection is clear from what has been said.

AD 7. Although there is a certain likeness of creature to God, there is no adequation. Therefore it does not follow that if God's unity is entirely without multitude and composition, the same must therefore be true of the creature's unity.

AD 8. [Although] an effect cannot exceed its cause, nevertheless a cause can exceed its effect. And so, although many effects can proceed from one cause, one effect cannot immediately proceed from several causes.

AD 9. Although in God the generative and the creative powers are really the same, nevertheless they do not connote the same relations,[34] but the generative power connotes relation to that which

34. *respectu.*

proceeds naturally, which is therefore necessarily only one, while the creative power implies relation to that which proceeds voluntarily, and so it is not necessary that it be one.

AD 10. As has been said, it is not necessary that the same kind of unity be in the creature and in God, although the creature does imitate God's unity.

AD 11. Although God's action is one and simple because it is his essence, it follows not that there is only one effect, but [that there are] many, because effects proceed from the divine action according to the order of his wisdom and the decree of his will.

AD 12. When the exemplate represents the exemplar perfectly, there can be only one exemplate from one exemplar, except accidentally inasmuch as exemplates are distinguished materially. But creatures do not imitate their exemplar perfectly, and so it can be imitated in different ways and there can be different exemplates. There is only one perfect way of imitating something and that is why the Son, who imitates the Father perfectly, can be only one.

AD 13. Although the form of the divine intellect is really only one, it is logically many with respect to the different relations [it has] to creatures,[35] inasmuch as creatures are understood to imitate the form of the divine intellect in different ways.

AD 14. These different relations to creatures are not only in our intellect but also in the divine intellect. Nevertheless, there are not different [ideas] in the divine intellect by which God understands, since he understands by only one, which is his essence, but there are many which are understood by him. For just as we understand that creatures can imitate God in many ways, so also does God understand this, and consequently he understands the various relations of creatures to him.

AD 15. Just as God understands all things by one,[36] so [does he understand them all] by one apprehension, for the act of the intellect must be one or many, according to the unity or multiplicity of the principle of understanding.

AD 16. Although multitude exists apart from many things only in

35. *est tamen multiplex ratione secundum diversos respectus ad creaturam.*
36. I.e. by his own essence.

the mind, nevertheless multitude is really in many things, just as animal in general exists only in the mind, but animal nature is in individual [animals]. And because of this, multitude and animal nature must be traced to God as [their] cause.

AD 17. The universe which God produced is the best with respect to the things that are, but not with respect to what God could make.

AD 18. That argument holds when that which conduces to the end can totally and perfectly attain the end by way of adequation, which is not the case here.

AD 19. This is Origen's argument[37] and it is not very strong. For it is not unjust that unequal gifts be given to equals except when something is owed to them, which cannot be said of the first creation of things. <For> that which is given out of pure liberality can be given more or less according to the will of the giver and what his wisdom requires.

AD 20. Although other creatures are beneath the angel, nevertheless their production requires infinite power in the producer, inasmuch as they are produced in being by creation, since they are not made from pre-existing matter. And thus one must say that all creatures that are not made from pre-existing matter are immediately created by God.

AD 21. Since creation terminates in being as its proper effect, it is impossible to say that those things created by God receive their forms from angels, since *all being is from form*.[38]

AD 22. Although whatever God makes is one in itself, nevertheless as we have said this unity does not exclude all multitude, since that [multitude] of which one is a part remains.

AD 23. When the Philosopher says that God understands nothing besides himself, this should not be understood to mean that God does not understand those things which are other than himself,

37. Origen, *On First Principles*, I 7, no. 4; I 8, nos. 1, 2.

38. I have been unable to trace a reference for this text. For a recent discussion of the principle *"forma dat esse,"* see Msgr. Wippel's "Thomas Aquinas on Creatures as Causes of *esse*," in *Metaphysical Themes in Thomas Aquinas II*, 175–79. See also Lawrence Dewan, O.P., "St. Thomas and the Distinction between Form and *Esse* in Caused Things," in *Gregorianum* 60 (1999): 353–70; reprinted in *Form and Being: Studies in Thomistic Metaphysics* (Washington, D.C.: The Catholic University of America Press, 2006), 188–204.

but that even those things which are other he understands not outside himself but in contemplating himself, since he knows all others through his own essence.

AD 24. A creature is said to be in God in two ways. First, as in its governing cause and the preserver of its being, and in this sense the being of the creature is understood to be distinct from the creator, so that the creature is said to be in God. For the creature is not understood to be preserved in being unless it already has being in its own nature, by which being the creature is distinguished from God.[39] And so the creature existing in God in this sense is not the creative essence. Secondly, a creature is said to be in God as in the power of an active cause or as in a knower. And in this sense a creature in God is the divine essence itself, as is said in John 1, *What was made, was life in him.*[40] But while in this sense a creature existing in God is the divine essence, nevertheless, there is in this sense not one creature but many, for God's essence is a sufficient medium for knowing different creatures and a sufficient power for producing them.

39. *non enim intelligitur creatura conseruari in esse nisi secundum quod iam habet esse in propria natura, secundum quod esse creatura* [*sic*] *a Deo distinguitur.* This is a text where the Marietti and Leonine differ in a philosophically significant way. The Marietti has: *Non enim intelligitur creatura conservari in esse nisi secundum quod jam habet esse in propria natura, secundum quod esse creaturae* [*sic*] *a Deo distnguitur.* I would translate this as "For the creature is not understood to be preserved in being unless it already has being in its own nature, according to which [nature] the being of the creature is distinguished from God." I very much appreciate Kevin White's help in teasing out the difference between the editions here.

40. John 1:3–4. Thomas' use of this same text above in the respondeo of article 15 sheds further light on his interpretation of it.

ARTICLE 17

The seventeenth point of inquiry is whether the world has always existed. And it seems that it has.[1]

OBJ. 1. For a thing always does what is proper to it.[2] But, as Dionysius says in the fourth chapter of The Celestial Hierarchy, It is *proper to* the divine *goodness to call those things which exist to* communicate in it.[3] This he does by producing creatures. Therefore, since the divine goodness has always been, it seems that it has always produced creatures in being, and so it seems that the world has always been.

OBJ. 2. God does not deny a creature that which it is capable of according to its nature. But there are creatures, such as the heaven, whose nature is capable of having always existed. Therefore it seems it was granted to the heaven always to have been. But given that the heaven existed, we must hold other creatures existed, as the Philosopher proves in On the Heavens.[4] Therefore it seems that the world has always been. The second premise is proved as follows. Everything that is incorruptible has the power to exist always, since, if its power to be were limited to a certain time, it could not always be, and thus it would not be incorruptible. But the heaven is incorruptible. Therefore its nature is to exist always.

OBJ. 3. But one might say that the heaven is not absolutely incorruptible, for it would fall into nothingness if God's power did not sustain it in being. On the contrary, we should not consider something to be [only] possibly or contingently because its destruction would follow from the destruction of its consequence. For although it is necessary for man to be an animal, nevertheless its destruction would follow the destruction of the consequence that man be a substance. Therefore it seems we cannot conclude that the heaven is corruptible because it would cease to exist if God withdrew his sustaining power from creatures.

1. For parallel texts, see article 14, note 1 above.
2. *quia proprium semper consequitur id cuius est proprium.*
3. *proprium est divine bonitatis ad communicationem sui ea que sunt vocare.*
4. Aristotle, *On the Heavens,* II 3, 286a3–b9.

OBJ. 4. As Avicenna proves in his Metaphysics, every effect is necessary in comparison with its cause because, if given the cause the effect does not necessarily follow, then even given the cause it is possible that the effect will be or not be.[5] For that which is in potency is not reduced to act except through that which is in act. And so it will be necessary that besides the cause mentioned there be another cause which makes the effect come forth[6] in act from the potentiality whereby it was possible for it to be or not be, given the cause. From this we can see that, given a sufficient cause, the effect is necessary. But God is the sufficient cause of the world. Therefore, since God has always been, the world also always was.

OBJ. 5. Everything that is prior to time is eternal (for eviternity is not before time but begins when time begins). But the world was before time, for it was created in the first instant of time, which was clearly before time, for it is said in Genesis 1, *In the beginning God created heaven and earth,*[7] that is, in the beginning of time, according to a gloss.[8] Therefore the world existed from eternity.

OBJ. 6. One thing always makes the same thing unless it is impeded. But God always remains the same, as we read in the Psalm: For you are always the self-same.[9] Therefore, since his action cannot be impeded, because of the infinity of his power, it seems he would always make the same thing. And so, since he did produce the world at some time, it seems that he always produced it from eternity.

OBJ. 7. Just as man necessarily wills his own happiness, so does God necessarily will his own goodness and whatever pertains to it. But the production of creatures in being pertains to the divine goodness. Therefore God necessarily wills this, and so it seems that he has willed to produce creatures from eternity, just as he willed his own goodness to be from eternity.

OBJ. 8. But one might say that it pertains to God's goodness to produce creatures in being but not to produce them in being from eternity. On the contrary, it is more generous to give something

5. Avicenna, *Liber de Philosophia Prima sive Scientia Divina,* IX 4. See also IV 1, VI 2, and IX 1.

6. *prodire.*

7. Genesis 1:1.

8. *Biblia Latina cum glossa ordinaria,* Genesis 1:1.

9. Psalm 102:27.

sooner rather than later. But the generosity of the divine goodness is infinite. Therefore it seems that it has given creatures being from eternity.

OBJ. 9. Augustine says, What you will, that you do if you can.[10] But God willed from eternity to produce the world, for otherwise he would have changed if the will to create the world came to him as new. Therefore, since no inability is proper to God,[11] it seems that he produced the world from eternity.

OBJ. 10. If the world was not always, then before the world existed it was either possible for it to exist or not [possible]. If it was not possible, then it was impossible, and therefore necessary that it not be, and thus it would never have been produced in being. But if it was possible, then there was some potency with respect to it, and thus there was some subject or matter, since potency can only be in a subject. But if there was matter, there was also form, since matter cannot be entirely without form. Therefore there was some body composed of matter and form and consequently there was the whole universe.

OBJ. 11. Everything which comes to be in act after having been possible is educed from potency into act. Therefore, if the world was possible prior to coming to be, we must say that the world is educed from potency into act, and thus that matter preceded and had existed eternally, from which the same conclusion follows as before.

OBJ. 12. Every agent that begins anew to act is moved from potency to act. But this cannot be said of God, since he is entirely unmoveable. Therefore it seems that he did not begin anew to act but that he produced the world from eternity.

OBJ. 13. If a voluntary agent begins to do what he previously willed but had not yet done, we must conclude that there is now something inducing him to act which did not induce him earlier, which in some way arouses him. But we cannot say that there was something other than God before the world which induced him to new action. Therefore, since he willed to make the world from eternity (otherwise his will would have been augmented by something), it seems that he made it from eternity.

10. *Illud dico te velle quod facis si potes.* This seems to refer to Augustine, *Confessions,* VIII 9.

11. *nulla inpotencia ei conveniat.*

OBJ. 14. Nothing moves the divine will to act except God's goodness. But the divine goodness is always the same. Therefore the divine will concerning the production of creatures is also always the same. And thus God produced creatures from eternity.

OBJ. 15. That which is always at its beginning and end never begins or ceases, since everything is after its beginning and before its end. But time is always at its beginning and at its end, for time is nothing but an instant which is the end of the past and the beginning of the future. Therefore time never begins or ceases but always is, and consequently movement also and moveable things and the whole world always [are]. For there is no time without movement, or movement without the moveable, or the moveable without the world.

OBJ. 16. But one might say that the first instant of time is neither the end of the past nor the ultimate beginning of the future. On the contrary, the now of time is always considered as flowing, and in this it differs from the now of eternity. But that which flows, flows from one thing into another. Therefore every now must flow from a prior now into a later one. Therefore it is impossible that there is a first or last now.

OBJ. 17. Motion follows the moveable and time follows motion. But because the first moveable thing is circular, it has neither beginning nor end, since in a circle we can observe no actual beginning or end. Therefore neither motion nor time has a beginning, and so the same conclusion follows as before.

OBJ. 18. But someone might say that, although a circular body has no beginning of magnitude, it nevertheless has a beginning of duration. On the contrary, motion's duration follows the measure of magnitude since, according to the Philosopher, the greater the magnitude, the greater the motion and the time.[12] Therefore, if there is no beginning of the magnitude of a circular body, neither will there be a beginning of magnitude of motion and time, and consequently [no beginning] of their duration, since their duration, especially that of time, is their magnitude.

OBJ. 19. God is the cause of things by his knowledge. But knowl-

12. I.e. motion and time are proportionate to magnitude.

edge connotes a relation to the knowable thing. Therefore, since related things are simultaneous by nature and God's knowledge is eternal, it seems that things are produced by him from eternity.

OBJ. 20. God precedes the world either in nature only or in duration [as well]. If in nature only, as a cause [precedes] a simultaneous effect, then it seems that, since God has been from eternity, creatures have been from eternity. But if he precedes the world in duration, then there must have been some duration prior to the duration of the world, which is related to the world's duration as earlier to later. But a duration <which> has earlier and later is time. Therefore there was time before the world, and consequently [before] motion and moveable things. And thus the same conclusion follows as before.

OBJ. 21. Augustine says, I will not *say that God was not lord* from eternity.[13] But whenever he was lord he had creatures subject to him. Therefore we cannot say that creatures have not been from eternity.

OBJ. 22. God could have produced the world before he did produce it; otherwise he would have been impotent. He also knew it before he produced it; otherwise he was ignorant. Therefore it seems that he willed it; otherwise he would have been envious. Therefore it seems that he did not begin anew to produce creatures.

OBJ. 23. Every finite thing is communicable to creatures. But eternity is finite, otherwise there would be nothing beyond eternity. Yet it is said in Exodus XV, *The Lord reigned in eternity and beyond.*[14] Therefore it seems that creatures were able to be eternal. And thus it was fitting to the divine goodness to have produced creatures from eternity.

OBJ. 24. Everything which begins has a measure of its duration. But time cannot have a measure of its duration, for it is not measured by eternity, since thus it would always have been, nor by eviternity, for thus it would always endure, nor by time, since nothing is its own measure. Therefore time did not begin to be, and thus neither did moveable things, nor the world.

OBJ. 25. If time began to be, it began to be either in time or in an

13. This seems to refer to Augustine, *The Trinity,* V 16.
14. Exodus 15:18.

instant. But it did not begin to be in an instant, since in an instant there is not yet time. Nor [did it begin] in time, because thus no time would precede the term of time, since before a thing begins to exist it is nothing. Therefore time does not begin to be, and thus the same conclusion follows as before.

OBJ. 26. God was the cause of things from eternity; otherwise it would be necessary to say that first he was a cause in potency and later in act, and thus that there was something already existing[15] which reduced him from potency to act, which is impossible. But nothing is a cause unless it has an effect. Therefore the world was created by God from eternity.

OBJ. 27. *Truth and being are convertible.*[16] But many truths are from eternity, as for example that a man is not an ass and that the world will be and many similar [truths]. Therefore it seems that many beings are from eternity and not only God.

OBJ. 28. But one might reply that all these things are true by the first truth, which is God. On the contrary, the truth of the proposition "the world will be" is different from that of the proposition "man is not an ass," since if we grant the impossible claim that one is false, the other will still be true. But the first truth cannot be one thing and another. Therefore these are not truths by the first truth.

OBJ. 29. According to the Philosopher in the Categories, *a statement is true or false based on whether a thing is or is not.*[17] Therefore if many propositions are true from eternity, it seems that the things they signify exist from eternity.

OBJ. 30. In God, to speak is the same as to make, whence the Psalm says, *He spoke and they were made.*[18] But God's speech is eternal; otherwise the Son, who is the word of the Father, would not be coeternal with the Father. Therefore God's making is eternal, and thus the world was made from eternity.

On the contrary (1) it is said in Proverbs VIII in the words of divine Wisdom, *The depths were not yet and I was already conceived,* and *the fountains of the waters had not yet sprung out, the mountains not yet estab-*

15. *aliquid prius.*
16. Cf. Aristotle, *Metaphysics,* II 1, 993b30.
17. Aristotle, *Categories,* 5, 4a34–36.
18. Psalms 33:9 and 148:5.

lished in their weighty immensity; before the hills I was brought forth, he had not yet made the earth or the rivers and poles of the orb of the earth.[19] Therefore, the poles of the orb of the earth and the rivers and the earth were not always.

Further (2) according to Priscian, *the younger* in time, *the more penetrating* in intellect.[20] But human penetration is not infinite. Therefore, neither was the time in which penetration increases infinite, and neither, consequently, is the world.

(3) According to the Book of Job, *the earth is gradually consumed by inundation.*[21] But the earth is not infinite. Therefore, if time had been infinite, it would now be entirely consumed, which is clearly false.

(4) It is certain that God is naturally prior to the world, as cause to effect. But in God duration and nature are the same. Therefore God is prior to the world in duration and thus the world was not always.

I answer that it must be firmly held that the world has not always been, as the Catholic faith teaches. This cannot be disproved by any philosophical demonstration.

In order to understand this we should note, as we have stated in another question,[22] that in God's operation there can be found no necessity on the part of a material cause or [on the part of] an active power of the agent or on the part of the ultimate end, but only on the part of the form which is the end of his operation, the presupposition of which is required in order that a certain thing be fit for that form.

And so we cannot speak in the same way about the production of one particular creature and about the coming forth[23] of the whole universe from God. For when we speak of the production of a single creature, we can assign a reason for its being thus from some other creature or at least from the order of the universe, to which every creature is ordered as a part to the form of the whole. But when we speak of the whole universe being educed into being, there is no other creature from which we can draw a reason why it is one way or another. And so since we cannot draw a reason for the defi-

19. Proverbs 8:24–26.
20. I have been unable to trace the source of this reference.
21. Job 14:19.
22. In article 16.
23. *exitu.*

nite disposition of the universe from the divine power, which is infinite, or from the divine goodness, which needs nothing, the reason for it must be drawn from the mere will of the producer. And so if we ask why the heavens are a certain size and no larger, the only reason that can be given is that the producer willed it. And because of this, as Rabbi Moses says, divine Scripture leads men to consider the heavenly bodies, whose disposition shows most clearly that all things are subject to the will and providence of the creator.[24] For one can give no reason why a particular star is a given distance from another or for any of the things which occur in the disposition of the heavens, except the order of God's wisdom. And so it is said in Isaiah XL, *Lift your eyes on high and see who has created these things.*[25]

Nor does it matter if it be said that this quantity[26] results from the nature of the heavens or heavenly bodies, even as some definite quantity *belongs to every constancy by nature,*[27] because just as the divine power is not limited to one quantity rather than to another, so is it not limited to a nature which requires a certain quantity rather than to a nature which requires another quantity. And thus it comes down to the same question whether concerning nature or quantity, although we concede that the nature of the heavens is not indifferent to any particular quantity, nor is there a possibility in them of a quantity other than that which they have. But this cannot be said of time or the duration of time, for time is extrinsic to a thing, just as place is. And so also in the heaven, in which there is no possibility with respect to another quantity or inherent accident, there is nevertheless possibility with respect to place or position, because it is moved locally, and also with respect to time, since time always succeeds time, just as there is succession in movement and in place. And so it cannot be said that neither time nor place results from [the heavens'] nature, as was said concerning quantity. And so it is clear that the predetermination of the universe to a definite quantity of duration[28] depends only on the will of God, just as the definite quantity of dimension does. And so nothing can be necessarily concluded

24. Moses Maimonides, cf. *The Guide of the Perplexed* III, 23.
25. Isaiah 40:26.
26. I.e. distance
27. Cf. Avicebron, *The Fountain of Life,* II 8.
28. *prefigatur uniuerso determinata quantitas durationis.*

concerning the duration of the universe, so as to show demonstratively that the world has always been.

Some however, not realizing that the universe came forth from God, could not avoid erring concerning the beginning of the world. For some, like the ancient natural philosophers, overlooked the agent cause and held that uncreated matter alone was the cause of everything. They necessarily maintained that matter always existed, for since nothing educes itself from non-being to being, that which begins to be must be caused by something else. And these [thinkers] held either that the world always existed continuously (because they posited only natural agents which were determined to one [effect], from which it follows that the same effect always resulted), or [that it always existed] with interruption (as for example Democritus, who held the world, or rather worlds, to have been frequently formed and dissolved by chance, because of the random motion of atoms).[29]

But since they are found always or in most cases, it seemed unfitting that all the congruities and utilities in natural things be by chance, which would necessarily follow if one maintained only matter [to be a cause]. And especially since certain effects are found for which material causality does not suffice, others posited an agent cause, as Anaxagoras [posited] intellect, and Empedocles, friendship and strife.[30] But they did not hold these to be causes of the sort to be the agent cause of the universe, but rather causes in the way that other particular agents are which act by transmuting matter from one thing into another. And so it was necessary for them to say that matter was eternal, because it has no cause of its being, but that the world began to be, since every effect of a cause acting through motion follows its cause in duration; and this is because the effect exists only at the term of motion, before which is the beginning of motion, which must be simultaneous with the agent who begins the motion.

Now Aristotle realized that if one held that the cause which established the world[31] acted through motion, it would follow that this would proceed to infinity, since before any motion there would be

29. Democritus, Diels-Kranz 68A37, 57.

30. Anaxagoras, Diels-Kranz, 59B12–13; Empedocles, Diels-Kranz, 31B17, 21, 22, 26, 35.

31. *causa constituens mundum.*

motion.[32] He therefore held that the world had always existed. He proceeded not from the position that the universe comes from God, but from the position that an agent begins to operate through motion, which is the case with particular causes but not the universal cause. Because of this he argued for the eternity of the world from the actuality and immobility of the prime mover. And so, when his arguments are carefully considered, they seem like arguments against a position; so that at the beginning of Physics VIII, having posed the question of eternal motion, he first presents the opinions of Anaxagoras and Empedocles, against which he intends to argue.[33]

Those who came after Aristotle, however, realizing that the whole universe comes forth from God through his will and not through motion, tried to prove the eternity of the world based on the fact that, though it be necessary to imagine it in the succession of time, when it wills to do something at a certain time and not sooner, the will does not delay doing what it intends except because of some alteration or change. But these [thinkers] fell into the same error as those already discussed. For they considered the first agent to be like an agent that performs its action in time though it acts voluntarily. But such an agent is not the cause of time itself, but presupposes time. God, on the other hand, is the cause of time itself, for even time itself is included in the universality of those things made by God. And so, since we are speaking of the coming forth of universal being from God, that he made it at a certain time and not sooner is not to be considered. For such consideration presupposes time for making, rather than subjecting it to making.

But when we consider the production of the universe of creatures, among which is time itself, we must consider why a certain measure was affixed to time, not why it was made at a certain time. Now the fixing of measure to time depends only on the will of God, who willed that the world not always be but begin to be at some time, just as he also willed that the heaven be neither greater nor smaller than it is.

AD 1. It is proper to goodness to produce things in being by means of the will, whose object it is. And so it does not follow that

32. Aristotle, *Metaphysics*, II 2 and VIII 5.
33. Aristotle, *Physics*, VIII 1, 250b25–251a8.

whenever the divine goodness was, things were produced in being, but [that they were produced] according to the disposition of the divine will.

AD 2. Since the body of the heaven is incorruptible it has the power to exist always. But no power, either of being or of operation, regards the past but [it regards] only the present or the future. For no one has power over past actions, since what was not done cannot [be made to] have been done, but one does have the power to do something now or in the future. And so also the power of always existing, which is in the heaven, regards not the past but the future.

AD 3. Speaking absolutely, the heaven cannot be said to be corruptible [merely] because it would fall into nothingness if God did not sustain it. But nevertheless, since God's preserving the creature in being depends on the immobility of the divine rather than on [the creature's] natural necessity (in which case it would be absolutely necessary), and [the creature] is necessary only on the supposition of the divine will which establishes it immovably, it can be conceded that in this sense the heaven is corruptible under this specific condition: "if God does not sustain it."

AD 4. Every effect has a necessary relation to its sufficient cause, whether it be a natural or a voluntary cause. But we hold that God causes the world voluntarily, not out of natural necessity, as was said above.[34] And so it is necessary that the divine effect follow, not whenever the divine nature was, but when the divine will decreed that it be and in the way that it willed it to be.

AD 5. That "something is prior to time" can be understood in two ways. First, it can mean prior to the whole of time and everything belonging to time. In this sense the world did not exist before time, since the instant in which the world began, though not time, is something belonging to time, not indeed as a part but as a term. Second, it can mean something is before time because it is before the completion of time, which is completed only in an instant before which there is another instant, and in this sense the world is prior to time. But from this it does not follow that it is eternal, since the instant of time which is before time is not itself eternal.

34. In article 15.

AD 6. Since every agent produces its like, an effect must follow from an effectively operating cause in such a way that it bears a likeness to the cause.[35] Now just as that which is from a naturally acting cause bears its likeness by having a form like the agent's form, so does that which is from a voluntary cause bear a likeness to its cause in the sense that what is produced in the effect is according to the disposition of the will, as is clear in the work produced by the craftsman. But the will determines not only the form of the effect but also its place, duration, and all its conditions. And so it is necessary that the effect of the will follows when the will determines, not [as soon as] the will exists. For the effect is likened to the will, not according to being, but according to what the will determines. Therefore, although the will is always the same, it is not necessary that its effect eternally follow from it.

AD 7. God necessarily wills his own goodness and everything without which his goodness cannot be. But such is not the production of creatures, and so this argument does not follow.

AD 8. Since God made creatures in order to manifest himself, it was better and more fitting that they be produced in such a way that they might more fittingly and clearly manifest him. Now he is more clearly manifested by creatures if they have not always been, because this makes it apparent that they are brought into being by another and that God does not need creatures and that creatures are entirely subject to the divine will.

AD 9. God has willed the making of the world from eternity, not that the world should always be made, but that it should be made when he did make it.

AD 10. Before the world was, it was possible for the world to be made, not indeed by some passive potency, but by the active potency of an agent. Or we can reply that it was not possible through some potency, but because the terms of the proposition "the world exists" are not contradictory to each other. For in this way something is said to be possible without reference to any potency, as the Philosopher makes clear in Metaphysics V.[36]

35. See article 1, note 10.
36. Aristotle, *Metaphysics*, V 12, 1019b28–35.

And so the solution to the eleventh objection is clear.

AD 12. This argument concerns an agent who begins a new action. But God's action is eternal, since it is his substance. However, he is said to begin to act because of the new effect which follows from his eternal action according to the determination of his will, which is understood to be the principle of action in relation[37] to the effect. For the effect follows from the action according to the condition of the form which is the principle of action, just as something is heated by the action of a fire according to the measure[38] of heat in the fire.

AD 13. This argument concerns an agent who makes his effect in time and is not the cause of time. This does not apply to God, as is clear from what is said above.[39]

AD 14. If we take motion in the proper sense, the divine will is not moved, but speaking metaphorically it is said to be moved by the willed object. And thus only God's goodness moves his will, in accordance with Augustine's statement in On the Literal Interpretation of Genesis VIII that God *moves himself independently of time* and *space.*[40] Nevertheless it does not follow that whenever his goodness was, the production of creatures occurred, since creatures proceed from God by sheer will and not out of obligation or necessity of goodness, for the divine goodness has no need of creatures, nor do they add anything to him.

AD 15. Since the succession of the beginning[41] of time is caused by the succession of motion, as is said in Physics IV,[42] it is true that every instant is a beginning and end of time insofar as it is true that every movement is a beginning and end of motion. And so, if we suppose that motion has not always been and will not always be, it will not be necessary to say that every instant is a beginning and end of time, but there will be some instant which is only a beginning and one which is only an end. And so it is clear that this argument is circular and therefore not a demonstration. Nevertheless, it serves Aris-

37. *in ordine.* 38. *modum.*
39. I.e. in the respondeo of this article.
40. Augustine, *De Genesi ad litteram libri XII,* VIII 22.
41. *primi.*
42. Aristotle, *Physics,* IV 12, 220b15.

totle's purpose when he uses it to rebut a position, as has been said.[43] For many arguments serve to rebut a position held by the adversary, [but] are not effective in themselves.[44]

AD 16. An instant is always considered as flowing, not however always as flowing from one thing into another but rather sometimes as only flowing from something, as for example the last instant of time, and sometimes as only flowing into something, as for example the first instant.

AD 17. This argument proves not that motion has always been but that circular motion can always be, because we cannot conclude anything definitive concerning motion from mathematics. And so Aristotle does not prove the eternity of motion from its circularity but, supposing that it is eternal, he demonstrates that it is circular, since no other motion can be eternal.[45]

And through this the response to the eighteenth objection is clear.

AD 19. As the knowable thing is related to our knowledge, so is God's knowledge [related] to creatures. For God's knowledge is the cause of creatures just as the knowable thing is the cause of our knowledge. And so, just as the knowable thing can exist without our knowledge, as is said in the Categories,[46] so can God's knowledge exist without creatures.

AD 20. God precedes the world by duration not of time but of eternity, because God's being is not measured temporally. Nor was there any real time before the world, but only imaginary. Thus we can now imagine an infinite space of time,[47] existing in eternity, and able to have unwound before the beginning of time.

AD 21. If the relation of lord is understood to follow the action by which God actually governs creatures, then in this sense he is not lord from eternity. But if it is understood to follow the power to govern itself, then it belongs to him from eternity. It does not, however, follow that creatures existed from eternity, except in potency.

AD 22. Augustine uses this argument to prove the Son is coeter-

43. I.e. in the respondeo of this article.
44. *simpliciter.*
45. Aristotle, *Physics,* VIII 8, especially 261b27–28.
46. Aristotle, *Categories,* 7, 7b27–28.
47. *temporum spacia.*

nal and coequal with the Father,[48] but this argument does not apply to the world. Since the Son's nature is the same as the Father's, it requires eternity and equality with the Father, [and] if this were denied to it, that would smack of envy. But the creature's nature does not require this, and thus the cases are not comparable.

AD 23. According to the Greek text, The Lord shall reign in age upon age and still. The Gloss, citing Origen, says that "age" means the space of one generation, the end of which is known to us, "age upon age" means an immense space of time which has an end unknown to us, but "still" the reign of God extends beyond that.[49] Thus "eternity" is explained to mean the duration of time. In his Proslogion, however, Anselm takes "eternity" to mean eviternity, which has no end and yet God is said to be beyond it, for these reasons: first, because eviternal things can be understood not to be; second, because they would not be if God did not sustain them and they do not exist of themselves; third, because they do not have their whole existence at once, since there is some succession of change in them.[50]

AD 24. That which begins must have a measure of duration insofar as it begins through motion. But time does not begin in this way [but] by creation, and so the argument does not succeed. Nevertheless it can also be said that every measure is measured by itself in its own genus, as for example, a line by a line, and likewise time by time.

AD 25. Time does not have being as permanent things do whose substance is entirely simultaneous. And so it is not necessary that the whole of time be when it begins to be, and so nothing prevents us from saying that time began to be in an instant.

AD 26. God's action is eternal but his effect is not eternal, as was said above.[51] And so, although God has not always been a cause, since his effect has not always been, nevertheless unless the potency is referred to the effect, it does not follow that he was a cause in potency, because his action always was.

AD 27. According to the Philosopher in Metaphysics VI, *truth* is *in*

48. Augustine, *Answer to Maximinus*, II 7 and 23.
49. *Biblia Latina cum glossa ordinaria*, Exodus, XV 18.
50. Anselm, *Proslogion*, 20.
51. See ad 12 above. See also ad 6, 9, 14, and 21.

the mind, not *in things,* for it is *an adequation of the intellect to the thing.*[52] And so everything which has been true from eternity has been true through the truth of the divine intellect, which is eternal.

AD 28. All of those things which are said to be truths from eternity are true not by differing truths but by one and the same truth of the divine intellect. Nevertheless they are related to different things in their own future being.[53] And so from these diverse relations some distinction can be designated in that truth.

AD 29. The Philosopher's words refer to mental or spoken statements, for the truth of our intellect or our words is caused by the existence of things. But conversely the truth of the divine intellect is the cause of things.

AD 30. On the part of God, to make connotes nothing other than to speak, for God's action is not an accident but rather his substance. But to make connotes the effect actually existing in its proper nature, while to speak does not.

Although the arguments presented to the contrary conclude to the truth, they are not necessary, except for the first, which proceeds from authority.

AD CONTRARY 2. The argument regarding [intellectual] penetration over the course of time does not show that time must have begun at some point, for it could have been that the study of the sciences was often interrupted and later after a long time begun again anew, as the Philosopher says in Metaphysics XI.[54]

AD CONTRARY 3. Again, the earth is not consumed by inundation in one part in this way without also being augmented in another part by corresponding conversion of elements.

AD CONTRARY 4. And although God's duration is really the same as his nature, they differ nevertheless logically. And so it does not follow that if he is prior by nature he is prior in duration.

52. Aristotle, *Metaphysics,* VI 4, 1027b25–34.

53. *ad diversas tamen res in proprio esse futuras relata.*

54. This seems to be a reference to Aristotle, *Metaphysics,* XII 7, 1072b24.

ARTICLE 18

The eighteenth thing to ask is whether angels were created before the visible world. And it seems that they were.[1]

OBJ. 1. In Book II [of his Exposition of the Orthodox Faith], Damascene notes that *Gregory* Nazianzen *says* God *first devised the angelic and heavenly powers, and the devising was the doing.*[2] Therefore he made the angels before he produced the visible world.

OBJ. 2. But someone might say that "first" here denotes the order of nature, not of duration. On the contrary, in the same place Damascene cites two opinions on this, of which the first posits that angels were created first, while the other says the contrary. But no one ever held the opinion that the angels were not prior to visible creatures by nature. Therefore this must be understood to refer to the order of duration.

OBJ. 3. At the beginning of the Hexameron, Basil says, *Before this world there was a certain* nature *that our intellect can behold.*[3] And shortly after he discusses angels. Therefore it seems that angels were created before this world.

OBJ. 4. At the beginning of Genesis, Scripture describes those things which were made with the visible world, but it makes no mention of angels. Therefore it seems that angels were not created with the world, but before the world.

OBJ. 5. That which is ordered to the perfection of another as its end is posterior to that other. But the visible world is ordered to the perfection of intellectual nature, since, as Ambrose says, God, who is invisible by nature, made a visible work through which he could be

1. Here in article 18, Thomas argues that the angels were not, in fact, created before the visible world. Then, in article 19, he argues that while that is arguably the factual case, it is nevertheless true that the angels could have been created before the visible world. For parallel discussions of issues raised in both of these articles, see *ST* I Q. 61 and Thomas' *Treatise on Separate Substances,* XVII.

2. *et excogitatio fuit opus eius.* John Damascene, *Exposition of the Orthodox Faith,* II 3. John Damascene may be referring to Gregory Nazianzen's *Second Theological Oration,* XXXI.

3. Basil the Great, *Homilies on the Hexameron,* Homily 1, no. 5.

known.[4] But [he could be made known] only to a rational creature. Therefore a rational creature was made before the visible world.

OBJ. 6. Anything prior to time is prior to the visible world, since time began with the visible world. But the angels were created before time, for there was no time before the day, and angels were created *before the day,* as Augustine says in On the Literal Interpretation of Genesis I.[5] Therefore the angels were created before the visible world.

OBJ. 7. Concerning the Epistle to Titus, Jerome says, *Six thousand years of our time are not yet complete, and how many prior ages, how much time ... was there to be considered in which the angels ... served* God *and were under* his *orders.*[6] But the visible world began with our time. Therefore the angels existed before the visible world.

OBJ. 8. A wise person is orderly in the production of his effects. But the angels precede visible creatures in nobility. Therefore, they ought to have been produced in being first by God, the supremely wise craftsman.

OBJ. 9. Insofar as God is good, he makes others share[7] his goodness. But angels were capable of the dignity of preceding visible creatures in duration. Therefore it seems that this was granted to them by God's sovereign goodness.

OBJ. 10. Man is called a lesser world since he bears a likeness to the greater world. But in man the more noble part, namely the heart, is formed before the other parts, according to the Philosopher.[8] Therefore it seems that angels, who are the more noble part of the greater world, were produced before visible creatures.

OBJ. 11. As Augustine says in the second book On the Literal Interpretation of Genesis, in the work of the second and following days, Scripture recounts the making of things in three ways.[9] For first it says, "God said: Let the firmament be made"; and next, "And thus it was made"; and finally, "God made the firmament." The first of these refers to the being of things in the Word; the second to the

4. Ambrose, *The Six Days of Creation,* I 5.
5. Augustine, *De Genesi ad litteram libri XII,* I 9.
6. Jerome, *Commentariorum in Epistolam ad Titum,* I 2.
7. *alios participes.*
8. Aristotle, *On the Generation of Animals,* II 4, 740a4.
9. Augustine, *De Genesi ad litteram libri XII,* II 7 and 8.

being of things in the angelic mind, as angels understand creatures to be made; and the third [refers] to the being of the creature in its proper nature. But when the visible creature was to be made, it did not yet exist. Therefore the angels existed and had knowledge of visible nature before the latter existed.

OBJ. 12. But one might reply that here he means the making of creatures in terms of their formation, not in terms of their initial creation. On the contrary, it is Augustine's opinion that the creation of visible nature does not precede its formation temporally. Therefore, if angels existed before the formation of visible creatures, they also existed before their creation.

OBJ. 13. God's speaking is the cause of a creature's being made. [Now] it seems this cannot be said in reference to the eternal birth of the Word, since that was from eternity and not repeated in the course of time, while nevertheless Scripture reports that God said something each day. Nor can this refer to corporeal speech, both because man, who would hear the voice of God speaking, was not yet [created], and because it would have been necessary for some other body to have been formed before the formation of light, since corporeal voice could be only through the formation of some body. Therefore it seems that it refers to the spiritual speech by which God speaks to the angels. And thus it seems that the angels' knowledge is presupposed as a cause in the production of visible creatures.

OBJ. 14. As was said above, sacred Scripture recounts the making of things in three ways, the first of which pertains to the being of things in the Word, the second to the being of things in the angelic mind, the third [to the being of things] in their proper nature. But the first of these precedes the second in both duration and cause. Therefore the second, namely the existence of the visible creature in the angelic mind, likewise precedes the third in duration and cause.

OBJ. 15. Order is required in things coming forth from their principle no less than in their return to their end. But as Dionysius says, in bringing things to their end, *this is the* fixed *law of the divine,* that the last be brought to the end through the intermediate.[10] Therefore corporeal creatures, which are lower, likewise also proceed to God

10. Cf. Pseudo-Dionysius, *The Celestial Hierarchy,* 5; 10, no. 12.

through angelic creatures, which are intermediate. And thus angels precede corporeal creatures as cause precedes effect.

OBJ. 16. Things which are entirely disparate are not fit for association. But angels and visible creatures are entirely disparate. Therefore they are not associated in creation by being made at the same time. And it would be contrary to order if angels were made after visible creatures. Therefore they were produced before visible creatures.

OBJ. 17. In Ecclesiasticus I it is said, The first *of all things wisdom was created.*[11] This cannot refer to the Son of God, who is the wisdom of the Father, since he is not created but generated. Therefore angelic wisdom, which is created, is made before all other things.

OBJ. 18. In his book On the Trinity, Hilary says, Is it any wonder that we believe our lord Jesus Christ was before the ages, since God also made the angels before the world?[12] But the Son of God preceded every age, not only in order of dignity, but also in that of duration. Therefore, so do angels precede the visible world.

OBJ. 19. Angelic creatures are intermediate between divine and corporeal nature. And eviternity, which is the measure of the angels, is intermediate between eternity and time. But by his eternity God was before the angels and visible creatures. Therefore the angels also by their eviternity were before the visible world.

OBJ. 20. In On the City of God XI, Augustine says that angels have always been.[13] But it cannot be said that corporeal creatures have always been. Therefore angels existed before corporeal creatures.

OBJ. 21. The movements of the corporeal creature are executed through the ministrations of the spiritual creature, as Augustine makes clear in On the Trinity III[14] and Gregory in Dialogue IV.[15] But the mover precedes the moveable. Therefore angels existed before visible creatures.

11. Ecclesiasticus 1:4.

12. Hilary of Poitiers, *The Trinity,* XII 37.

13. Augustine, *City of God,* XI 9.

14. This seems to refer to Augustine, *The Trinity,* III 1. The passage in *The Trinity* reads: *"Pervenit enim potentia voluntatis Dei per creaturam spiritalem usque ad effectus visibiles atque sensibiles creaturae corporalis."*

15. Gregory the Great, *Dialogues,* IV 6.

OBJ. 22. Dionysius likens the divine action on things to the action of fire on bodies which are flammable. But fire acts on nearer bodies before those which are distant. Therefore the divine goodness also produced the angelic creatures nearer to itself before the corporeal creatures more distant from it. And thus angels existed before the world.

On the contrary (1) in the beginning of Genesis it is said, *In the beginning God created heaven and earth.*[16] Augustine's gloss says that here heaven means angelic nature, while earth means corporeal nature.[17] Therefore angels and corporeal nature were made at the same time.

2. Strabo's gloss on the same text says that heaven here means the *empyrean heaven,* which was filled with holy angels as soon as it was made.[18] Therefore angels were made at the same time as the empyrean heaven, which is a visible creature.

3. Man is said to be a lesser world because he bears a likeness to the greater world. But in man body and soul are made at the same time. Therefore in the greater world angelic and corporeal creatures are made at the same time.

I answer that all Catholic doctors agree that angels have not always existed, seeing that they are produced in being from nothing.

Some, however, held that angels were not made at the same time as the visible world but before the visible world. They were led to this position for various reasons. For some believed that corporeal creatures were not at first intended by God, but their production was occasioned by the merit and demerit of spiritual creatures. Indeed, Origen held that in the beginning all invisible and rational creatures were made at the same time, and they were equal, as divine justice requires. For it did not seem that they could in justice be granted unequal gifts except based on diversity of merit and demerit. And so [he maintained that] the diversity we see in creatures is preceded by diversity of merit and demerit so that, inasmuch as certain spiritual creatures adhered more closely to God, they were promoted to higher ranks of angels, while those who sinned more were bound to grosser and more ignoble bodies, as though the very diversity of

16. Genesis 1:1.

17. Augustine, *De Genesi ad litteram libri XII,* I 17.

18. *Biblia Latina cum glossa ordinaria,* Genesis, I 1.

merits required that diverse grades of bodies be produced by God.[19]

Augustine, however, disproves this position in On the City of God XI. For the cause of the production of creatures, both spiritual and corporeal, is none other than God's goodness, inasmuch as his creatures, created by his goodness, represent uncreated goodness according to their own modes.[20] For this reason, at the beginning of Genesis Scripture speaks of each individual work of God and later of all at once: *God looked at all that he had made and it was very good,*[21] as though to say that God made creatures in order that they have goodness. On the other hand, according to the opinion discussed above, corporeal creatures were made not because it was good for them to be but in order to punish the wickedness of spiritual creatures. It would even follow that the order of the universe we now see exists by chance, inasmuch as different rational creatures happened to sin in different ways. For according to these thinkers, if they had all sinned equally, there would be no diversity of natures in corporeal things.

And so, this position being rejected, others held that spiritual substances were made before corporeal substances because they observed that the nature of spiritual substances is more noble than any corporeal nature. In this way, just as the created spiritual nature is intermediate between God and the corporeal creature in the order of nature, so is it also intermediate in duration. Now since this was the opinion of great doctors, including Basil, Gregory Nazianzen, and certain others, it is not to be rejected as erroneous. But, carefully considered, the opinion of Augustine and other doctors, which is also more widely accepted, seems to be more rational. For angels are to be considered not only absolutely but also insofar as they are part of the universe, and this consideration of them should command more attention, inasmuch as the good of the universe outweighs the good of any particular creature, just as the good of the whole outweighs the good of the part. Considered as part of the universe, it is appropriate for angels to be made at the same time as corporeal creatures. For it seems that there is one production of one whole. But if angels were created separately, they would seem to be entirely alien

19. Cf. Origen, *On First Principles,* I 5, no. 3; I 7, no. 4; I 8, nos. 1, 2, 4.
20. Augustine, *City of God,* XI 23.
21. Genesis 1:31.

to the order of corporeal creatures, as though they constituted another universe in themselves.

And so we must say that the angels were made at the same time as corporeal creatures, but without prejudice to the other opinion.

And through this the response to the first three objections is clear, since they proceed along the lines of the second opinion.

AD 4. As Basil says in Hexameron I, at the beginning of Genesis Moses the lawgiver began to explain the origin of visible creatures, omitting the spiritual creatures that were produced earlier. These he did not mention because he wrote for ignorant[22] people incapable of grasping spiritual things.[23] On the other hand, according to Augustine, when [Moses] said, *In the beginning God created heaven and earth,* he meant by heaven spiritual creatures and by earth corporeal creatures.[24] Now the reason [Moses] related the creation of angels under the metaphor of heaven and not expressly may be the same as the reason given above, namely the ignorance of the people. A further reason may be to avoid the idolatry to which they were prone and for which they might be given occasion if they believed in many spiritual substances, other than God, which were more noble than the heavens. [They might err in this regard] especially since the gentiles called substances of this sort gods. But according to Strabo and others after him, in this text heaven signifies the empyrean heaven, which is the abode of the holy angels,[25] and so the creation of angels is also to be understood in its creation by metonymy, as when the container stands for the contents.

AD 5. As Augustine says in On the Literal Interpretation of Genesis IV, angels do not know God through visible creatures.[26] And so visible creatures were made to make God manifest not to angels, but to the rational creature which is man, whence man is proved to be the end of creatures. But although the end is first in intention, it is nonetheless last in operation, and so man was made last.

AD 6. According to Augustine, the creation of heaven and earth

22. *rudi.*
23. Basil the Great. *Homilies on the Hexaemeron* Homily 1, nos. 5 and 6.
24. Augustine, *De Genesi ad litteram libri XII,* I 17.
25. *Biblia Latina cum glossa ordinaria,* Genesis, I 1.
26. Augustine, *De Genesi ad litteram libri XII,* IV 6/7.

did not precede the formation <or> production of light in duration,[27] and thus he does not mean that the creation of spiritual nature was prior to the first day in [the order of] duration, but in a certain order of nature, since spiritual substance and even formless matter considered according to its essence are not subject to the alteration of time. As a result, we cannot hold that the spiritual creature was made before the corporeal, since even before the production of light, the creation of the corporeal creature, which is denoted by earth, is mentioned. But according to other thinkers, the creation of heaven and earth pertains to the first day, since time was created with heaven and earth, although the distinction of time into day and night began through light.[28] And so time is held to be one of the four things first created: the angelic nature, the empyrean heaven, formless matter, and time.

AD 7. Jerome speaks according to the opinion of the early doctors.

AD 8. This argument would succeed if each creature were produced as existing absolutely *per se.* For thus it would be fitting that each be created separately according to the degree of its goodness. But since all creatures were produced as part of one universe, it was fitting that all be produced at once in order to form one universe.

AD 9. Although the spiritual creature might attain a certain dignity if it were created before visible creatures, nevertheless this would not be appropriate for the dignity and unity of the universe.

AD 10. Although the heart is formed before the other parts, there is nevertheless one continuous generation of the animal's whole body, not a separate generation in which the heart is formed and later other successive generations of other parts at various times. But it cannot be said that angels and corporeal creatures are formed in one [continuous] production, with the spiritual creature [formed] before the corporeal, as though the universe were produced continuously. For successive procession of production is proper to those things which are produced from matter, in which one part is nearer to the final completion than another. And so succession has no place in the first creation of things, although it may have a place in the formation of things from created matter. And so the doctors who held

27. Augustine, *De Genesi ad litteram libri XII,* I 5.
28. I have been unable to trace a reference for this text.

that the angels were created before the world maintained that the creation of angels was entirely distinct from that of bodies and that there was a long interval between them. Moreover, the heart is necessarily formed first in an animal, since the power of the heart works for the formation of the other parts. But no spiritual creature operated in the creation of corporeal creatures, since only God can create. And so in his Metaphysics XI, the Commentator faults Plato for saying that God first *created the angels* and later committed to them the creation of corporeal creatures.[29]

AD 11. Augustine is speaking of the making of corporeal creatures not in terms of their initial creation, but in terms of their formation.

AD 12. In maintaining that all things were created in form and matter at once, spiritual creatures are said to have had knowledge of corporeal creatures yet to be made, not because their formation was temporally yet to be, but because they were known as yet to be as considered in their cause, in which they existed in the sense that it was possible for them to proceed from it. In the same way, someone who knows a box in the principles from which it is made can be said to know it as something to be made.

AD 13. God's speaking refers to the eternal generation of the Word of God, in whom the type[30] of all creatures to be made was from eternity. Nor is the frequent repetition in each work of *God said* to be understood to mean that he spoke temporally, but rather that although the word in itself is one, nevertheless there is in it the proper type of each individual creature. Therefore each individual work is set out in advance in the word of God as the proper type of the work to be made, in order that, the work being done, it not be necessary to ask why such work was done, since before the making of the work it was said, *God said.* In the same way, when someone wants to identify the cause of a thing, he begins by identifying the cause.[31]

AD 14. The being of things in the Word is the cause of the being

29. Averroës, *Metaphysicorum libri XIV,* XI, com. 44.

30. *ratio.*

31. *cum aliquis volens assignare alicuius rei causam, incipit a cause assignatione.* This is an odd text. The Leonine and Marietti are the same. Fr. Shapcote translates it: "When we wish to indicate the cause of a thing we begin with knowledge of the cause."

of things in their proper nature and in the angelic mind. <But the being of things in the angelic mind> is not a cause of the being of things in their proper nature, and thus there is no comparison.

AD 15. A thing is ordered to its end through its own operation, but it is not produced in being through its own operation but only through the operation of the agent cause. And so it is more fitting that higher creatures cooperate with God in bringing lower creatures to their end than in their production.

AD 16. Although corporeal and spiritual creatures are disparate in their proper natures, nevertheless they are connected in the order of the universe, and thus it was necessary that they be created at the same time.

AD 17. According to Augustine,[32] that passage in Ecclesiastes refers to the created wisdom which is in the angelic nature, which nonetheless in itself is the first created, not in time, but in dignity. But according to Hilary, in his book On the Synods,[33] it refers to the uncreated wisdom which is the Son of God, which is indeed called both created and generated simultaneously, as is clear in Proverbs VIII[34] and in various other places in Scripture, in order that every imperfection be excluded from the birth of the Son of God. For creation implies imperfection on the part of the created thing inasmuch as it is brought into being from nothing, but it implies perfection on the part of the creator, who produces creatures without any change in himself. But in birth it is the converse, since it implies perfection on the part of the offspring, inasmuch as it receives the nature of the generator, but in generation among lower things, [it implies] imperfection on the part of the generator, inasmuch as generating entails change or division of substance in it. And thus the Son of God is said to be at once both created and generated, in order that creation exclude change in the generator and birth [exclude] imperfection in the offspring, and from both one perfect sense is constituted.

AD 18. Hilary is speaking according to the opinion of the early doctors.

32. Augustine, *Confessions,* XII 15.

33. This may be a reference to Hilary of Poitiers, *Liber de Synodis,* IX 23, but the discussion in Hilary's *The Trinity,* I 35, IV 21, and XII 1 seems more to the point.

34. Proverbs 8:22–25.

AD 19. God is the cause of the angelic nature, but the angelic nature is not the cause of corporeal nature, and so there is no comparison.

AD 20. Angels are said always to have been, not in the sense that they have existed from eternity but in the sense that they have been for all time, since, whenever time was, the angels were. And in this sense corporeal creatures also have always been.

AD 21. The mover does not necessarily precede the moveable in time, but [only] in dignity, as is clear in the soul and body.

AD 22. In fire's action on bodies a twofold order is to be considered, that of position and [that of] time. There is order of position in all its actions because they are all situated and it operates more fully on bodies closer to it. And so when [fire] spreads, its effect is so diminished that in the end it is totally spent. The order of time, however, is not found in all [fire's] actions, but only in those which act through motion. And so, when fire illuminates and heats bodies, the order of position and of time is observed in heating, but in illumination, which is not a motion but a term of motion, only the order of position is observed. Therefore, because God's action in creation is without motion, there is no comparison in the order of time but only in that of position. For there is the same variety of grades of nature in spiritual action as there is variety of position in corporeal action. Therefore Dionysius' comparison extends thus far, that as fire diffuses its power more fully on bodies near to it, so does God bestow his goodness more copiously on things nearer to him in degree of dignity.

ARTICLE 19

The nineteenth thing to ask is whether angels could have existed before the visible world. And it seems they could not.

OBJ. 1. Any two things whose distinction requires diversity of place cannot be in one place. But it is commonly held that two angels cannot be in one place. Therefore it makes no sense that there be two distinct angels unless there are two distinct places. But before visible creatures there was no place, since according to the Philosopher in Physics IV, place is nothing but the *innermost boundary of what contains* a body.[1] Therefore angels could not exist before the visible world.

OBJ. 2. The production of corporeal creatures cost the angels nothing of their natural power. Therefore if angels could exist without place before the visible world was made, then now that the visible world is made they can exist without place. But this seems to be false since, if they were not in place, they would be nowhere, and thus they would seem not to be.

OBJ. 3. Bernard says that every created spirit needs a body.[2] But the angel is a created spirit. Therefore it needs a body and thus could not exist before corporeal creatures.

OBJ. 4. But one might reply that [the angel] needs a body not to exist but only for his ministry. On the contrary, the ministry of angels is performed where we are, namely in this world. But angels also have corporeal place beyond our realm, namely the empyrean heaven. Therefore it is not only because of their ministry to us that they need a body or a corporeal place.

OBJ. 5. It is impossible to imagine before and after without time. But if angels already were before the world, the beginning of the angels' existence was before the beginning of the visible world. Therefore time would have begun before the visible world. But that is impossible, since time follows motion and motion the moveable. Therefore it is impossible that the angels were before the world.

1. *ultimum corporis continentis.* The reference is to Aristotle, *Physics,* IV 4, 212a20.

2. Bernard of Clairvaux, *Sermons on the Song of Songs,* Sermon 5, sec. 1.

On the contrary, that which does not entail a contradiction in creatures is possible for God. But no contradiction is entailed if angels exist while visible creatures do not. Therefore it was not impossible for God to produce angels before the world.

I answer that, as Boethius says in his book On the Trinity, in divine matters we must not be misled by our imagination,[3] and likewise in all incorporeal things, because since the imagination follows the senses, as the Philosopher makes clear in his book On the Soul,[4] imagination cannot be extended beyond quantity, which is the subject of sensible qualities.

But certain thinkers, failing to note this and not able to transcend the imagination, could not conceive of anything not situated somewhere, and because of this, certain early thinkers said that what is not in a place is not, as is said in Physics IV.[5] And through the same error some moderns say that angels cannot be without a corporeal creature, thinking of angels as if they were things we imagine to be in distinct places.

This biased the position of early thinkers who held that angels existed before the world. It also diminished the dignity of the angelic nature for, since it is naturally prior to the corporeal creature, it in no way depends on the corporeal creature.

And thus, speaking absolutely, angels could have existed before the world.

AD 1. Although it would confuse their operation, two angels being in one indivisible place would not impede their distinction. And so the argument does not follow.

AD 2. Even now nothing prevents angels not being in a place if they wish, although they are always in a place according to the order by which the spiritual creature presides over the corporeal, according to Augustine in On the Trinity III.[6]

AD 3. As Bernard himself explains, angels need the body only for their ministry, not for the completion of their nature.[7]

3. Boethius, *On the Trinity,* II.
4. Aristotle, *On the Soul,* III 3, 427b15 and 428b10–16.
5. Aristotle, *Physics,* IV 1, 208b32–36.
6. This may be a reference to Augustine, *The Trinity,* III 1.
7. Bernard of Clairvaux, *Sermons on the Song of Songs,* Sermon 5, sec. 1.

AD 4. Angels are in the empyrean heaven as in a place which is suited to contemplation but not necessary for contemplation.

AD 5. This priority and posteriority do not compel us to posit real time before the world, but only imaginary time, as was said in the question about the eternity of the world.[8]

8. In article 17, ad 20, above. See also article 1, ad 10, and article 2.

BIBLIOGRAPHY

Primary Sources

1. Latin Editions of St. Thomas' *De potentia Dei*

Questiones disputate de potentia Dei, Q. 3. Ed. R.-A. Gauthier, O.P. Leonine edition, vol. 21. Paris, in preparation. [This is the text from which this translation has been made.]

De potentia Dei. Ed. P. Bazzi et al. In *Questiones Disputatae,* vol 1. Rome: Marietti, 1942. [English translation of Marietti edition: *On the Power of God.* Translated by Lawrence Shapcote, O.P. Westminster, MD: The Newman Press, 1952; reprinted by Wipf & Stock Publishers, 2004.]

2. Other Works of St. Thomas Cited in Footnotes

De aeternitate mundi contra murmurantes. In *Opuscula Philosophica,* Turin: Marietti, 1954.

[English translation: *On the Eternity of the World.* 2nd ed. Trans. C. Vollert, L. H. Kendzierski, and P. M. Byrne. Medieval Philosophical Texts in Translation, vol. 16. Milwaukee: Marquette University Press, 1984.]

De Physico Auditu sive Physicorum Aristotelis. Ed. A. Pirotta, O.P. Naples: M. D'Auria Editore Pontificio, 1953.

[English translation: *Commentary on Aristotle's Physics.* Trans. R. J. Blackwell, R. J. Spath, and W. E. Thirlkel. New Haven: Yale University Press, 1963.]

De substantiis separatis. In *Sancti Thomae de Aquino opera omnia,* Leonine edition, vol. 40. Rome: 1969.

[English translation: *Treatise on Separate Substances.* Trans. Francis J. Lescoe. West Hartford, CT: St. Joseph College, 1963.]

In Aristotelis Librum de Anima. In *Sancti Thomae de Aquino opera omnia,* Leonine edition, vol. 45.1. Rome: 1984.

[English translation: *Commentary on Aristotle's De Anima.* Trans. K. Foster, O.P., and S. Humphries, O.P. Notre Dame, IN: Dumb Ox Books, 1951.]

In Quattuor Libros Sententiarum. Ed. R. Busa, S.J. In *S. Thomae Aquinatis Opera Omnia,* vol. 1. Stuttgart: Frommann-Holzboog, 1980.

[Italian translation: *Commento alle sentenze di Pietro Lombardo e testo integrale di Pietro Lombardo.* Trans. R. Coggi. Bologna: ESD, 2001.]

Metaphysicorum Aristotelis Expositio. Ed. M. R. Cathala, O.P., and R. M. Spiazzi, O.P. Turin: Marietti, 1950.

[English translation: *Commentary on the Metaphysics of Aristotle,* vols. 1 and 2. Trans. J. P. Rowan. Chicago: Henry Regnery Co., 1961.]

Summa contra gentiles. Leonine edition. Rome: Desclée & Co., 1934.

[English translation: *Summa Contra Gentiles.* Notre Dame: University of Notre Dame Press. Bk. I, Trans. A. C. Pegis, F.R.S.C., 1955; Bk. II, Trans. J. F. Anderson, 1956; Bk. III, Trans. V. J. Bourke, 1956; Bk. IV, Trans. C. J. O'Neil, 1957.]

Summa theologiae, 4 vols. Leonine edition. Turin: Marietti, 1950.

[English translation: *Summa theologica*. Trans. English Dominican Fathers. Westminster, MD: Christian Classics, 1948.]

Super librum de causis expositio. Ed. H.-D. Saffrey, O.P. Fribourg: Société Philosophique, 1954.

[English translation: *Commentary on the Book of Causes*. Trans. V. A. Guagliardo, O.P., C. R. Hess. O.P., and R. C. Taylor. Washington, D.C.: The Catholic University of America Press, 1996.]

3. Works Cited by St. Thomas

Algazel. *Tahâfot al-falâsifat* (*The Incoherence of the Philosophers*). Ed. M. Bouyges. Frankfurt am Main: Institute for the History of Arabic-Islamic Science at the Johann Wolfgang Goethe University, 1999.

Ambrose. *Exameron*. In CSEL, vol. 32, Part 1. Ed. C. Schenkl. Prague: Tempsky-Freytag, 1897.

[English translation: *The Six Days of Creation*. Trans. John Savage. In FOTC, vol. 42. New York: The Fathers of the Church Inc., 1961.]

Anselm. *Monologion* and *Proslogion*. *Opera Omnia S. Anselmi Cantauariensis archiepiscopi*, vol. 1. Ed. F. S. Schmitt. Edinburgh: T. Nelson and Sons, 1946.

[English translation: *Monologion*. Trans. S. Harrison. In *Anselm of Canterbury: The Major Works*. Ed. B. Davies and G. R. Evans. Oxford: Oxford University Press, 1998.]

[English translation: *Proslogion*. Trans. M. J. Charlesworth. In *Anselm of Canterbury: The Major Works*. Ed. B. Davies and G. R. Evans. Oxford: Oxford University Press, 1998.]

Aristotle. *Aristoteles Graece*. Ed. I. Bekker. Berlin: Reiner, 1931.

[English translation: *The Complete Works of Aristotle*, 2 vols. Revised Oxford Translation. Ed. J. Barnes. Princeton: Princeton University Press, 1984.]

Augustine. *Confessionum*. In PL, vol. 32. Ed. J. P. Migne. Paris: 1841.

[English translation: *Confessions*. Trans. V. Bourke. In FOTC, vol. 21. New York: Fathers of the Church Inc., 1953.]

———. *Contra Maximinum Arianum*. In PL, vol. 42. Ed. J. P. Migne. Paris: 1841.

[English translation: *Answer to Maximinus*. In *Arianism and Other Heresies*. Trans. R. Teske. Hyde Park, NY: New City Press, 1995.]

———. *De Anima et eius Origine*. In PL, vol. 44. Ed. J. P. Migne. Paris: 1841.

[English translation: *On the Soul and Its Origin*. In NPNF, series 1, vol. 5. Trans. P. Holmes and R. Wallis. Reprinted, Grand Rapids, MI: Eerdmans, 1978.]

———. *De Civitate Dei*. In CCSL, vol. 47. Turnholt: Brepols, 1955.

[English translation: *City of God*. Trans. D. B. Zema, S.J., and G. G. Walsh, S.J. (Books 1–8); G. G. Walsh, S.J., and G. Nonahan, O.S.U. (Books 8–16); G. G. Walsh, S.J., and D. J. Honan (Books 17–22). In FOTC, vols. 6 (1950), 7 (1952), and 8 (1954), respectively. New York: Fathers of the Church, Inc.]

———. *De Doctrina Christiana*. In CCSL, vol. 32. Ed. J. Martin. Turnholt: Brepols, 1962.

[English translation: *On Christian Doctrine*. Trans. D. W. Robertson, Jr. Indianapolis: Library of Liberal Arts, 1958.]

———. *De Duabus Animabus contra Manichaeos*. In PL, vol. 42. Ed. J. P. Migne. Paris: 1845.

———. *De Genesi ad litteram libri XII*. In CSEL, vol. 28, part 1. Ed. I. Zycha. Prague: Tempsky-Freytag, 1894.

[English translation: *De Genesi ad litteram libri XII*. Trans. J. H. Taylor. Dissertation. St. Louis: St. Louis University, 1948.]

———. *De Inmortalitate Animae*. In CSEL, vol. 89. Ed. W. Hormann. Vindobonae: Hoelder-Pichler-Tempsky, 1986.

[English translation: *The Immortality of the Soul*. Trans. L. Schopp. In FOTC, vol. 2. New York: Cima Publications, 1947.]

———. *De Peccatorum Meritis et Remissione et de Baptismo Parvulorum ad Marcellinum*. In CSEL, vol. 60. Ed. C. Urba and I. Zycha. Vondobonae: Tempsky-Freytag, 1913.

———. *De Spiritu et Anima*. In PL, vol. 40. Ed. J. P. Migne. Paris: 1845.

———. *De Trinitate*. Ed. W. J. Mountain and Fr. Glorie. In CCSL, vols. 50 and 50A. Turnholt: Brepols, 1968.

[English translation: *The Trinity*. Trans. S. McKenna, C.SS.R. In FOTC, vol. 45. Washington D.C.: The Catholic University of America Press, 1963.]

———. *De Vera Religione*. In CCSL, vol. 32. Ed. J. Martin. Turnholt: Brepols, 1962.

[English translation: *Of True Religion*. Trans. J. H. S. Burleigh. In *Augustine: Earlier Writings*. Ed. J. H. S. Burleigh. Philadelphia: The Westminster Press, 1953.]

———. *Enchiridion ad Laurentium de Fide et Spe et Caritate*. Ed. E. Evans. In CCSL, vol. 46. Turnholt: Brepols, 1969.

[English translation: *Faith, Hope and Charity*. Trans. B. M. Peebles. In FOTC, vol. 4. New York: Cima Publications, 1947.]

———. *In Joannis Evangelium*. In PL, vol. 35. Ed. J. P. Migne. Paris: 1841.

[English translation: *Tractates on the Gospel of John*, 5 vols. Trans. J. W. Rettig. In FOTC, vols. 78 (1988), 79 (1988), 88 (1993), 90 (1994), 92 (1995). Washington D.C.: The Catholic University of America Press.]

Averroës (Ibn Rushd). *Metaphysicorum libri XIV*. In *Aristotelis opera cum Averrois commentariis*. Ed. Marco Antonio Zimara, vol. 8. Frankfurt am Main, Minerva, 1962.

[French translation: *Etude du livre zay (dzêta) de la «Métaphysique» d'Aristote dans sa version arabe et son commentaire par Averroès*. Trans. Ahmed Elsakhawi. Paris: Atelier National de Reproduction des Thèses, 1994.]

[English translation: *Commentary on Aristotle's Metaphysics*. Book Lām. Trans. C. Genequand. Leiden: E. J. Brill, 1986.]

———. *De anima libri tres*, in *Aristotelis opera cum Averrois commentariis*. Ed. Marco Antonio Zimara, supp. 2. Frankfurt am Main, Minerva, 1962.

Avicebron (Ibn Gabirol). *Fons Vitae*. Ed. Clemens Baeumker. In *Beiträge zur Geschichte der Philosophie des Mittelalters*. Münster, 1985.

[English translation: *The Fountain of Life*. Trans. Alfred B. Jacob. Stanwood, Washington: Sabian Publication Society, 1987.]

Avicenna (Ibn Sina). *Liber de Philosophia Prima sive Scientia Divina* (medieval Latin translation from Arabic). Ed. S. Van Riet. Louvain: E. Peeters, vol. 1 (1977), vol. 2 (1980).

[French translation: *La Metaphysiqu du Shifa* (contemporary translation from Arabic). Trans. G. C. Anawati, O.P. Paris: Librarie Philosophique J. Vrin, vol. 1 (1978), vol. 2 (1985).]

Basil the Great. *Homilae in Hexaemeron*. In PL, vol. 17. Ed. J. P. Migne. Paris: 1857.

[English translation: *Homilies on the Hexaemeron*. Trans. A. C. Way, C.D.P. In FOTC, vol. 46. Washington, D.C.: The Catholic University of America Press, 1963.]

Bede. *In Genesim*. In CCSL, vol. 118A. Ed. C. W. Jones. Turnholt: Brepols, 1967.

Bernard of Clairvaux. *Sermones in Cantica*. In PL, vol. 183. Ed. J. P. Migne. Paris: 1879.

[English translation: *Sermons on the Song of Songs*. In *Bernard of Clairvaux, Selected Works*. Trans. G. R. Evans. New York: Paulist Press, 1987.]

Biblia Latina cum glossa ordinaria: facsimile reprint of the editio Princeps Adolph Rusch of Strassburg 1480/81. Turnhout: Brepols, 1992.

Boethius. *De Arithmetica*. In CCSL, vol. 94A. Ed. H. Oosthout and J. Schilling. Turnholt: Brepols, 1999.

———. *De Persona et Duabus Naturis*. In PL, vol. 64. Ed. J. P. Migne. Paris: 1891.

———. "De Hebdomadibus." A.k.a. "Quomodo substantiae in eo quod sint bonae sint cum non sint substantialia bona." In PL, Vol. 64. Ed. J. P. Migne. Paris: 1891.

[English translation: "How Substances May Be Good in Their Essence Without Being Good of Their Essence." Trans. John F. Wippel. In *Medieval Philosophy*. Ed. J. F. Wippel and A. B. Wolter, O.F.M. New York: The Free Press, 1969.]

———. *De trinitate*. A.k.a. *Quomodo Trinitas unus Deus ac non tres Dii*. In PL, vol. 64. Ed. J. P. Migne. Paris: 1891.

[English translation: *On the Trinity*. In *The Theological Tractates*. Trans. H. F. Stewart and E. D. Rand. In *Loeb Classical Library, Latin Series*. London: Heinemann, 1918.]

———. *Philosophiae Consolatio*. In CCSL, vol. 94. Ed. L. Bieler. Turnholt: Brepols, 1957.

[English translation: *The Consolation of Philosophy*. Trans. R. Green. Indianapolis: The Library of the Liberal Arts, 1962.]

John Damascene. *Expositio Fidei Orthodoxae*. In PG, vol. 94. Ed. J. P. Migne. Turnholt: Brepols, n.d.

[English translation: *Exposition of the Orthodox Faith*. Trans. S. D. F. Salmond. In NPNF, series 2, vol. 9. Ed. P. Schaff and H. Wace. Reprinted, Grand Rapids, MI : Eerdmans, 1976.]

Diels, H. ed. *Fragmente der Vorsokratiker*, 6th ed. Revised by W. Kranz. Berlin: 1952.

[English translation: Kathleen Freeman. *Ancilla to the Pre-Socratic Philosophers*. Cambridge: Harvard University Press, 1978.]

Fulgentius. *Ad Monimum*. In CCSL, vol. 91. Ed. J. Fraipont. Turnholt: Brepols, 1968.

[English translation: *To Monimus*. Trans. R. B. Eno, S.S. In FOTC, vol. 95. Washington, D.C.: The Catholic University of America Press, 1997.]

Gennadius Massiliensis. *De Ecclesiasticis Dogmatibus*. In PL, vol. 58. Ed. J. P. Migne. Paris: 1862.

Gregory the Great. *Dialogorum*. In PL, vol. 77. Ed. J. P. Migne. Petit Montrouge: 1862.

[English translation: *Dialogues*. Trans. O. J. Zimmerman, O.S.B. In FOTC, vol. 39. New York: Fathers of the Church. Inc., 1959.]

Gregory Nazianzen. *Oratio XXVIII, Theologica Secunda, De Theologia*. In PG, vol. 20. Ed. J. P. Migne. Petit Montrouge: 1857.

[English translation: *The Second Theological Oration*. Trans. C. G. Browne and J. E. Swallow. In NPNF, series 2, vol. 7. Ed. P. Schaff and H. Wace. Reprinted, Grand Rapids, MI: Eerdmans, 1979.]

Gregory of Nyssa. *De Anima*. In PG, vol. 45. Ed. J. P. Migne. Petit Montrouge: 1863.

———. *De Hominis Opificio*. In PG, vol. 44. Ed. J. P. Migne. Petit Montrouge: 1863.

[English translation: *On the Making of Man*. Trans. W. Moore and H. A. Wilson. In NPNF, series 2, vol. 5. Ed. P. Schaff and H. Wace. Reprinted, Grand Rapids, MI: Eerdmans, 1979.]

Hilary of Poitiers. *De Trinitate*. In PL, vol. 10. Ed. J. P. Migne. Paris: 1845.

[English translation: *The Trinity*. Trans. Stephen McKenna, C.Ss.R. In FOTC, vol. 25. New York: Fathers of the Church Inc., 1954.]

———. *Liber de Synodis* seu *De Fide Orientalium*. In PL, vol. 10. Ed. J. P. Migne. Paris: 1845.

Hippocrates. *Places in Man*. In *Hippocrates* VIII, Loeb Classical Library, vol. 482. Trans. and ed. Paul Potter. Cambridge: Harvard University Press, 1995.

Jerome (Eusebii Hieronymi). *Commentariorum in Epistolam ad Titum*. In PL, vol. 26. Ed. J. P. Migne. Paris: 1866.

———. "Epistola CXXIV, ad Avitum." In PL, vol. 22. Ed. J. P. Migne. Petit Montrouge: 1864.

[English translation: *Letters and Select Works*. In NPNF, series 2, vol. 6. Ed. P. Schaff and H. Wace. Reprinted, Grand Rapids, MI: Eerdmans, 1952.]

Liber de causis. Ed. A. Pattin, O.M.I. In *Tijdschrift voor Filosofie* 28 (1966): 90–203.

[English translation: *The Book of Causes*. Trans. D. J. Brand. Milwaukee: Marquette University Press, 1984.]

Macrobius, Ambrosius Aurelius Theodosius. *Commentarii in Somnium Scipionis*. Ed. J. Willis. Leipzig: B. G. Teubner, 1970.

[English translation: *Commentary on the Dream of Scipio*. Trans. W. H. Stahl. New York: Columbia University Press, 1952.]

Moses Maimonides. *The Guide of the Perplexed*. Trans. Shlomo Pines. Chicago: University of Chicago Press, 1963.

Nemesius. *De Natura Hominis*. In PG, vol. 40. Ed. J. P. Migne. Paris: 1857.

[English translation: *A Treatise on the Nature of Man*. Ed. W. Telfer. In Library of Christian Classics, vol. 4. London, 1955.]

Origen. *Peri Archon*. In PG, vol. 11. Ed. J. P. Migne. Petit Montrouge: 1857.

[English translation: *On First Principles.* Trans. G. W. Butterworth. Gloucester, MA: Peter Smith, 1973.]

Peter Lombard. *Sententiarum Libri IV.* In PL, vol. 192. Ed. J. P. Migne. Paris: Garnier Brothers, 1880.

[English translation: *The Sentences.* Trans. Giulio Silano. Toronto: Pontifical Institute of Mediaeval Studies, vol. 1 (2007), vol. 2 (2008), vol. 3 (2008), vol. 4 (forthcoming 2010).]

Pseudo-Dionysius. *Opera Omnia quae exstant.* In PG, vols. 3 and 4. Ed. J. P. Migne. Petit Montrouge: 1857.

[English translation: *Pseudo-Dionysius: The Complete Works.* Trans. C. Luibheid. New York: Paulist Press, 1987.]

Secondary Sources Cited in Footnotes

Allen, Prudence, R.S.M. *The Concept of Woman,* vol. 1. Grand Rapids, MI: Eerdmans, 1985.

Asma, Stephen. "Abortion and the Embarrassing Saint." *The Humanist* 54 (1994): 30–33.

Berger, H. H. "Der Partizipations-gedanke im Metaphysik-Kommentar des Thomas von Aquin." *Vivarium* 1 (1963): 115–40.

Blanchette, Oliva. *The Perfection of the Universe according to Aquinas: A Teleological Cosmology.* University Park, PA: The Pennsylvania State University Press, 1992.

Bobik, Joseph. *Aquinas on Matter and Form and the Elements.* Notre Dame, IN: University of Notre Dame Press, 1998.

Bradley, Denis. "'To Be or Not To Be': Pasnau on Aquinas's Immortal Human Soul." *The Thomist* 68 (2004): 1–39.

Brown, Montague. "The Relation between God and Human Beings: The Difference It Makes to Human Happiness." *Proceedings of the American Catholic Philosophical Association* 66 (1992): 163–73.

Clarke, W. Norris, S.J. *The One and the Many: A Contemporary Thomistic Metaphysics.* Notre Dame: University of Notre Dame Press, 2001.

———. *Person and Being.* Milwaukee: Marquette University Press, 1993.

Collins, James. *The Thomistic Philosophy of the Angels.* In The Catholic University of America Philosophical Studies, vol. 89. Washington, D.C.: The Catholic University of America Press, 1947.

Condic, Maureen. "When Does Human Life Begin? A Scientific Perspective." *National Catholic Bioethics Quarterly 9 (2009): 131–49.*

de Finance, Joseph. *Etre et agir dans la philosophie de Saint Thomas,* 3rd ed. Rome: Presses de l'Université Grégorienne, 1965.

de Nys, Martin J. "Aquinas and Kierkegaard on the Relation between God and Creatures." *American Catholic Philosophical Quarterly* 75 (2001): 389–407.

Dewan, Lawrence, O.P. "St. Thomas and the Distinction between Form and *Esse* in Caused Things." *Gregorianum* 60 (1999): 353–70. Reprinted in *Form and Being: Studies in Thomistic Metaphysics,* 188–204. Washington, D.C.: The Catholic University of America Press, 2006.

Eberl, Jason. "Aquinas's Account of Human Embryogenesis and Recent Interpretations." *Journal of Medicine and Philosophy* 30 (2005): 379–94.

———. "Aquinas on the Nature of Human Beings." *Review of Metaphysics* 58 (2004): 333–65.

Flannery, Kevin L., S.J. "Applying Aristotle in Contemporary Embryology." *The Thomist* 67 (2003): 249–78.

Gauthier, R.-A. *Saint Thomas d'Aquin, Somme contre les gentils. Introduction.* Paris: Éditions Universitaires, 1993.

Gilson, Etienne. *The Spirit of Mediaeval Philosophy.* Trans. A. Downes. New York: Charles Scribner's Sons, 1940.

Grygiel, Wojciech F.S.S.P. "The Metaphysics of Chaos: A Thomistic View of Entropy and Evolution." *The Thomist* 66 (2002): 251–66.

Haldane, John, and Patrick Lee. "Aquinas on Human Ensoulment and the Value of Life." *Philosophy* 78 (2003): 255–78.

Hankey, Wayne. *"Ab uno simplici non est nisi unum."* In *Divine Creation in Ancient, Medieval, and Early Modern Thought.* Ed. M. Treschow et al., 316–28. Leiden: Brill, 2007.

Henle, R. J., S.J. *Saint Thomas and Platonism.* The Hague: Martinus Nijhoff, 1956.

Hershenov, David, and Rose Koch. "How a Hylomorphic Metaphysics Constrains the Abortion Debate." *National Catholic Bioethics Quarterly* 5 (2005): 751–64.

Hyman, A. "From What Is One and Simple Only What Is One and Simple Can Come." In *Neoplatonism and Jewish Thought.* Ed. L. E. Goodman, 111–35. Studies in Neoplatonism 7. Albany: State University of New York Press, 1992.

Ide, Pascal. "Le zygote: est-il une personne humaine?" *Nova et vetera* 76 (2001.1): 45–88 and (2001.2): 53–88.

Johnson, Mark. "Did St. Thomas Attribute a Doctrine of Creation to Aristotle?" *New Scholasticism* 63 (1989): 129–55.

Jones, D. A. *The Soul of the Embryo: An Enquiry into the Status of the Human Embryo in the Christian Tradition.* London: Continuum, 2004.

Liske, Michael-Thomas. "Kann Gott reale Beziehungen zu den Geschopfen haben? Logisch-theologische Betrachtungen im Anschluss an Thomas von Aquin." *Theologie und Philosophie* 68 (1993): 208–28.

Litt, Thomas. *Les corps célestes dan l'univers de Saint Thomas d'Aquin.* Louvain: Publications Universitaires, 1963.

Meyer, John. "Embryonic Personhood, Human Nature, and Rational Ensoulment." *Heythrop Journal* 47 (2006): 206–25.

O'Rourke, Fran. *Pseudo-Dionysius and the Metaphysics of Aquinas.* Leiden: E. J. Brill, 1992. Reissued by University of Notre Dame Press, 2005.

Pasnau, Robert. *Thomas Aquinas on Human Nature.* Cambridge: Cambridge University Press, 2002.

Rosemann, Philipp. *Omne Agens Agit Sibi Simile. A "Repetition" of Scholastic Metaphysics.* Leuven: Leuven University Press, 1996.

Schioppetto, Dario. "L'Ombra dell'Eterno: Note sul Tempo degli Angeli." In *Il Tempo in Questione: Paradigmi della Temporalità nel Pensiero Occidentale.* Ed. L. Ruggiu, 155–81. Milan: Guerini, 1997.

Selner-Wright, Susan. "Aquinas on Acts of Creation and Procreation." *National Catholic Bioethics Quarterly* 3 (2003): 707–16.

Serra, Angelo, and Roberto Colombo. "Identity and Status of the Human Embryo: The Contribution of Biology." In *Identity and Statute of Human Embryo: Proceedings of the 3rd Assembly of the Pontifical Academy for Life*. Ed. J. Correa and E. Sgreccia, 128–77. Rome: Libreria Editrice Vaticana, 1998.

Shanley, Brian. "Eternity and Duration in Aquinas." *The Thomist* 61 (1997): 525–48.

Sweeney, Leo, S.J. "Doctrine of Creation in *Liber de Causis*." In *An Etienne Gilson Tribute*. Ed. C. J. O'Neil, 274–89. Milwaukee: Marquette University Press, 1959.

Tomarchio, John. "Aquinas's Division of Being According to Modes of Existing." *Review of Metaphysics* 54 (2001): 585–613.

———. "Four Indices for the Thomistic Principle *Quod recipitur in aliquo est in eo per modum recipientis*." *Medieval Studies* 60 (1998): 315–67.

———. *The Modus Principle in the Writings of St. Thomas Aquinas*, Ph.D. dissertation, The Catholic University of America, 1997.

Torrell, J.-P., O.P. *Saint Thomas Aquinas. Vol. 1: The Person and His Work*. Trans. Robert Royal. Washington, D.C.: The Catholic University of America Press, 1996.

van Steenberghen, Fernand. "Le problème de l'existence de Dieu dans les questions disputées 'De potentia Dei.'" *Pensamiento* 25 (1969): 249–57.

———. *Le problème de l'existence de Dieu dans les Écrits de S. Thomas d'Aquin*. Louvain-la-neuve: l'Institut Supérieur de Philosophie, 1980.

Weisheipl, James, O.P. "The Date and Context of Aquinas' *De aeternitate mundi*." In *Graceful Reason: Essays in Ancient and Medieval Philosophy presented to Joseph Owens, CSsR*. Ed. L. P. Gerson, 239–71. Toronto: Pontifical Institute of Mediaeval Studies, 1983.

Wilhelmsen, Frederick D. "Creation as a Relation in St. Thomas Aquinas." *Modern Schoolman* 56 (1979): 107–33.

Wippel, John F. *Metaphysical Themes in Thomas Aquinas II*. Washington, D.C.: The Catholic University of America Press, 2007.

———. "Thomas Aquinas on God's Freedom to Create or Not." In *Metaphysical Themes in Thomas Aquinas II*, 218–39.

———. "Thomas Aquinas on Our Knowledge of God and the Axiom That Every Agent Produces Something Like Itself." *Proceedings of the American Catholic Philosophical Association* 74 (2001): 81–101.

———. "Thomas Aquinas on Creatures as Causes of *esse*." *International Philosophical Quarterly* 50 (2000) 197–213.

———. "Truth in Thomas Aquinas." *Review of Metaphysics* 43 (1989): 295–326.

———. "Thomas Aquinas and the Axiom 'What Is Received Is Received according to the Mode of the Receiver." In *A Straight Path: Studies in Medieval Philosophy and Culture*. Ed. R. Link-Salinger, 279–89. Washington, D.C.: The Catholic University of America Press, 1988.

———. *Metaphysical Themes in Thomas Aquinas*. Washington, D.C.: The Catholic University of America Press, 1984.

———. "Did Thomas Aquinas Defend the Possibility of an Eternally Created World?" *Journal of the History of Philosophy* 19 (1981): 21–38.

INDEX OF SUBJECTS

INDEX OF SOURCES

On Creation [Quaestiones Disputatae de Potentia Dei, *Q. 3*] was designed and typeset in Meridien by Kachergis Book Design of Pittsboro, North Carolina. It was printed on 50-pound Natural and bound by Versa Press of East Peoria, Illinois.